The British
Tax System

THE BRITISH TAX SYSTEM

BY

J. A. KAY

M. A. KING

OXFORD UNIVERSITY PRESS

1978

Oxford University Press, Walton Street, Oxford OX2 6DP

OXFORD   LONDON   GLASGOW
NEW YORK   TORONTO   MELBOURNE   WELLINGTON
IBADAN   NAIROBI   DAR ES SALAAM   LUSAKA   CAPE TOWN
KUALA LUMPUR   SINGAPORE   JAKARTA   HONG KONG   TOKYO
DELHI   BOMBAY   CALCUTTA   MADRAS   KARACHI

British Library Cataloguing in Publication Data

Kay, J A
 The British tax system.
 1. Taxation – Great Britain
 I. Title   II. King, M A
 336.2′00941   HJ2619   78-40085

 ISBN 0-19-877104-5
 ISBN 0-19-877105-3   Pbk

*Typeset by Gloucester Typesetting Co. Ltd.,
and printed in Great Britain by
Billing & Sons Ltd., Guildford and Worcester*

Fantastic grow the evening gowns;
Agents of the Fisc pursue
Absconding tax-defaulters through
The sewers of provincial towns.

Caesar's double-bed is warm
As an unimportant clerk
Writes I DO NOT LIKE MY WORK
On a pink official form.

From W. H. Auden, 'The Fall of Rome'
(*Collected Shorter Poems*,
Faber & Faber, 1966)

PREFACE

WE should like to thank the many people who have directly or indirectly helped us to write this book. We could not have written it without the knowledge and experience we gained as members of the Meade Committee on the Structure and Reform of Direct Taxation between 1975 and 1977. We are indebted to all those who worked on that project and to the Institute for Fiscal Studies which made it possible. We know that they will not think it invidious if we express our special gratitude to James Meade, not only for what we learnt from him about taxation but also for the influence of his combination of unfailing personal sympathy and understanding and uncompromising intellectual rigour on both the content of our work and our approach to it. The impact which the contents of the Meade Report have had on our thinking is obvious: but the analysis and opinions expressed here are our own and do not represent the contents of the Meade Report nor the views of any of its other members. The reader who attributes our errors to the Meade Committee, or who believes that he will find here a substitute for reading that Report, is quite mistaken.

We are grateful to P. J. Thompson for research assistance. We have received help on particular problems from J. A. Beath, M. B. E. White, and representatives of the Inland Revenue, Central Statistical Office, and the Bundesministerium der Finanzen; also from the finance directors of a number of the companies cited in Table 12.1. An earlier version of the manuscript was read by A. B. Atkinson, J. S. Flemming, P. M. S. Hacker, R. W. Houghton, E. F. King, R. I. McKibbin, J. A. Mirrlees, J. K. Rutter, and S. M. Waldman, and without their comments there would have been many more obscurities and errors in our presentation. It is hardly necessary for us to say that not all of these organizations and individuals share the views we express; we hope that some of them do but we cannot commit any of them. We should also like to thank Miss B. Atkinson, Mrs. P. Hawtin, and Mrs. J. Saxby for organizing the preparation of the manuscript.

Since many of the properties of a tax system depend on the rates of taxes and benefits and the relations between them, a book like this would be incomprehensible if we did not use specific figures in our description and analysis. But it is rare for more than a few weeks to pass without some changes in these rates, and rare for more than a few months to pass without some structural changes. We have attempted to ensure that the information given here was correct on 1 January 1978.

CONTENTS

LIST OF TABLES

LIST OF FIGURES

INTRODUCTION

IN this book we seek to use economic analysis to examine the problems facing the British tax system. We try to do this in a practical way by looking at real day-to-day problems. We were ourselves surprised that economics was useful to us not only in analysing the economic effects of taxes, but also in thinking about administrative problems. The reason for this is that much of the muddle and complexity of the present system derives from the absence of any clear view as to what principles do or should underlie it.

This is not to suggest that economics provides all the answers. Public finance is one of the most rapidly developing branches of economic theory, but we found much traditional theory of little help in dealing with the everyday problems of the British tax system and it is instructive to consider why. Much of this material is concerned with evaluating the economic effects of taxes, and this is quite properly done by contrasting the characteristics of different theoretical taxes. But the ways in which actual taxes differ from these theoretical taxes are often of much greater economic significance than the ways in which theoretical taxes differ from each other. We pursue in this book the question of whether income or expenditure should be the major component of the tax base: the extent to which savings should or should not be taxed. It is conventional to think of this in terms of how aggregate savings respond to changes in taxes. But there is little evidence to suggest that aggregate savings are likely to be very sensitive to tax changes. What is more significant is that the ways in which people save are very sensitive indeed to the ways in which different savings media are taxed. The present tax system, in effect, exempts some forms of saving from tax but not others; and this, we think, has more marked economic effects than a structure in which all forms of savings are taxed or one in which none of them is taxed. We pursue this argument, and others like it, in more detail below; but we note at this stage that the loopholes and anomalies in the tax system can often be much more significant in their effects on behaviour than the taxes themselves. The economist who thinks that because the main U.K. personal direct tax is called an income tax it has the same characteristics as income taxes he encounters in public finance texts is likely to be seriously misled.

These observations are not in any way intended to question the need for any analysis of applied economic problems to be rooted firmly in economic theory: indeed it is because we are convinced of this that we offer, in Chapter 1, a crash course in some simple, but central, economic concepts. We would like to stress that we shall only make proposals for change if we believe them to be practicable. It is necessary to spell out what this means. The most usual definition equates the impracticable with the unfamiliar. This definition is convenient for those who find adaptation to new ideas difficult or disturbing, but it is not very useful for a discussion of the tax system. It is perfectly clear that there are many other systems of all kinds which differ from those presently in operation which would work, and it would be surprising if some of them would not work better than existing systems. Those who believe that being practical involves confining attention to minor modifications of the *status quo* are simply showing that their minds, or the minds of those to whom they are reporting, are closed.

A related error is to confuse a practical outlook with an obsession with detail. As an example, the Inland Revenue in its memorandum on local income tax to the Layfield Committee was apparently exercised by the problem of people who live in caravans. It would be foolish to deny that there is such a problem. It would also be foolish to deny that the problem is, like the number of people who live in caravans, small. It is very unlikely that anyone would say 'I would be in favour of a local income tax if only I could think of a way of dealing with people who live in caravans'. Given that this is so, it is pointless to discuss the matter further at this stage. Not only is it unnecessary to consider the difficulty in advance of making basic decisions about the structure of such a tax (such as whether to have one); it is positively undesirable to do so, since this kind of problem can be more sensibly tackled in the light of other, more important, decisions that would need to be taken first. The enumeration of endless lists of unimportant objections is a common administrative tactic for resisting change, and the man who seeks to deal with it by answering them is lost. Since most people are—rightly—uninterested in the minutiae of hypothetical tax systems, we shall not take our description of alternatives beyond the point at which we are confident that we, or a competent firm of management consultants, could fill in the remaining details. It is extremely unfortunate that the Inland Revenue has cried wolf so often on the impossibility of administering reforms—including several which were subsequently implemented—that its views on what is and what is not feasible can no longer be regarded as reliable.

All this said, it must be recognized that administrative feasibility is an important constraint on tax policy, and we have given it due weight in our discussion. We shall regard measures as practicable if we believe they can be operated reasonably cheaply and simply in a manner which corresponds to the underlying intention of the measure. Most things can be made to work, after a fashion, if we are prepared either to spend a good deal of effort on policing them or to accept many *ad hoc* expedients and anomalies in their operation. Practicability is therefore a matter of degree (so that it is not easy to make firm statements about it) and we judge something to be impracticable if it would cost too much in one or other of these directions; too much administrative burden or too extensive compromise with the original objective. It should be clear from this definition that it is not only not necessary for a measure to be part of the *status quo* for it to be practicable; it is not sufficient either. There are substantial parts of the British tax system which do not work satisfactorily and could not, without great difficulty and expense, be made to do so. We shall return to this point in various specific contexts.

We begin our discussion in Chapter 1 with a brief explanation of some basic economic concepts which we believe to be of fundamental importance to an understanding of the tax system. The style of this chapter is necessarily rather different from the rest of the book and we suggest that if it poses difficulty the reader should move on to Chapter 2, referring back to Chapter 1 when necessary. Chapter 2 describes the evolution of income tax and the main features of the tax as it operates today. The economic effects of taxes on earnings are analysed in Chapter 3, and in Chapter 4 we discuss the taxation of investment income and the tax treatment of savings. The arguments of these two chapters suggest the need for a reappraisal of the personal tax base, and this question is examined in Chapter 5 where we look at the claims of a tax based not on income but on individual expenditure. An explanation of how such a tax might operate in practice is provided in Chapter 6.

Two of the most controversial of current issues are the interaction between taxation and social security benefits, and the role of indirect taxes. We discuss these issues in Chapters 7 and 8 respectively. Problems of rates, local authority finance, capital taxes, and the taxation of companies are dealt with in Chapters 9–12. The final two chapters discuss the tax system as a whole. Chapter 13 looks at the question of the distribution of the tax burden among different groups and individuals in society and at how progressive the tax system should be. We conclude the book with a description of some reforms which are worth pursuing and others which are not.

There are two aspects of the tax system about which we shall have little to say, its use to stabilize fluctuations in the economy and relations with other countries. Following the Keynesian revolution much attention was directed to the use of fiscal policy as a way of controlling fluctuations in aggregate demand. Stabilization policy based on marginal changes in Government expenditure and taxation was to be the means of eliminating the business cycle. Indeed Musgrave in his classic work on public finance (1959) explains that he began with the idea of producing a tract on 'compensatory finance' dealing with the question of how the public budget affected certain key macroeconomic variables such as the level of unemployment. But the gaps in the theory of public finance which he discovered, many of which still exist today, lay in the more traditional areas of the effect of taxes on income distribution and economic efficiency. In the end stabilization policy occupied less than one-third of his treatise. This trend has continued. In his latest book (Musgrave and Musgrave, 1976) only 100 out of 750 pages are devoted to fiscal stabilization.

Part of this decline in interest is due to the realization that macroeconomic policy is more complicated than the simple textbook Keynesian models led us to believe and that 'fine-tuning' of the economy is considerably more difficult than we might have hoped. This is because there is uncertainty as to what will happen to the economy in the future in the absence of any change in policy, and because there are long delays between when a decision is made to alter taxes and when the desired effect on spending or unemployment becomes apparent. First of all there is the inevitable delay in collecting statistics, so we may only have an adequate idea of what was happening to the economy some months or even a year ago. Even when the Government has looked at the statistics, deliberated, and then decided to, say, reduce taxes there are still more lags in the system. Individuals will take time to adjust their spending decisions and, at least initially, the impact will be felt on the level of stocks in shops. Producers will probably wait before increasing their output rather than running down stocks, and the extra output will be met by overtime working until firms are convinced it is worth expanding their labour force on a more permanent basis. These lags in conjunction with uncertainty about the future make stabilization policy a hazardous business.

It has been seriously argued that the net effect of British Government policies has been to destabilize rather than to stabilize the economy, and that they have in any case been motivated more by electoral factors than by considerations of demand management ('the political business cycle'). (See Worswick, 1971; Nordhaus, 1975.) We shall not attempt to assess these views. For our purposes we may simply note that it is unlikely that the choice of the *structure* of the tax system will make these problems any easier. It is with the structure of the system that we shall be concerned and to say that we shall not answer every question is not to say that we shall not tackle the most pressing.

Another issue about which we shall say little is the international aspect of taxation. This may surprise some people who regard harmonization as one of the most important practical issues in the determination of tax policy. We do not share this view, but we consider issues of tax harmonization in the E.E.C. where they arise in three specific contexts—for corporation tax, value added tax, and the duties on tobacco products. In each of these cases, we show that harmonization has been a purely cosmetic activity. We share the widespread desire to break down barriers to trade and capital movements within Europe, but these efforts at tax harmonization have contributed absolutely nothing to this, and we do not expect much change in the foreseeable future. In practice, it is clear that harmonization is always used as a secondary argument—as a reason why we can, or cannot, do something which is proposed, or opposed, on other grounds.

I

THE ECONOMICS OF TAXATION:
SOME BASIC CONCEPTS

Tax incidence

ECONOMISTS have long been concerned with the question of who actually pays any particular tax: the *incidence* of the tax. At first sight, it may seem surprising that this is a problem. The house-owner who is required to write out a cheque in payment of rates to his local authority, or the employee who sees income tax deducted from his wages, knows very well who is paying the tax. But things are not really so simple. The tax on tobacco is paid by the trader who withdraws it from a bonded warehouse, at some intermediate stage of the process which turns tobacco leaves into cigarettes. But no one imagines that he really pays the tax, in the sense that he is personally worse off by the amount of the duty which he regularly pays over to the Customs and Excise. The tax is paid by those who ultimately smoke the cigarettes. There is no law which requires or even entitles the tobacco distributor to recover his liabilities from them—indeed in all probability he has no direct dealings with them and does not know who they are. He simply adjusts the terms on which he sells in order to reflect the tax which he is required to pay: so, in turn, do those who buy from him: and the final result is that the tax burden is passed on to the consumer.

We can therefore usefully distinguish the formal incidence of a tax from its effective incidence. The formal incidence falls on those who have the actual legal liability for paying the tax. The effective incidence identifies those who are, in the end, the people who are out of pocket as a result of the imposition of the tax. Naturally enough, it suits traders to encourage some confusion between the two. Suppliers will from time to time express regret that they are obliged to charge V.A.T. on a particular invoice. But the truth of the matter is that they are not obliged to charge V.A.T. at all: they are merely obliged to pay it, and in adding it to a bill they are seeking (as those who devised the tax intended they should) to pass that burden of payment on to someone else. The formal incidence of V.A.T. is on the supplier: the effective incidence (subject to some qualification) is on the purchaser.

Even where popular usage distinguishes the formal and effective incidence of tax, we tend to make 'all-or-nothing' assumptions about the incidence of a tax. Thus it is assumed that V.A.T. is essentially a tax on consumers, and there is no doubt that this is basically true. But it is not completely true. When a special discriminatory rate of V.A.T. was imposed on television sets and some other electrical goods in 1975, their price rose and purchasers of television sets suffered accordingly. But the demand for television sets fell: so did profit margins in the manufacture and distribution of television sets, and the profits of companies engaged in these activities were reduced: the earnings of those who worked in these industries were lower, and some of them lost their jobs. Thus the major part of the incidence of the tax was on consumers, but some of it fell on the owners of, and workers in, activities related to the supply of television sets.

Income tax is assumed to be paid by those who earn the income, and this is a good first approximation to the effective incidence of the tax. But it is only a first approximation. This is especially true at higher income levels: when the Board of Directors ponders on the appropriate differential between the Chief Executive and his deputy it is unlikely that they are entirely oblivious to the fact that six-sevenths of it will be absorbed in tax, and if this induces them to make the pre-tax margin a little wider than they would have done in the absence of the tax, then the company is sharing some of the incidence of the tax with its employee. (It is also, as we shall suggest later, likely to encourage them to think of some more efficient way of paying him.) Nor are these problems confined to higher income levels. When a householder meets a tradesman who offers to work for £100 in cash or £120 by cheque he is faced with a useful reminder that on taxable transactions part of the effective incidence falls on the employer rather than the employee.

Although the general notion of incidence is an indispensable concept in the analysis of taxation, it is one which cannot easily be given a precise meaning. The reason is that it implicitly requires a counterfactual hypothesis: what would have happened if the tax had not been imposed? It is not sufficient to say 'there would have been no tax' since public expenditure would have had to be financed in some other way. So we must specify either what other tax would have been imposed, or which item of public expenditure would have been reduced, or how the Government would have met its borrowing requirements, and the answer to our incidence question will depend on the alternative assumption which we make. For this reason the issue is sometimes described as 'differential incidence' because we examine differences between alternative tax systems which raise the same revenue. Several different concepts of incidence can be found in the theoretical literature on public finance, each reflecting different counterfactual hypotheses; while, as we see in Chapter 13, empirical studies of tax incidence either make intolerably crude assumptions or become impossibly complicated.

Thus we noted above that a consequence of imposing a heavy tax on television sets was that some of those employed in their manufacture suffered reduced earnings, and others lost their jobs: had the same tax revenue been raised in some different way, other groups of workers would probably have suffered similar hardships. But without exploring these issues in detail—as a rigorous answer would require—we can say that a significant part of the incidence of this tax fell on those who were previously employed in making televisions.

What factors govern the incidence of any particular tax? We can set out two basic principles. First, the formal incidence of a tax is generally irrelevant to its effective incidence. It makes little practical difference to the incidence of the tobacco tax whether it is levied on importers, wholesalers, manufacturers, retailers, or individual smokers: and the sensible decision is to impose the legal liability at the point at which the tax can be collected most cheaply and conveniently. Second, the harder it is for someone to substitute other things for the taxed activity, the greater the proportion of the incidence of the tax which he will bear. V.A.T. is imposed on most goods: and since there is not very much (except leisure) that can be substituted for consumption in general most of the burden of V.A.T. falls on consumers. But if a specially heavy rate of V.A.T. is imposed on one or two items, as with television sets, the situation is rather different. Consumers can substitute other things for television sets, and if the price rises sufficiently they will tend to do so. Producers, on the other hand, are in the short term stuck with capacity for manufacturing television sets: and if the only way to sell them is to keep down the price and absorb part of the tax themselves then that is what they must do.

If the tax were more discriminatory still—if it were imposed on a single manufacturer of television sets in isolation, for example— then that manufacturer would have no alternative but to hold down his price, accept the resulting losses, and grin and bear it until in the long run he could try to move into a less adversely treated business. For most people, there is no alternative to work which is both attractive and feasible and that is why the major part of the incidence of the income tax falls on the employee. But there are alternatives to effort, to overtime, and to increased responsibility: and to the extent that these are important and valuable components of the package which a particular employer is buying that employer will have to pay the price, at least to some extent, by raising the gross wage which he pays to a level which takes some account of the burden of taxation on the employee.

The first principle—the irrelevance of formal incidence—is easy to understand in abstract, but has some wide-ranging implications. For instance, it suggests that it is a matter of no practical importance whether national insurance contributions are levied on employees or employers (see pp. 23–25 below). It is not too easy to determine what the effective incidence of such a tax is—though the argument above has suggested that it mostly falls on the employee —but whatever it is, it will be the same for both kinds of contribution. When wages come to be renegotiated, the employer's concern will be with gross labour costs, inclusive of any pay-roll taxes to which he may be subject: and that will determine the level of employment which he will provide at any particular wage and the offer he will be prepared to make to avoid industrial trouble. On the other side of the table, the employee's interest is in his take-home pay, net of any deductions imposed on him: and that should determine the amount of quality or work which he will provide at particular wage rates and the minimum he will accept in preference to incurring the costs of a strike or other action against the employer. None of these calculations is in any way affected by the proportions in which a given tax is divided between employers' and employees' contribution, and this will therefore not have a significant effect on the final outcome.

Of course, none of this denies that the nature of formal incidence may have significant short-term effects. If a shift from employees' to employers' contributions were to be made, then next week workers would be better off and firms worse off. But this is simply to say that adjustments may take time, and that the incidence of a tax may differ in the short and long run. In practice the restoration of net real wages to their initial level might come about as much through an uncompensated rise in prices as through a diminution in the rate of increase of money wages. But the proposition that effective incidence is independent of formal incidence in the long run is true generally. The invoice that says £50+£4 V.A.T., or the pay-slip that says £50 less £15 deductions gives £35 net, may in the short run mean what they appear to say. However, it is erroneous to suppose that if these tax items were not there the price or the wage from which these computations start would necessarily remain unchanged, and likely that the price might be £51 or £52 and the wage £44 or £47.

Tax capitalization

The easiest way to see *tax capitalization* in operation is to start with a rather artificial example. Suppose there exists a range of bonds, each of which sells for £100 and yields 10 per cent in perpetuity: income tax on this yield is levied at 50%, so that the after-tax return on each bond is £5. Now suppose that the Government decides, for some reason, that among these bonds there is one particular one that should be tax exempt. As a result, this bond—let us call it bond X—now returns £10 per annum after tax as well as before it. Because of this, it is worth twice as much to any taxpayer, and so its price rises to £200. Now look ahead a few years. By this time, most of the holders of bond X will be people who have purchased it since the tax concession was given—people who have paid £200 for it. They are only earning 5% on their investment—which is the same as they could earn from other bonds—and are therefore no better off than if this concession had never been granted. In spite of this, however, they would suffer if the concession were withdrawn—if they intended to continue holding the bond, their after-tax income would be halved, while if they intended to sell the bond, they would discover that its capital value had halved. As a result of this, even people who are deriving and have derived no direct benefit from the concession would lose if it were repealed. The holders of such a bond might include some pension funds and charities, who do not pay tax and therefore gain nothing from the apparent concession (such groups would not find bond X especially attractive, but they might have other reasons for wishing to hold it). They too would suffer capital losses as the price of bond X fell if it became again subject to tax: although they obviously gain nothing from the concession, they would suffer by its withdrawal.

This is a simple case of a capitalized tax exemption. The only people who gain from it are those who hold the favoured asset at the date when the concession is introduced (and perhaps their descendants). In the example above, the fortunate holders of bond X on the critical day when the Chancellor made his announcement saw the capital value of their asset double. Subsequent to that, no one derives any benefit from the concession at all. Nevertheless, later holders of the bond would lose if the concession were discontinued: in effect, they have bought the right to it from the former holders, and would have the part of their savings which they have invested in this form eliminated. Indeed, they would probably lose rather more than would be generally recognized. Not only would they be worse off by virtue of the extra tax they would themselves have to pay, but they would additionally be worse off because the asset they hold would fetch much less on resale. In other words, tax capitalization is a trap. In such a situation, almost everyone could agree that it would be better if the concession had never been given in the first place. But once it has been given, it is inequitable to withdraw it, and such a course is likely to cause real hardship. Thus the apparent beneficiaries of the concession will feel insecure: although their gains from it are small, their potential losses are significant, their position is anomalous and hence vulnerable. But once a concession of this kind has been made, there is not very much that can reasonably be done except to resolve not to fall into this particular trap in future. There is no point in considering the possibility of phasing out capitalized tax concessions, or any other method of retrieving the position. The Chancellor who has made such a move is almost literally in the position of a man who has unwisely given his assets away. After the first flush of gratitude, the original recipients will have spread ownership far and wide, and there is no method, except theft, by which he can ever get them back.

Needless to say, there are numerous examples of capitalized taxes in the British tax structure. It seems useful to give two concrete examples here. One, and probably the most important, is the effect of tax concessions to owner-occupied housing. These are discussed in more detail below. For present purposes, we may simply accept that investment in housing is very favourably treated relative to investment in other kinds of asset. As a result, house prices are higher than they would otherwise be. This means that the interest and capital repayments being made by current house-buyers are substantially greater than they would be if there were no tax concessions, and hence the concessions are of little net assistance to them. Nevertheless, they would be seriously injured if, for example, relief on mortgage interest were reduced or withdrawn: not only would they find they had to pay more in tax every year but the anticipated capital gains on their houses would fail to materialize and might well be turned into capital losses. New purchasers are not gaining much from the present tax system, nor indeed has this ever been true: those who have gained have been those who have owned houses, over the thirty or forty years in which the favoured position of housing has been built up, who have seen substantial real appreciation in value of their assets. They have not benefited much either, since the gain one derives from living in the same house of ever-appreciating nominal value has very little practical utility.

This analysis is well illustrated by the effects of the withdrawal in 1974 of tax relief on mortgages in excess of £25,000. It is probably no more difficult to buy expensive houses now than it was before 1974, since the loss of tax relief has been offset by a fall in the price of such houses. The losers from the change have been those who owned such houses in 1974. Moreover, people in this position have lost whether they actually had large mortgages or not, since the fall in prices has affected all property without reference to the personal tax position of the owner.

A second illustration of tax capitalization was provided at around the same time in the market for agricultural land. Under the pre-1974 estate duty, substantial reliefs were given for agricultural assets. Their nominal purpose was to assist working farmers. It is more likely that they damaged the interests of such farmers, since the capitalization of such concessions raised land prices to levels which were nonsensical in terms of any likely agricultural returns from the land and at which working farmers were squeezed out of the market by those avoiding estate duty. When the withdrawal of such concessions was proposed as part of the shift to capital transfer tax, land prices fell by a third or more. However, political pressures for the restoration of these reliefs have been largely successful, and land prices have regained their earlier levels.

Tax and welfare

.What are the costs of collecting tax revenue? Some costs are obvious. Any tax diverts resources from the taxpayer to the Government, and leaves him worse off by that amount. Of course, that is not the end of the story; these resources are presumably used to provide public services, which may be more or less valuable to him than the possibilities for private consumption which he loses. But there are bound to be administrative costs to tax collection, since it is necessary to provide inspectors to receive the revenues and gaols to receive those who do not pay them. There will also be 'compliance costs' for taxpayers, who will spend time and suffer distress completing tax returns, and who may employ advisers to help them fulfil their obligations and suggest how to minimize them. All these latter activities represent the necessary costs of tax collection and are pure social loss, simple subtractions from the total of goods and services—private and public—available to the community.

There is a less obvious cost, which has been called the 'excess burden' of taxation. Suppose I earn £2 per hour, and my employer is willing to give me as much, or as little, work as I require at this rate. However, a 25% income tax reduces my take-home pay to £1·50 per hour, and given this I choose to work 40 hours per week, thus paying £20 in tax each week. For £1·50 I do not think it worth working any more than this, but if I were paid a little more I might. (Premium payments for overtime often succeed in inducing additional effort.) In fact for £2 per hour I would stay late on one or two evenings and put in an extra three or four hours' work a week. My employer would be better off—why else would he allow this overtime? I would be better off—why else would I stay? And if the £20 which I pay in income tax were levied, not as income tax, but as a weekly contribution to public revenue which I was obliged to pay regardless of how much work I did that week or whether I did any at all, then my net earnings from overtime would be £2 per hour and I would decide to do it.

But with an income tax, I turn this opportunity away. The problem results from the way the tax depends on how much I choose to work. These disincentive effects imply that the losses imposed by the tax are greater than the £20 which I have to pay— if I had the opportunity to do so, I would prefer to pay the £20 as a lump sum, and everyone would be better off. The idea that income taxes have undesirable disincentive effects is of course familiar, and the 'excess burden' concept is simply the economist's formal expression of it. But the idea is quite general, and commodity taxes impose losses of just the same kind. If a bottle of whisky costs 50p to make but, because of tax, sells for £4 then it is easy to imagine that I do not buy it because I am willing to pay only, say, £2. If I were able to buy it at that price, I would more than cover production costs, be able to contribute something (though less than the regular £3·50) to the Customs and Excise, and enjoy a warm inner glow myself. Because of the tax, none of these things happens. There is a disincentive effect here too—a disincentive to consume whisky—and this imposes an 'excess burden' or welfare loss of the same kind as disincentives to work.

It is very important to recognize that the magnitude of such effects depends on the impact of taxation at the margin—on the tax implications of a decision to work a little more or a little less, or to buy slightly more or less of a particular commodity—and not on the over-all or average burden of taxation. My reluctance to put in more effort to obtain higher earnings arises because the Revenue will take such a high proportion of these additional earnings. Thus there are two basic components to the welfare effects of a tax. There is an 'income effect', which reflects the reduction in the taxpayer's net income which occurs when part of it is compulsorily transferred to the Government, and which depends on the average rate of tax. There is also an 'excess burden', which reflects additional losses arising from the way in which the tax is levied. This depends on the marginal tax rate and the way in which behaviour responds to that marginal rate. The total loss is the sum of these two.

Tax and incentives

We have considered the question 'How do the disincentive effects of taxation on effort affect welfare?' We now look at a different but closely related question: 'What effect would an increase in taxation have on the amount of work you do?' Any individual considering his answer would probably feel the influence of two conflicting pressures. On the one hand, he would realize that the tax change would make him worse off. As a result, given his commitments and expectations about the style of life which he aims to enjoy, he would feel some pressure to do more work in order to earn sufficient to live up to these expectations. This effect (the *income effect* of the tax change, so called because it results from the fall in his real income) depends on the *average* rate of tax: on the total size of the burden imposed by the tax structure. On the other hand, he will also be conscious that the tax change reduces the amount of additional consumption which he can enjoy as a result of additional work, so that increased effort becomes less attractive relative to idleness or staying at home and redecorating the bedroom. This effect (the *substitution effect* of the tax, so called because it implies a substitution of leisure for work) depends on the *marginal* rate of tax—on the proportion of any additional earnings which are absorbed in tax. The net impact of such a tax change on the work done by any individual therefore depends on the balance of these two factors—one, tending to increase effort, which is related to the average rate of tax, the other, tending to reduce it, which depends on the marginal rate of tax.

We can illustrate this by returning to the example above. We were able to eliminate the excess burden in that case by transforming the 25% income tax which reduced gross earnings from £2 to £1·50 an hour into a fixed tax of £20 per week. This revision of the tax restored his overtime rate to £2 and persuaded him to do more work. In this way, we eliminated the substitution effect of the tax. We could now eliminate the income effect also by abolishing the tax of £20 per week. If we did, the worker would discover that he could achieve the same standard of living—which requires a net weekly income of £60—by working for 30 rather than 40 hours per week. It is very likely that he would in fact respond by reducing the amount of work he did, and this would tend to offset the increase which had resulted from the reduction in the marginal rate of tax. Thus the net effect of complete abolition of income tax on the amount of work he does may be small, and may even lead him to reduce it. This observation does not, however, upset our excess burden analysis at all. The gains we made from eliminating the excess burden—from encouraging him to do work which both he and his employer wanted—remain. Adding in the income effect— conferring on him an opportunity to take out increased income in the form of greater leisure—raises his welfare further. The disincentive effects of taxation, which discourage additional work effort or other kinds of economic activity, make society worse off; the offsetting incentive effects, which force people to greater effort to maintain living standards reduced by taxation, do not make anyone better off.

Care is therefore necessary in evaluating empirical evidence on the effect of taxation on incentives. In our normative analysis—where we asked how taxation affected welfare—there was an income effect and a substitution effect, and they both operated in the same direction. The income effect is the welfare loss which results from having to pay the tax—a loss which is offset by the benefits of public expenditure—and its size is determined by the average rate of tax paid. The substitution effect is the welfare loss which results from the disincentive effects of taxation at the margin and this depends only on the marginal rate of tax. This is a pure social loss, and there is no corresponding gain to anyone. The sum of these two components gives the total loss which any tax imposes on the individual who pays it.

In our positive analysis—where we asked how taxation affected the quantity of effort—we also identified an income effect and a substitution effect, but discovered that they generally worked in opposite directions. The income effect of taxation increases effort, the substitution effect reduces it, and the observed change in work effort is the net effect of the two. It follows that even if empirical studies show that tax has little effect on work effort, we cannot necessarily infer that incentive effects are not a matter for concern. Such an outcome might result from a small substitution effect, offset by a small income effect, in which case our inference would be justified; or from large income and substitution effects, in which case the effects on welfare would be correspondingly large. More sophisticated analyses are required to enable us to discriminate between these possibilities.

We have used as an expository device the possibility that a man might be subject to a tax of £20 per week rather than a 25% income tax on his earnings of £80. If such a tax were related to his earning potential rather than his earnings, it would take the form of a fixed weekly sum and would, as we have seen, have no disincentive effects at all. Economists have dreamt of such 'lump sum taxes' which eliminate the excess burden of taxation, but it is not easy to find taxes which have no disincentive effects. Nevertheless, they illustrate that it is possible to envisage a tax system where average rates are high but marginal rates are low. In practice, the easiest way to reduce marginal rates is to reduce average rates: but it is possible, by improving the structure, broadening the base, or altering the rate schedule, to achieve one without changing the other and hence to effect a more or less unequivocal improvement in the effects of the tax system on economic efficiency. We consider these effects and possibilities further in our discussion of particular taxes.

Neutrality

In discussing these issues, we shall use the concept of tax neutrality. A neutral tax system is one which seeks to raise revenue in ways which avoid the distortionary substitution effects we have described; it is designed to minimize as far as possible the impact of the tax structure on the economic behaviour of agents in the economy. This is a distinctly unfamiliar idea in the U.K., where it is widely thought that a major function of the tax system is to encourage good things and to discourage bad things. Even if one takes this view, there is much to be said for understanding the notion of neutrality and what a tax system which generally sought to achieve it would be like. Even if you know where you are going, it is generally valuable to know where you are starting out from, and if you are aiming to influence people in certain directions, it is useful to have an idea of what things would be like if you were not trying to do so. The neutral tax system, in effect, provides a bench-mark against which non-neutralities, intentional or otherwise, can be judged.

We have described one argument for neutrality—minimization of the excess burden of tax disincentives. But there is a more basic argument. The effects of taxation are generally not obvious, and are very often not what they seem. We will describe in subsequent chapters the ways in which behaviour and institutions have been moulded by the British tax system—and while there is room for argument about the desirability or undesirability of these effects, it is really very difficult to argue that many of them have ever been explicitly intended by anyone. The present state of the British tax system is the product of a series of unsystematic and *ad hoc* measures, many undertaken for excellent reasons—for administrative convenience or to encourage deserving groups and worthy activities

—but whose over-all effect has been to deprive the system of any consistent rationale or coherent structure. We should be rather content if a tax system can achieve its basic functions of raising revenue and relieving inequalities of income and wealth without doing too much damage in the process. Clearly, this is a good deal less than an ideal tax system, but it is a good deal better than what we have at the moment. We now turn to some description and analysis of what that is.

THE U.K. INCOME TAX

INCOME tax was first introduced to Britain during the Napoleonic
Wars, but it only became a permanent feature of the tax system in
1842. As part of Peel's economic reforms it was reintroduced to
replace in large part the revenue previously derived from tariffs and
from various archaic taxes. It was imposed at the single low rate
of 7*d*. in the £ (3%) and, although this varied from time to time
and ministry to ministry in the course of the nineteenth century,
these essential elements never changed. The highest rates were
reached during the Crimean War, when the tax threshold was an
annual income of £100 and the rate 1*s*. 4*d*. (7%): but even at this
time there were less than half a million taxpayers. Thus income
tax was then an impost of no interest or relevance to the great
majority of the population.

The numbers of taxpayers did not exceed a million until the
early years of the twentieth century. In 1909 effective progressivity
came to the income tax with Lloyd George's 'people's budget' in
which he proposed a 'supertax' on incomes over £5,000 per annum
(equivalent to about £80,000 at 1977 prices). This took the maximum rate to the unprecedented level of 1*s*. 8*d*. (8%). These proposals generated a constitutional crisis (the supertax was not the
most bitterly resisted element, although it was the most quanti-
tatively significant) and they were implemented only in association
with a fundamental reform of the House of Lords. During the
First World War enormously increased revenue requirements led
to top rates of tax in excess of 50%. Although there were reductions
thereafter, rates and revenue remained well in excess of pre-war
levels while the supertax, renamed surtax, became a permanent
and accepted feature.

Even then, however, liability to income tax was still confined to
a small and affluent minority. Average wages in 1939 were around
£180 per annum; there was no possible liability to tax for a married
couple with earnings below £225 at that time, and there were less

than four million taxpayers in a working population which exceeded 20 million. The decision that Second World War expenditure should be substantially financed from taxes changed this situation radically. Tax rates were increased and thresholds lowered at a time when money wages were rising rapidly. This brought about not only a quantitative change in the significance of income tax, but also a qualitative change in its method of operation. The number of taxpayers soon exceeded 12 million, so that the majority of working people now came within the ambit of the tax. These included large numbers of households lacking significant capital resources and accustomed to budgeting on a weekly basis: so the only practical method of enforcing tax liabilities was by deduction from wages before they were received. The Inland Revenue concluded that this was impracticable, and published a White Paper (Cmd. 6348) explaining that view: simultaneously, however, it was instructed to devise a scheme for doing so. P.A.Y.E. (pay-as-you-earn) was introduced and has remained the principal means of collecting income tax since then. By 1960 essentially the whole of the working population was covered by income tax.

Some caution is required in interpreting historical information on the rate structure and tax thresholds, since from 1920 to 1973 there operated a system of 'earned income relief', by which in addition to the basic personal allowance (the tax threshold) a fraction of earned income (lately two-ninths) was deducted in the computation of taxable income. This means that in measuring their effect on earned income, the nominal tax rates which applied during this period should be reduced by two-ninths: the rate of 8s. 3d. which applied from 1965 to 1971 was in fact equivalent to 32% on earned income. It also means that the real value of tax thresholds was actually nine-sevenths of their nominal value, since they were credited in full against only seven-ninths of earned income. Thus the indicated tax threshold of £325 in 1970 is equivalent to an effective tax threshold on earnings of £418. This mumbo-jumbo was swept away in 1973, and at the same time the separately assessed and administered surtax was integrated into a single system of unified income tax. In consequence, the essentials of the current structure of U.K. income tax are relatively easy to explain, and to this we now turn.

The taxation of individuals

First we set out the position for a single individual, later considering explicitly the relationship between the tax treatment of individuals and households. Everyone is entitled to a 'personal allowance', a fixed amount of income which can be received free of tax. This allowance is £945 p.a. (1977–8). It is virtually inconceivable that any adult in full-time work could have earned less than this figure, and most long-term recipients of social security benefits would receive more than this. It therefore follows that anyone who does not pay tax at at least the basic rate is likely to fall into one of four categories: (a) dependent on someone who is a basic rate taxpayer; (b) in receipt of considerable amounts of tax-exempt income (of which unemployment and sickness benefit, supplementary benefit or pension, and student grants are the most important examples); (c) having a very low income and living off capital (there cannot be many people in this category, since the capital would usually produce some income); (d) a pensioner (although the old age pension is taxable, a specially enhanced personal allowance for the elderly ensures that the national insurance pension is not in fact taxed in the hands of those with no other source of income).

All income in excess of this personal allowance is subject to tax at the *basic rate* of 34%. This rate is applied to the first £6,000 of taxable income. Thereafter (i.e. on total income in excess of £6,945) higher rates of tax apply, escalating rapidly to 65% on total income over £12,945 and a maximum rate of 83% on taxable income above £21,000. These rates are graphed against income in Fig. 2.1, as is the corresponding schedule of average rates of tax: the average rate of tax rises continuously, but is always below the marginal rate of tax (it is easy to check that each of these characteristics implies the other).

In Fig. 2.2 we show the average and marginal tax rates implied by the 1975 tax schedules of the U.K., U.S.A., and West Germany. The diagram illustrates the rates which apply to a single man with a given proportion of average earnings (these are much higher in the other two countries). In Britain the initial marginal rate of 34% is very high but persists over a wide range of income. This long basic rate band is exceptional; in the other two countries, the starting rate is much lower but rises more or less continuously. The rapid

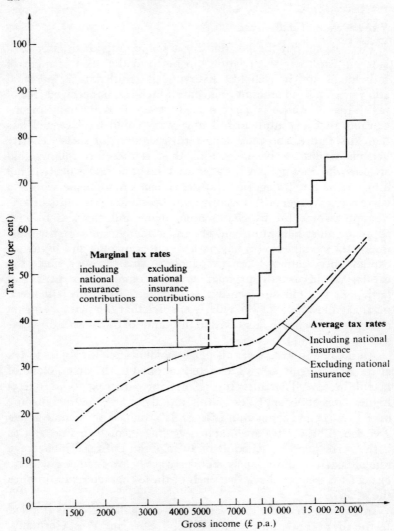

Fig. 2.1. Average and marginal rates of tax in the U.K.
(rates apply to a single man, with earned income and no other allowances)

escalation of marginal rates once the basic rate band is exhausted is not paralleled in the other countries. The resultant differences in the schedules of average rates are much less striking, and indeed the British and German systems look rather similar, except at very high levels of income, where the tax burden appears to be much greater in the U.K. The U.S. schedule is markedly lower throughout. It is, however, very important to note that the vast majority of taxpayers are clustered in a region close to 100 on the scale and it is from them that most revenue is raised; at this point, the average tax rate in Britain looks high.

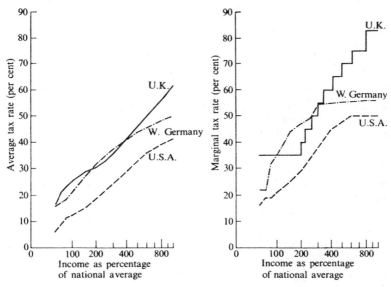

Fig. 2.2. Average and marginal rates of tax in different countries, 1975 (rates apply to a single man with no other allowances)

This description of the tax schedule ignores, however, the role of national insurance contributions. Employees' contributions are levied at a rate of 5¾%. Since the additional benefits which are received in return for additional contributions are negligible, and the administrative procedures for collecting these contributions are now integrated with those of income tax, there is no difference of substance between these contributions and income tax. Figure 2.1 shows how the basic income tax schedule is modified by national insurance contributions. Thus the effective basic rate of income tax is 39¾% on income up to £105 per week (£5,460 per year). National insurance contributions are not payable on earnings in excess of this figure, so there is an upper earnings limit. While everyone can earn £945 free of income tax, national insurance contributions are levied on every penny of earnings below the limit (though there is provision for complete exemption of those with negligible earnings). The complexity of these arrangements is increased further in 1978 with the introduction of the State Earnings Related Pension Scheme. Higher contributions are payable by those who are members of the scheme, but it is inappropriate to regard this simply as a tax since benefits are earned by the payment of contributions. Lower ('contracted-out') rates of contribution are payable by members of approved occupational pension schemes, and these 'contributions' are just a form of taxation.

National insurance contributions are not imposed on investment income. But such income is liable not only to income tax but also to a separate investment income surcharge. The first £1,500 of investment income is exempt from surcharge (and hence taxed as earned income). The next £500 of investment income is subject to a 10% surcharge (so that someone with £2000 of investment income must pay an extra £50), and additional amounts are surcharged at 15%. Thus the maximum rate of income tax in the U.K., which is levied on those with taxable income above £21,000 and investment income in excess of £2,000, is 98%: made up of the top rate of income tax of 83% plus the 15% surcharge. It is not easy to rationalize the combination of the two surcharges—5¾% on earned income below £5,460, 15% on investment income over £2,000.

We have still understated the effective rate of income tax, since as we noted in Chapter 1 there is in the long run no substantive difference between employees' and employers' contributions. It would be incorrect, however, simply to add on the 10¾% paid by employers to the basic 39¾% tax rate, since the employer pays his fraction without this being a taxable benefit for the employee.

Thus for every £100 paid in gross wages, the cost to the employer is £110·75 (£100+£10·75 employer's contribution): the taxes payable on this total £50·50 (£10·75+£5·75 in national insurance contributions and £34 income tax), so that the effective tax rate is £50·50÷£110·75 or 46%. It is worth pursuing this calculation a little further to see what the total tax burden on marginal income is likely to be. On spending the remaining £60·25 of the initial £110·75 our worker would have to pay consumption taxes. The size of these would of course depend on his consumption patterns, and if these were deemed sufficiently meritorious by the Government's expressed preferences (for books, bread, and British Rail) it would be possible (though boring) to pay no or even negative consumption taxes. But on a representative collection of commodities the average tax rate would be 10·8%[1] so that of the £60·25 some £6·50 would go in tax. This calculation raises the effective marginal tax rate to 51%: it still underestimates the true figure since there are several taxes (such as corporation tax and capital taxes) which have been left out of account, but it is clear that the figure exceeds 50% and that this is a minimum figure applicable to virtually everyone in the U.K.

Families and children

So far, we have described the system simply as it relates to a single individual. We should now consider how it is modified in its application to households. In general, the British tax system starts from the premiss that a wife is a dependent of her husband. Thus the husband is responsible for submitting a return of their joint income and is liable for their joint tax. Any income of the wife's is aggregated with his, and in recognition of these obligations he is given an addition (£510 in 1977–8) to his personal allowance. There are two modifications to this general principle. One is 'wife's earned income relief'. A working wife receives a personal allowance of her own, equal to the personal allowance of the single individual, and this is available against her earnings (but not her investment income). There is no consequential reduction in the additional personal allowance given to the husband. The second modification is the availability of an option for separate taxation of the earned income of the two partners. Investment income continues to be added to the income of the husband, who receives only the personal allowance of the single man. Since this option implies the loss of the increment to the married man's personal allowance, it is only advantageous to a couple who would otherwise pay substantial amounts of higher rate tax: i.e. if their joint income exceeds about £10,500. We consider further in Chapter 13 the appropriate treatment of the tax unit.

[1] Estimated from the Cambridge Growth Project model of the U.K. economy.

The household may also include children. Their dependent status has traditionally been recognized by conceding an additional allowance to a taxpayer who is responsible for the maintenance of a child. These allowances have for a long time interacted rather uneasily with family allowances, a system of weekly cash payments to the mother for her second and subsequent children. This interaction was complicated by the introduction of 'clawback', a device by which not only was tax payable on the family allowances themselves, but if family allowances were paid for a child the tax allowance for that child was reduced by £52. This meant that it was advisable for those subject to a sufficiently high marginal tax rate to renounce the allowance altogether (if they understood the system, which it is possible some may have done). It is proposed to replace both family allowances and tax allowances by a single tax-free weekly payment for all children (including the first) paid in the same way as family allowances. These proposals were incorporated in the 1975 Child Benefit Act, but the Government somewhat belatedly noticed that this meant transferring cash from the pay-packet of the wage-earner to the purse of his wife. Finding this unpalatable, it deferred the scheme, but after protest agreed to implement it in stages, and in 1977–8 both a limited cash benefit (of £1 or £1·50 per week) and a limited child allowance (of between £170 and £261) are payable. We return to this question in Chapter 7.

Children are taxed on their own income, as separate individuals. Obviously few children have amounts of income which exceed the exemption limits. To prevent avoidance of too blatant a kind, the investment income of children is taxed as if it had been received by the parents if it is derived from money which the child has been given by the parents. For a brief period, all investment income of children was taxed in this way, but this provision has now been repealed. In principle, the child allowance of the parent is reduced by any earnings of the child over a certain amount. It is likely that this income in fact generally remains unreported, and this has been tacitly recognized by raising the limit to a figure (£350) which exceeds the likely earnings of most children (if not students).

The tax base

For earned income, the definition of the income which is potentially subject to tax poses no particular problems. For investment income, the tax base primarily relates to interest, dividends, and net rents received. Capital gains are not subject to income tax; thus the dividend received from a share is subject to income tax, but any profit made on selling the share is not. Until 1965 such capital gains were generally exempt from tax: since then there has been a distinct capital gains tax, at a rate of 30%, administered in conjunction with the income tax. For small gains, the taxpayer may choose to have half of them taxed as his investment income; for those paying tax at basic or some of the higher rates this is clearly advantageous, while gains are free of tax if annual disposals do not exceed £1,000. The distinction between income and capital gains is blurred, and someone who generates capital gains in a regular way of business may be deemed a trader and find his profits subjected to income tax. Regularity is broadly a sufficient definition of trading, but not a necessary one: the classic case in English law is of a man who made a shrewd purchase of toilet-paper in Germany—once—and whom the Revenue successfully charged with income tax on the resulting profit (*Rutledge* v. *C.I.R.*, 1929).

The tax base is also modified by the existence of a number of minor allowances. In the U.S.A., where such allowances are much more extensive—taxpayers there can, for example, deduct the amount of their medical expenses and their losses from theft—they have become known as 'tax expenditures'. The implicit or explicit suggestion is that such exemptions require justification of much the same kind as is given to positive items of Government expenditure. Such allowances are available to the blind, for single-parent families, to those who need and use the services of a housekeeper. Apart from the basic single and married personal allowances, the items of most significance, in both the amount of the tax expenditure involved and the number of taxpayers affected, are the allowances for mortgage interest, life insurance premiums, and pension contributions. Historically, tax relief was available on all interest payments: and since interest receipts are taxable the logical case for permitting interest payments to be deductible is quite persuasive. In recent years, however, this relief has been systematically restricted, and it is now confined to interest on loans of up to £25,000 whose purpose is stated to be for the purchase or improvement of the taxpayer's main residence.

Tax relief is also available on regular payments for life insurance (which includes contractual savings programmes with minimal life insurance content). Such relief is given on half the premiums, and confined to the basic rate, so that it amounts (at current rates) to a 17% subsidy. There are some (modest) restrictions on qualifying policies to ensure that the life insurance element is not entirely bogus, and an over-all limit of one-sixth on the proportion of income which can be disposed of in this way. An employee's pension contributions to a scheme approved by the Inland Revenue can be deducted in full from his taxable income, and he incurs no liability in respect of contributions made by his employer on his behalf.

Administration

It is useful to begin by setting out the implicit premisses on which administrative arrangements for the British tax system are based. The central assumption is that the taxpayer is incompetent. The procedures therefore seek to ensure that as far as possible the correct amount of any tax liability is deducted from income before it is received, to ensure that the administrative burden on the taxpayer is reduced to a minimum, and that whenever possible such obligations are imposed on employers and other payers of income and on the Inland Revenue itself. As a result it is not only unnecessary for the taxpayer to understand what his liabilities are and how they are computed, but it is difficult for him to understand this even if he wishes to do so. Additionally, the system avoids reliance on the supply of accurate information by the taxpayer, and seeks to check individual returns and secure independent verification of the information supplied whenever possible. Thus while other jurisdictions—America is an extreme contrast—believe what the taxpayer says but penalize him rather heavily if he is found to be lying, in the U.K. prosecution for tax offences is very rare. In 1974–5, 126 people were convicted on income tax charges, including three cases of assault on Inland Revenue Officers. The Revenue prefers to nudge the taxpayer gently until he brings his own declaration into line with what it already knows.

For the vast majority of taxpayers, all or virtually all their earnings are from employment and tax is deducted by their employers under P.A.Y.E. procedures. People in this category, with simple incomes and modest earnings, are normally required to make a return of income only every five years. When they first become potentially subject to tax, they will be asked to file a tax return. This is in general somewhat confusing, since the form appears to be principally concerned with their past income when in fact its actual purpose is to elicit their present circumstances with a view to establishing their future allowances. On the basis of this information the Revenue issues a 'notice of coding' to the taxpayer, and to his employer. The notice of coding is a cryptic document, which concludes with a code number of the form 89H. The numerical part of this code is one-tenth of the taxpayer's total allowances for the year: the letter indicates marital status (H, higher, for married; L, lower, for single persons or married women). But no action is required from the taxpayer: his employer will now deduct tax in the light of this coding using the tax tables with which he is supplied.

Before describing how these tables work, we should notice an important administrative difference between the ways in which the two taxes on earnings—income tax and national insurance contributions—are levied. Income tax is levied on a cumulative basis, so that the whole year's income is taken into account. So in computing liability, low earnings in one week will be offset against high earnings in the next and vice versa. National insurance contributions are charged non-cumulatively, so that liability in each week depends only on earnings in that week, and is not affected by the amounts which are earned in earlier or later weeks. This is why students, who may have earnings which exceed the exemption limits for only a small number of weeks in the year, pay national insurance contributions but do not usually pay income tax; and why people who start work midway through a tax year pay less tax in the first months of employment than they do subsequently. An unusual feature of the British tax system is that income tax is not only levied on a cumulative basis, but also collected on a cumulative basis. In other countries it is common to levy tax cumulatively, but to collect it non-cumulatively. Tax is paid each week on the basis of earnings in that week and if an adjustment is necessary when the whole year's income is assessed (as is often the case for those with fluctuating earnings) this is done at the end of the year.

The British tax system, by contrast, tries to ensure that at each point in the tax year an appropriate proportion of the whole year's liability has been paid. A non-cumulative system credits the taxpayer each week with $\frac{1}{52}$ of his annual allowances. The cumulative system does this also: but if income in any week is less than the allowance for the week then the excess is credited against tax which has previously been paid in the year, and a tax refund becomes due. If all the tax previously paid has been refunded, or at the beginning of the tax year when little or no tax has been paid, these unused allowances cannot be credited against earlier tax payments and are carried forward to be offset against taxable income in future weeks. It is therefore necessary to maintain throughout the year for each taxpayer a record of the total tax he has paid so far and the total allowances ('free pay') for which he has already been given credit. If these procedures work well, they ensure that by the end of the year the taxpayer will have paid the right amount of tax and no significant adjustment to his liability will be required.

The advantages of a system which reaches the right answer in this automatic way are obvious. So are the problems; each taxpayer must carry with him from week to week and employment to employment records of his tax position for the year so far, and this is an expensive administrative operation. One curious aspect of it is the tax refunds which are paid to those who are sick, or unemployed, or on strike. The taxable earnings of a man in this position will generally fall to zero: provided the sickness, unemployment, or strike occurs sufficiently late in the tax year he will receive refunds of the tax he has already paid, at a rate equal to the amount of his average weekly tax allowance, multiplied by the basic rate of tax. (This is about £9·50 per week for a married couple with no other allowances in 1977–8.) Refunds can continue at this rate until all the tax paid has been refunded, or the tax year ends (on 5 April).

The system works less smoothly when an individual's allowances change during the year (perhaps a male taxpayer marries or his wife has children). He must then inform the Inland Revenue which will revise his coding. He receives an immediate refund which reflects the tax he has overpaid in each week of the tax year so far. This system cannot operate in reverse for someone whose allowances go down (because he gets divorced, for example); if it did the taxpayer might have no net income for several weeks as previously underpaid tax was recouped. Broadly, he will be credited with the tax he *should* have paid so far, and the deficiency collected by a reduction in his allowances in future tax years. Fortunately, allowances rise in practice much more often than they fall. An exception was when mortgage interest rates fell sharply in 1977 and tax allowances for many owner-occupiers were reduced correspondingly. Then the cumulative principle was in effect simply abandoned for taxpayers in this position.

Earnings from employment are taxed under what is known as schedule E. Earnings from business are taxed under schedule D. (The authors' salaries are taxed on schedule E but any royalties from this book fall under schedule D.) These terms, which derive from the income tax legislation of 1803, are not referred to in the forms or guidance supplied to the taxpayer, but are of some practical importance to him. A much wider range of expenses can be deducted under schedule D than E: under D the test is broadly that the expenditure was incurred for the purpose of earning the income, while under E it is necessary to suggest that one would be dismissed if one did not spend the money in that way—and in the case of expenditure on travel to work even that is not sufficient justification. Schedule D earnings are subject to a surcharge, described as national insurance contributions, of a flat weekly sum (£2·66 in 1977–8) plus 8% of earnings between £1,750 and £5,500. The administrative procedures for collection are quite different. Tax under schedule D is paid in two lump sums—for the tax year 1977–8 these would be due on 1 January 1978 and 1 July 1978. Liability is calculated on a 'preceding year' basis: thus these assessments would be based on earnings in the year 1976–7. Since business accounts take time to compile there is some reason for this. The tax therefore appears to be paid a year in arrears, which sounds a rather favourable option. However, the system is in fact much more complicated and less advantageous to the self-employed, than this would suggest. It is impossible to provide a brief and intelligible —or indeed lengthy and intelligible—description of the rules but a consequence is that in the early years of a business some components of income may be taxed two or even three times while others will not be taxed at all. This is obviously a licence for abuse, and a number of accountants live well on the proceeds of manipulating these procedures for the benefit of their clients.

The principle of getting hold of the money before the taxpayer has a chance to spend it is applied as far as possible to investment income also. Most payers of interest (though not commercial banks or the National Savings Bank) are required to deduct and transmit to the Revenue the basic rate tax due before sending the balance to the lender. It is interesting to note that one security, War Loan, is exempt from this requirement and stands at a premium in consequence. This tax can be reclaimed by anyone not liable to tax: higher rate taxpayers will be assessed for an additional charge. The treatment of company dividends is more complicated (see pp. 188–90 below) but the effect is the same. A different arrangement is applied to building society interest: in return for a negotiated tax payment by the building society (the so-called composite rate) their interest is exempted from basic rate tax. No refund is available to those who pay no tax, who would therefore be well advised to deposit their money elsewhere (but are often not well advised). Investment income is also taxed on a preceding year basis, though there are some minor differences between the methods used here and those for schedule D income.

These administrative procedures are rather complicated, given the basic simplicity of the system. We consider in subsequent chapters the costs which result and the means by which they might be reduced and procedures simplified.

3

THE TAXATION OF EARNINGS

In Chapter 2 we described the present structure of the U.K. income tax, and we now try to assess its economic effects. It is not obvious that earnings and investment income should both be taxed in the same way, and we consider them separately. In Chapter 3 we deal with some problems in the taxation of employment incomes, first considering the disincentive effects of income tax and then examining increasingly prolific fringe benefits. We show how inflation has affected the rate structure—the problem of 'fiscal drag'—and consider the costs of British tax administration.

In Chapter 4 we illustrate the mechanisms by which the well advised can escape the apparently confiscatory maximum rates of tax on investment income. 'Fiscal drag' is not the only problem which inflation raises for an income tax, and we examine income indexation—the implications of the failure to take account of inflation in the determination of taxable income. We conclude this somewhat dispiriting account with an assessment of the effects of income tax on savings behaviour and the distribution of wealth.

Taxation and effort

The effects of income taxation on work effort are a continuing subject of concern and discussion. This is not surprising—'reduce my taxes so that I can work harder' is generally a more winning argument than 'reduce my taxes so that I can be better off'. Unfortuntely, this makes this an area in which it is hard to disentangle rhetoric from evidence.

In Chapter 1 we described how an income tax would affect work effort in two ways. The income effect describes the way in which tax reduces the taxpayer's real income. It leads him to take less leisure and to do more work, in order to maintain his standard of living, and is a function of the average rate of tax. The substitution effect depends on the way in which tax makes additional work less attractive than additional leisure and is related to the marginal tax rate. This analysis suggests that if we wish to identify those people on whom the effects of taxation on effort is likely to be greatest, we should look at cases where the substitution effect dominates the income effect—typically, where the marginal tax rate substantially exceeds the average rate. It is not necessarily there, however, that most economic damage is likely to be done by taxation. This will occur at the points where the marginal rate of tax is highest and hence the substitution effects are greatest. The total damage done will depend on the numbers of people falling into such categories as well as the size of the effect.

We now turn to the actual British tax structure. High marginal rates are encountered in Britain at income levels where higher rate tax begins to bite effectively—at incomes of £7,000 and above at 1977–8 rates—and increasingly at higher incomes. But they arise also at below-average income levels (those below £3,000 p.a.). The reason why this latter group may pose a problem is not due solely to the operation of the income tax—the rate faced by people in this category is around 40%, the same as that for those on somewhat higher incomes—but to its interaction with the wide range of *ad hoc* means-tested benefits which exists in the U.K. Since these benefits are gradually (or in some cases suddenly) withdrawn as income increases, there is an 'implicit tax rate' applicable to each benefit. This 'implicit tax rate' is the proportion of any rise in income which is lost as a result of an offsetting reduction in benefit. These rates vary from item to item. They include 50% for family income supplement (F.I.S.), 17–25% for rent rebates, and 6–8% for rate rebates, and it is quite possible for several to be operating simultaneously. Each of these involves a different means test, with somewhat different criteria, so that the actual marginal tax rate faced by a low-paid worker may be anything between zero and a figure in excess of 100% depending in an arbitrary way on his particular combination of income and family and other circumstances. (This is the so-called 'poverty trap', discussed in Chapter 7.) But the typical rate is clearly in excess of those applicable at higher incomes. So the function which relates the marginal tax rate to the income of a U.K. employee is U-shaped: the rate of tax he pays on additional earnings is high at low incomes, falls as income grows towards average income, where it stabilizes at around 40%, before rising again with higher rates of tax.

Figure 3.1 illustrates (somewhat schematically) the pattern of marginal rates described above and the average rates which this implies. It enables us to identify the regions in which net disincentive effects are largest (those in which the marginal rate greatly exceeds the average rate) and those in which they are most economically significant (where the marginal rates are high). While there is considerable overlap between these regions, this overlap is not complete: disincentive effects may be fairly large at around average income levels but these may not be as economically important as those whose net effect on effort is smaller and which may arise at very high income levels where high marginal rates are experienced. But the central point is that disincentives will be most marked at the lowest and the highest levels of income. It is to these —especially the former—that most attention has been given in empirical studies.

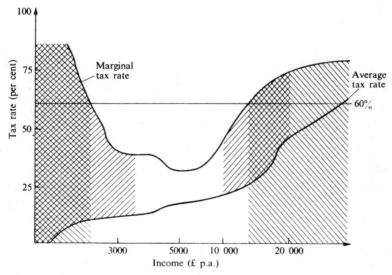

Fig. 3.1. Disincentive effects of taxation

There are a number of econometric studies of the effect fo changes in wages on the number of hours worked and since taxation alters the effective wage we can infer its likely significance from

them. These analyses raise rather difficult technical issues of interpretation, which are by no means fully resolved, and we refer the
reader to the surveys by Stern (1976) and Godfrey (1975). Here we
can only summarize the currently prevailing assessment, which is
that the effect is not very large, and that it is probably negative—
that an increase in a worker's wage leads him to do less work rather
than more. This implies that the income effect of higher earnings
in permitting increased leisure is greater than the substitution
effect's encouragement to additional effort. This may seem startling, but it should not to anyone who has observed that better-paid
workers tend to work shorter hours and receive longer holidays
than those who are poorly paid: and that as the general level of
earnings has increased over the last century or more hours of work
have tended to diminish.

This does not, however, show that a progressive tax system has
little disincentive effect nor, as we have argued above, that such
effects are unimportant. A change in wages leads to both income
and substitution effects, while it is the substitution effect which
matters in assessing the welfare consequences of progressive taxation. By estimating the sizes of these two effects separately we can
judge the likely impact of various taxation systems, and this distinction can be achieved with these econometric methods. Nevertheless, there is still little evidence for large substitution effects.
This position is supported by some of the few experimental studies
to have been undertaken in economics. The Penn-New Jersey
N.I.T. (negative income tax) studies were undertaken in the late
1960s by the U.S. Office of Economic Opportunity, which offered
a selection of low-income families fixed lump sum payments in
return for a fraction of their earnings, and compared their activities
with those of a matched control group. The results of these studies
have been generally interpreted as indicating that the effect of taxation on work incentives is small.

Although this evidence is suggestive, it cannot be regarded as
decisive. We have noted that there are technical problems involved
in statistical studies of this kind and these may bias the conclusions
towards insignificant results. Moreover, the studies are necessarily
concerned with easily measurable dimensions of performance at
work, such as hours of work or earnings in a particular occupation.
If workers are deterred from seeking or accepting promotion by the
effects of taxation, then this will not be adequately measured by

these methods (though it seems improbable that incentive effects, if large, would be confined to those items which cannot easily be appraised). Further, the hours and the effort which people put in at work are closely related to group norms: if these norms are influenced by the existence of taxation, as seems quite likely, then there may be effects on group behaviour which are not fully observable in the actions of individual workers. Although an individual may not be able to choose to work a seven- or a nine-hour shift rather than one which lasts for eight hours, the reason for adopting some particular shift length will be related to the wishes of workers generally; if taxes were different, it is very possible that most people would want to work for longer or shorter periods and that the normal shift length would be changed.

A final, but very important, reservation is that all our discussion so far—theoretical and empirical—relates to what we might describe as 'primary' workers: people who may decide to work more or less but for whom the question of whether or not they enter the labour force is not in doubt. But there are also 'secondary' workers—married women are the most important group in this category—who may choose to work or not according to a range of considerations which will clearly include financial ones. For such workers, what affects their decision to enter the labour force is not any marginal rate of tax but the average rate of tax on the whole of their earnings. This may, depending on the treatment of the tax unit, be affected by the earnings of their husband (in the U.K. it is). The influences on these work/leisure decisions are rather different, although the operation of income and substitution effects may be similar in its end result—taxation by reducing the net earnings of the husband encourages the wife to work but by reducing the net earnings of the wife has a disincentive effect also. The empirical evidence suggests that this aspect of labour supply is much more sensitive to changes in wage rates or taxes than the hours or effort of primary workers: there are determined mainly by conventional expectations and fixed commitments of the family, while it is the wife's labour supply that provides the margin at which adjustments are made and where the main effects of changes in incentives are likely to be observed.

Somewhat different considerations arise in evaluating incentive effects at the other point in the income distribution at which they may potentially be important—near the top. Here we are primarily concerned with managers. We are also more concerned with the quality of effort than with its quantity. The performance of a senior manager may often depend less on how long he spends in the office than on how well he works when he is there—though there may, but need not, be some correlation between the two. His incentive to do better lies not in overtime payments for extra hours but in the hope of promotion and, to a much greater extent than for lower-paid workers, in the intrinsic satisfaction of the job itself. These factors mean that it is much harder, and more subjective, to assess the effects of taxation on managerial effort. Experimental studies are excluded, and there is no body of data which is even potentially available for econometric assessment. Such evidence as exists is derived from interview surveys, which are not (here as in many other economic contexts) a very satisfactory method of investigation: they can reveal attitudes to taxation, but these are not necessarily good indicators of what people actually do. Thus a recent survey (Opinion Research Centre, 1977) established that those with high incomes were more likely to consider the present income tax 'not sensible', but that is neither surprising nor very helpful.

The most carefully designed surveys of the impact of taxation on the higher-paid are those of Break (1957) and Fields and Stanbury (1971). Both these are studies of British solicitors and accountants. These groups are likely to be relatively well informed about the tax system, and are also in a better position than most to vary their effort and hours of work. Break found that only 13% of his sample made plausible reports of disincentive effects of taxation and that the proportion credibly describing incentive effects was almost as great. However, the former (though not the latter) proportion rose substantially with income, as the theoretical analysis would suggest it should, and reached 30% for those with incomes over £5,000 a year. (This is equivalent to between £15,000 and £20,000 at 1977 prices, and someone earning this would, like the £5,000-a-year man of 1956, face a marginal tax rate of about 70%.) Fields and Stanbury replicated Break's work in 1968, and found that disincentive effects had significantly increased: the proportion of their sample reporting these was 19%, and this increase occurred primarily among those on moderate incomes: the fraction among the highest income group remained at 30%. These figures tell us the number of people who plausibly claim that taxation affects their work effort. They do not, however, tell us the magnitude of the effect on those who are influenced: and they are difficult to interpret adequately because they fail to distinguish income and substitution effects. Nevertheless, they are consistent with the hypothesis which was supported for low-income earners; disincentive effects exist, but they are not substantial. A further indication is provided by the observations of both Break and Fields and Stanbury that the hours of work of those reporting disincentives differed little from the rest of their sample. They interpreted this as implying that those most affected were by nature more hard-working: there are alternative, and less disturbing, explanations.

Our discussion of disincentive effects so far relates to the amount of work which people do, given that they choose some particular occupation. But the effects of taxation on whether they choose that occupation at all may be of as much or more practical importance. There are three levels of choice in this decision. First, there is the issue of whether people choose to live in the U.K. rather than in some more lightly taxed jurisdiction—the effects of taxation on the decision to emigrate. We defer a brief discussion of this issue to Chapter 13. Second, given that people live in the U.K. there is the question of whether they choose to work at all or not; we have already noted this possibility for 'secondary' workers, but retirement is also a decision which may be postponed or brought forward in the light of financial considerations influenced by taxation: and this was one of the effects noted by Break. Unlike other disincentives, which depend on the marginal rate of tax, the effects of taxation on the decision to enter or leave the country or the labour force altogether will depend on the average rate of tax on the whole of earnings.

A further issue is the way in which taxation affects choices between jobs. It is well known (for example, Goldthorpe et al., 1970) that car factories, as one example, tend to recruit workers who attach especially great importance to financial rewards and give low priority to a satisfying work environment. Income taxes reduce substantially the differential between jobs like these and others which are less well paid but more congenial. Some friends of the authors are badly paid academics rather than well-paid tax inspectors because they do not feel that the net addition to their income would compensate them for the loss of their friends and fulfilment in their work. High marginal tax rates will make it more difficult to recruit people to these less attractive occupations;

though it is important to note that a society which feels it needs to recruit a certain number of tax inspectors will therefore be forced to raise their pre-tax salaries and thus part of the incidence of the income tax will fall on the employer rather than the employee.

It is widely believed that disincentive effects have increased rather substantially in recent years. This is certainly credible. The basic rate of tax on earned income has risen from around 30% in the early 1960s to about 40% in the mid-1970s: slightly more than half of this increase is due to the introduction of earnings-related national insurance contributions, the rest to increases in the rates of tax. The number of higher rate taxpayers has risen very sharply from 400,000 in 1970–1 to 1·7 million in 1975–6 (out of a total number in the region of 25 million). Thus the marginal rate of tax faced by everyone has increased, and for a significant number of people it has risen substantially. But firm evidence of damage which this has done is very limited. The Opinion Research Centre survey (1977) found that 18% of managers would not accept a job in a different part of the country for a pre-tax pay increase of £5,000 p.a. But three-quarters of them would not subscribe to the view that 'it isn't worth taking promotion because of the effects of taxation on pay increases'. Significantly, a much higher proportion of supervisors and foremen than of more senior managers agreed with that proposition: these may include those starting to face marginal tax rates much in excess of their average rate, but a more probable explanation is that they represent a group for whom financial rewards are more important than non-material aspects of work such as increased responsibility. Indeed for senior managers promotion will often be desired for itself and no net financial inducement is needed to persuade them to accept it.

It is true, however—and this is well documented in the O.R.C. survey—that there has been a major decline in the state of managerial morale in the U.K. in recent years. It seems likely that taxation is an element in this, but it is doubtful whether it is more than one possibly rather minor element in what is in fact a complaint about a decline in real incomes. To the extent that such effects do arise, the average rate of tax probably contributes as much as the conventional disincentive effects of marginal rates. It is impossible to judge the magnitude of these factors, or their effect on management performance. Yet if tax changes could alter this situation at little cost, the case for them would be made. Such a case is difficult to argue, however, on the basis of available evidence of disincentives.

Fringe benefits

High marginal rates of income taxation lead to income being sought and given in untaxed or lightly taxed forms. Thus the employers of well-paid workers in the private sector will tend to offer, not a salary, but a 'total remuneration package', which will include a range of fringe benefits. Such benefits are generally provided on a more extensive scale in Britain than in most other countries: and as a proportion of salary they tend to rise sharply at the same points in the scale as do marginal rates of tax.

TABLE 3.1

Total remuneration, excess over basic salary, 1975

Grade	Median earnings, U.K. (£)	U.K. %	France %	W. Germany %
Foreman	3200	13	5	4
Superintendent	5150	16	7	8
Production manager	7080	29	7	15
Works manager	9170	32	7	21
Manufacturing manager	13 200	33	8	27
General manager	16 950	29	13	29

Source: Hay-M.S.L. Ltd. (1976)

What are these fringe benefits? It is difficult to determine any sensible borderline between conditions of work and benefits. The employer who provides a congenial wash-room for his employees is presumably simply offering a reasonable working environment, while the one who installs a coloured suite in the bathroom of their homes is providing a fringe benefit; but there is a spectrum of benefits in between, and taxation will lead to a tendency for all of them to be substituted for earned income. The cruder forms of fringe benefit, such as the coloured bathroom suites, are liable to be taxed. Holidays are clearly a means by which managers can substitute leisure for taxed income, and their incidence increases with status and remuneration: 42% of top managers have over 21 working days' holiday in the year, compared with 4% of clerical workers and a negligible proportion of manual workers (B.I.M., 1974). Most companies provide meals in some form for their employees while on duty—indeed, large firms are legally obliged to do so. They are not obliged to subsidize them, but implicitly or explicitly most do. This benefit is generally available to all workers but tends to be on a significantly more lavish scale for the higher-paid.

Most firms provide some form of medical and life insurance benefits for managerial employees (and not, in the main, for lower-paid employees). But the most significant benefits provided for them are usually company cars and pensions. The expectation that an employer will provide a car for his top employees is confined to the U.K., where it is more or less universal: 94% of top managers were provided with a company car for their personal use in 1975 (Diamond Commission Report No. 3, 1976). A survey of company attitudes showed clearly that the main motivation for this is the provision of a tax-efficient fringe benefit rather than any transport requirement (B.I.M., 1974). From 1978 such benefits are to be somewhat more heavily taxed. More stringent provisions are now also applied to loans at low interest rates; the best known of these are the cheap mortgages provided by many financial institutions to their employees, although since the interest on these loans would generally be eligible for tax relief the tax advantages to such arrangements are limited. Nothing of the sort, however, applies to pension provisions. Contributions by employees are fully tax-deductible and no liability arises from the value of the employer's contribution. These benefits are limited only by a restriction of the pension which can be paid (before inflation adjustment) to a (tax-free) lump sum of one and a half times final salary and a pension of two-thirds (one-half if the lump sum is taken) of this salary, taxed as earned income.

These provisions are so generous that it is not surprising that the term 'deferred remuneration' has been coined to replace 'pension' as a description of these benefits at high income levels. It is now the case that at top managerial levels high salaries have become more important for the pension entitlements which they confer than for the net of tax value of the salary itself. An addition of £1,000 to the final salary of an 83% taxpayer is worth £170 to him in cash: but it permits the company (if his service with it exceeds twenty years) to make him a tax-free retirement payment of £1,500 and an annual pension of £500 p.a. thereafter (taxable, but in most cases at lower rates). We shall discuss pensions further below: but these provisions not only represent a significant erosion of the tax base but involve a restructuring of remuneration in a form whose impact on incentives is dismal. Whatever view one takes of managerial motivation, it is difficult to believe that it is encouraged in desirable directions by a system in which the most important form of payment to senior employees is their pension. And while it is clearly desirable that retiring employees should be provided with adequate pensions, there is nothing to be said for an outcome in which this becomes hopelessly confused with measures for tax avoidance.

This is reflected rather generally. Partly because incentive payments are often not pensionable, the British tax system encourages benefits such as cars and pensions which are status-related rather than incentives which are performance-related. Table 3.1 showed how Britain runs ahead of an international league in the former kind of supplement to salary; Table 3.2 shows how it runs behind in the latter.

How seriously should we take this proliferation of fringe benefits? It is an inevitable consequence of high marginal tax rates, and while the scope for it can be reduced it cannot be eliminated since in the end no tax authority can or should hope to prevent employers making the lives of their workers more congenial. These benefits do represent a significant erosion of the apparent progressivity of the tax schedule but it is probably only in small firms, where the distinction between personal and corporate expenditure is often unclear, that the erosion is very substantial. The most serious objection is their distorting effect on the ways in which remuneration is paid. First, since many employees do not greatly want these benefits and would, if they could get it, prefer cash in their pockets, they represent a straightforward source of economic inefficiency. Indeed the more stringent the tax regime is in outlawing more attractive fringe benefits the greater these losses are likely to be. But perhaps more serious is that by diverting money which might otherwise be paid as salary into conspicuous items of consumption—company cars, longer holidays, and lavish expenditure on offices, accommodation and travel for senior executives—high tax rates may well serve to increase the visibility of differentials and the extent to which they are resented. Many people would find it easier to see why their employer should pay more to those with

TABLE 3.2

Bonuses and incentive payments as % of basic salary, 1975

Grade	Median earnings, U.K. (£)	U.K.	Australia	France	W. Germany	Canada	U.S.A
Foreman	3200	2	5	1	0	1	2
Superintendent	5150	1	0	3	2	3	4
Production manager	7080	4	2	5	5	4	6
Works manager	9170	4	5	6	8	9	12
Manufacturing manager	13 200	5	4	6	16	13	18
General manager	16 950	6	10	13	11	15	23
Managing director	22 570	4	1	n.a.	n.a.	20	30

Source: Hay-M.S.L. Ltd. (1976)

greater responsibilities than why he should offer them larger desks and plusher carpets, and it is difficult to disagree. Pensions are a much more serious problem, and we return to this below.

Inflation

In many ways, inflation has been a more potent influence for change in the structure of British taxation than any explicit reforms in recent years. Income tax has been subject to a phenomenon which has been somewhat inelegantly christened 'fiscal drag'. This arises from the effect of a progressive tax structure in an inflationary environment. In these circumstances, higher and higher levels of money income correspond to fixed levels of real income. If tax brackets are fixed in terms of money incomes, someone who is no better off after adjustment for price changes finds himself paying higher and higher effective rates of tax. Thus the revenue's take, as a proportion of total personal income, will increase steadily: and this is precisely what has happened. Figures 3.2 and 3.3 show why. If we look at the average tax rates shown in Fig. 3.2, the rate

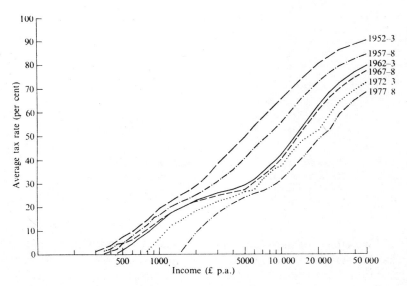

Fig. 3.2. Tax rates payable at various income levels, 1952–1978
(tax payable by a married man with no other allowances)

schedule appears to have slowly drifted downwards at each level of money income. If, as in Fig. 3.3, one adjusts for the change in average earnings over the period, the picture is dramatically changed. Although tax thresholds have frequently been raised in money terms, they have generally declined in real terms. In 1952–3 a married man had to earn almost £800 per year to be liable for standard rate tax. If his salary kept pace with average earnings over the next twenty-five years, it would have risen to around £6,500 and he would have been on the verge of paying the higher rates.

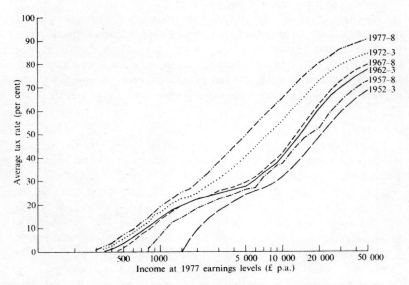

Fig. 3.3. Tax rates payable at various real income levels, 1952–1978 (data as in Fig. 3.2, adjusted to 1977 using Index of Average Weekly Earnings from D.O.E. Gazette)

Two effects of fiscal drag merit special attention. One is that it has substantially shifted the balance between direct and indirect taxation. This feature is more marked because several major U.K. indirect taxes are specific monetary amounts, which therefore decline in real value with inflation. For example, there are taxes of o·9p per cigarette and 30p per gallon of petrol. In 1965 income tax (including national insurance contributions) raised 45% of total Government current receipts and indirect taxes 29%. In 1975 these proportions were 53% and 23% respectively: income tax revenue rose by 300% over a period in which prices generally went up by 125%. The second effect is that the percentage wage increase required to maintain a given real income net of tax is for all individuals higher than the rise in the cost of living, and higher by an amount which varies depending on the initial level of income. In fact the ratio of the required rise in wages to the increase in the cost of living depends on the ratio of the marginal tax rate to the average. Thus in Fig. 3.1 the ranges in which we noted the probability of major disincentive effects, because of high marginal rates relative to average, are also precisely those in which fiscal drag is most marked—at below-average and fairly (but not very) high incomes. Even if the over-all tax burden is not increased—by adjustment to the rates of these or other taxes—there will be redistribution away from those with incomes in these ranges in the distribution towards the rest of the community. It is therefore not surprising that it is at these points in the distribution that recent dissatisfaction with the income tax structure has been greatest.

There is only one answer to the problem of fiscal drag; indeed, there is only one way of ensuring that inflation does not by accident change things which there is no deliberate intention to change, and that is indexation. Measures of this kind have been adopted in Canada, Denmark, Holland, and Sweden. In the course of debate on the 1977 Finance Act, pressure by back-benchers secured the passage of an amendment requiring indexation of the basic single and married (and some other) personal allowances in the U.K. This required the Government to increase these allowances each year by the amount of the increase in retail prices over the preceding year. Scepticism about the strength of the Treasury's commitment to this policy was fully justified when subsequent changes in personal allowances for 1977–8 were described as reductions due in 1978–9 but backdated one year, thus nullifying the effect of the indexation provisions and fully restoring administrative discretion. Despite this disingenuous manoeuvre, we retain some hope that it will be more difficult in future to describe what are in fact increases in income tax as reductions. We give some examples in Table 3.3, which demonstrates clearly why despite repeated assertions in budget statements that changes in tax allowances will exempt large numbers of low-paid workers from tax the actual number of tax-payers has not fallen.

TABLE 3.3

Inflation and taxation, 1972–1978

($£$)

Year	Single personal allowance	Stated increase	Required figure	Actual increase
1972–3	460	135	345	115
1973–4	595[1]	—	645	50 reduction
1974–5	625	30	685	60 reduction
1975–6	675	50	760	85 reduction
1976–7	735	60	803	68 reduction
1977–8	945	210	863	82

Note: Required figure' is previous year's allowance adjusted for price changes.
[1] Note change to unified tax system in 1973 (p.20).
Source: Own calculations using April–April change in index of retail prices.

Administration

The administration of any tax system is an inevitable butt of criticism, but there are two characteristics of British tax administration which can be given objective description: it is very expensive, and very few people understand how it works. Collection costs absorb about 2% of income tax receipts; while this proportion may not seem high, tax revenue is such that it represents a large absolute figure and a fraction which is high judged either by historical or international standards. Inland Revenue costs rose rather more than fourfold between 1966–7 and 1975–6, from £78 m. to £354 m. During this period, prices generally doubled, so that the real increase in Revenue costs was around 100%. This increase is more worrying because unexplained: while the costs of collecting indirect taxes have risen even more dramatically (see p. 138 below), this is in part attributable to the shift to less efficient collection methods (the replacement of purchase tax by V.A.T.), but nothing of the kind has happened with income tax. As noted above, income tax receipts have risen much faster than prices generally—though still not as rapidly as the costs of collection—but in any case this can provide little explanation. The number of taxpayers has not increased significantly and it should not cost twice as much—or even much more—to collect twice as much tax by the same methods from the same individual. Progress in introducing computerized systems has been extremely limited, and retarded by technical problems and frequent changes in plans.

As a proportion of tax receipts, British collection costs are now much higher than in comparable countries: twice as high as in Sweden or Canada, four times as high as in the U.S.A. (Barr *et al.* 1977). The Inland Revenue employs about 86,000 people; slightly more than the number who work for the U.S. Internal Revenue although the latter deals with about four times as many taxpayers. These calculations leave out administrative costs imposed on taxpayers (which are certainly higher in the U.S.A.) and on employers (which are probably higher in the U.K.). Sandford (1973) suggests that the total administrative costs of U.K. income tax are in the range of 4%–6% of revenue.

We saw in Chapter 2 that an advantage of this elaborate administrative machinery is that the taxpayer is required to do comparatively little tax work for himself, but a consequence of that is that he knows very little about what is being done to him. In the 1950s the Government Social Survey concluded that 'our evidence suggests that if productivity is related to income tax in any way it can only be related to misconceptions about the system. It cannot be related to the system because only 3 or 4% are sufficiently informed of the system' (Radcliffe Report, 1954, App. 1, para. 129). More recently, Brown (1968) found that only 3% of a sample of workers could even tell him what the basic rate of tax was (although all of them were paying it), and less than half of a group of managers possessed even this elementary information. (It is possible that understanding may have increased since the administrative changes in 1973.) And in spite of the apparent advantages to him of a wholly automatic system of tax deduction, the bewildered British taxpayer is in contact with the Inland Revenue more frequently than his American counterpart (four times as often, according to the estimates of Barr *et al.*). The American taxpayer must complete a return every year, but normally that is the only correspondence with the Internal Revenue which he has.

In its central elements, the British tax structure is simpler than that of most other countries, with a rather limited range of deductions and a very straightforward rate structure. It is peripheral aspects of its operation which preclude understanding. Whatever the merits of the cumulative P.A.Y.E. system, it has the effect that the weekly deductions made from wages are computed on a basis which is not explained or in practice explicable to the average worker. The interaction of cumulative income tax deductions with non-cumulative national insurance contributions computed on different principles aggravates this. The schedular system and the preceding year basis require professional tax expertise for adequate comprehension, and indeed description of them is to be found only in technical literature. The representative taxpayer rarely makes a tax return, and as a rule does not see any statement of how his liabilities have been computed. Filling in such a return is not a purposive activity: it does not enable the recipient to check how much tax he owes or is owed, or indeed to do anything except post the form back to the tax inspector, and it is therefore not surprising that this generates irritation rather than understanding. It is extraordinary that the design of tax forms which do allow the respondent to check his liabilities is left to commercial organizations such as the magazine *Money Which*. The appearance of both the tax return and the accompanying instructions compare very unfavourably with similar documents in other countries. It is difficult to resist the conclusion that the Inland Revenue does not feel that its work could be helped if the taxpayer had a better understanding of the basis or methods of collection of the taxes involved.

4

THE TAXATION OF
INVESTMENT INCOME AND SAVINGS

WE described in Chapter 2 how investment income is taxed as ordinary income but is subject to a surcharge which rises to 15%. Thus the top rate of income tax in the U.K., payable on investment income by those with total taxable income in excess of £21,000 p.a., is 98%. It must be obvious to anyone who stops to think about the matter for a few minutes that it is entirely impracticable to tax things at 98%. The pressure to avoid tax becomes so strong that virtually any avoidance scheme becomes worth while, and no aspect of the activity in question is of any importance other than its tax implications. Even if as a result of measures for avoidance four-fifths of the receipts disappear, the after-tax returns have been multiplied tenfold. If actions yield 49 times as much to the Inland Revenue as they do to the taxpayer, then no one will engage in them, except by accident or mistake: and if finding loopholes is so profitable then it will prove impossible to stop them up. But in Britain no one has tried very hard to stop them up anyway. There are three major methods of getting round the taxation of investment income in this country, and together they enable those potentially liable to this tax to drive a coach and horses, or perhaps a large Rolls Royce, through the structure of the tax.

The first of these methods arises because capital gains are not taxed as income but at a maximum rate of 30%. Since many forms of investment income can be turned without difficulty into capital gains (and back again if desired), this is what any sensible higher rate taxpayer will do. Consider the case of a 98% taxpayer wishing to invest £100 for a secure return over a period of five years. He might consider investing this in Treasury 14% Stock 1982, which could on 1 January 1977 be bought for around £100 and which would have paid him £14 gross in interest in each of the next five years—on which he would have paid £13.72 in tax, leaving him a net 28p per annum—and have returned his £100 in 1982. Before doing this, however, he would have been wise to consult a competent stockbroker, who would have advised him to purchase Treasury 3% Stock 1982 instead. £100 in nominal value of this stock yields £3 per annum till 1982, when it will also be repaid at £100. But because of the low interest rate it offers, the price of this stock is well below £100: it could have been purchased on the same day for around £73 per £100 nominal. Thus he could have purchased for his £100 stock with a face value of £137. This would pay £4·11 in gross annual interest, from which he would retain a net 8p which would just about cover the cost of the ink used in completing his annual tax returns. But he would make over the five years a capital gain of £37 (which on Government Stock is tax-free), since his stock will be redeemed in 1982 for £137. This is equivalent to an annual income of £6–£7. It is a minor nuisance to receive income in a lump sum at the end, but since the stock is readily marketable and can be relied on to appreciate steadily in value from 1977 to 1982, he can if he wishes receive an annual income by selling off each year sufficient of the stock to maintain at about £100 the capital value of the amount invested.

Thus by a suitable choice of investment, the 98% taxpayer could earn a perfectly secure annual income of between 6% and 7% per annum, or just under half the 14% which is available to someone who pays no tax. The effective rate of tax is therefore not 98%, but something in the range 50%–60%. Everyone connected with the investment business knows this, and indeed it is universally assumed that the reason the Bank of England issued this Treasury 3% Stock is that it would be attractive to higher rate taxpayers. But it is in no way exceptional. Similar opportunities exist for either shorter- or longer-term investments. Nor would it matter if the Bank of England were to stop conniving at tax avoidance schemes. There is a similar stock issued by the World Bank, which promises at least as great security, and other stocks of first-rate private companies with similar characteristics: these are subject to capital gains tax (at 30%) but in compensation the capital gain which can be expected from them is somewhat greater. (This is an instance of capitalized taxes and tax exemptions, as described in Chapter 1.)

Higher rate taxpayers not only buy stocks such as these, but also property and ordinary shares in companies. All of these investments are also held by tax-exempt institutions (such as pension funds), and since property and shares regularly provide an income yield (rent or dividends) which has recently averaged between 5% and 10% less than the secure fixed income from Government stocks it follows that these institutions must expect capital gains of at least that amount. If these expectations materialized, then the higher rate taxpayer could anticipate a total return (after both income and capital gains tax) of perhaps 5%. In fact he should do better than this, since he can invest in so-called 'growth stocks' which offer particularly low incomes but high opportunities for capital gain: to pick a random example, Associated Dairies is a rapidly expanding hypermarket chain whose shares in January 1977 yielded less than 1% but whose profits (and hence share value) were expected to show a rapid increase. Similar opportunities— such as reversions, properties with low current rents due for eventual review—exist in other fields. Investment trusts exist whose objective is to eliminate taxable income by turning it into capital gains (which are then favourably taxed), though these have not had the success for which their promoters or investors had hoped.

It is of course true that these capital gains are in the main less certain than the income yield from investment. Thus this part of the tax system operates so as to more or less eliminate the secure component of the returns from wealth while leaving the variable component unscathed. It is therefore a substantial inducement to speculative investment. Paradoxically, this is a factor which tends to increase inequalities of income and wealth. But it is likely that in recent years with a volatile stock-market and collapsed property boom it has destroyed more fortunes than it has made. In consequence, private investors have shown strong inclinations to seek greater security, and in all recent years the personal sector has been a substantial net seller of equities and a net purchaser of fixed interest securities, as individuals seek the safer haven of secure capital gains from stocks like Treasury 3% 1982. At present, at least £3,000 m. is invested in Government stocks which are clearly unattractive to anyone who is not a higher rate taxpayer: some examples are shown in Table 4.1. The tax system has, in effect, pushed private investors out of traditional 'middle-of-the-road' investments like good-quality equities, properties, and bank deposits and into fringe activities like 'performance shares', geared investments in property, and portfolio investment abroad, as well as higher rate taxpayers' stocks, which promise—but do not necessarily deliver—above-average capital gains. This is part of the general mangling of patterns of savings and investment in this country by the tax system, to which we shall return.

TABLE 4.1

Government stocks for higher rate taxpayers

Stock	Yield to 98% taxpayer	Yield to non-taxpayer	Yield on comparable stock	Amount invested
	%	%	%	(£ m.)
Treasury 3% 1979	3·2	6·3	10·0	608
Electricity 3½% 1979	2·9	6·3	10·1	235
Treasury 3½% 1980	2·7	6·0	9·8	245
Treasury 3½% 1981	3·6	6·9	10·7	432
Treasury 3% 1982	3·9	6·9	11·2	340
Transport 3% 1988	5·4	9·6	11·3	591
Gas 3% 1995	5·6	11·2	13·6	81
Redemption 3% 1996	5·2	11·1	13·7	15
Funding 3½% 2004	4·5	12·4	13·3	138
				2685

Notes: (1) Based on prices on 27 July 1977.
(2) 'Comparable stocks' are similar stocks more suitable for those who do not pay tax: significantly higher yields are available in all cases.
(3) Short-dated stocks are assumed to be sold with maximal accrued interest.

Source: Own calculations.

The second difficulty in the taxation of investment income is that a good deal of income accrues to institutions rather than to people, and is consequently taxed on a different basis. The most important of these institutions are life insurance companies, corporations, and trusts. Since the income of these is, for obvious reasons, taxed at much less than 98%, it is clearly convenient for higher rate taxpayers to arrange for their income to be accumulated by an institution rather than by themselves. This is less convenient if they actually wish to spend the income, since it cannot be distributed to the ultimate beneficiary without being subject to tax: but this difficulty can be surmounted if the taxpayer spends his *capital* while using the accumulated interest to replace it over time. This system is so easy to operate that its most extreme abuses have been checked: the investment income of bogus companies is liable to be attributed to its owners, as is the income of a trust which is permitted to pay money out to the person who put it in. But there are so many variations on the theme that there are still many that can be played.

A simple example of how this works is as follows. Consider someone paying the top marginal tax rate of 98%. If he is able to earn 12% on £1 m. of his investments, he will obtain £120,000 per annum, which tax will reduce to £2,400. Instead, he might use £300,000 to set up a trust to accumulate for the benefit of his children. The income of this trust will generally be taxed at 49% (34% basic rate plus 15% investment income surcharge) so that if the trust can earn 12% before tax also, it obtains just over 6% after tax and will in twenty years' time be worth over £1 m. In the meantime, the settlor can spend the £700,000 which remains from his original £1 m. at a rate of rather more than £35,000 a year. He has therefore multiplied his spending power by 15 while preserving his wealth for his children. For people who are not rich enough to set up trusts, life insurance policies can be used in a rather similar way.[1]

The third loophole in the taxation of investment income is the simplest and probably the most widespread. This is simply to buy durable goods. If investment in shares, in bank deposits, or in investment property is very heavily taxed, it is not very surprising that many rich people buy large houses, or several houses, valuable pictures and furniture, cars, hobby farms, and so on. Such purchases yield no taxable income: their main return is the pleasure they give to the owner, his family, and his friends—which does not have to be very great to exceed the net of tax return they would obtain from more productive investments. These items can be expected broadly to maintain their real value in the long run: if they generate capital gains, these are lightly taxed, and then only if they are actually sold. Thus the tax system not only diverts private funds away from productive purposes, but into forms which encourage the kind of conspicuous display of wealth which its architects were presumably hoping to reduce.

The three methods we have described—the transformation of

---

[1] These measures will also have effects (normally advantageous) on capital transfer tax liability. See Chapter 10.

income into capital gains, the use of an institution to hide income while capital is spent, and the diversion of wealth into non-income-yielding forms—are by no means the only ways round the heavy taxes on investment income nominally imposed in the British tax system. But to list them is sufficient for our present purpose. This is to show that these taxes are entirely farcical, and despite the appearance of swingeing rates rising to 98% anyone who is paying an *effective* tax rate on such income of more than 50%–60% ought to obtain better professional advice. Given that this is so, it is interesting to speculate on the motives of those who are responsible for imposing these taxes. It is possible that they do not know how little they correspond to reality, but it seems unlikely. It is possible that although the politicians and administrators most closely involved know that the appearance of immense progressivity is a sham, they believe that this appearance will deceive others into thinking that such objectives are being achieved. It is hard to imagine that the deception is successful, and the explanation is not one which flatters either group. The hypocritical nature of the present situation reflects little credit on the British tax system or on the British political system.

Income indexation

The problems which inflation raises for an income tax are not confined to fiscal drag and the decline in the real value of tax thresholds. Inflation poses difficulties for the definition of income itself. When prices are stable, an investor who earns 3% on £100 he deposits in the bank is better off by that amount at the end of the year: £3 is the sum which he can prudently spend while maintaining his capital and his ability to earn a similar sum in future years. When inflation runs at 20% per annum, the man who earns 12% on his bank deposit is in a very different position: the interest he receives is significantly short of what he needs simply to stay as well off as he was when he deposited the money in the first place. Thus when inflation is taken into account his real income is negative, not positive: he cannot spend this £12 except by making himself worse off in future, and hence it is as much part of his capital as is his basic £100. Nevertheless, the taxman will present a demand for 34% (or up to 98%) of his nominal income of £12, so that the amount by which his receipts after tax fall short of what is required to keep pace with inflation is greater still.

While fiscal drag describes the impact of inflation on effective rates of tax, the problem of income indexation refers to the definition of the tax base. This difficulty has received some, but rather selective, attention. There has been widespread acknowledgement that many of the capital gains made in an inflationary environment are fictitious, and in 1977 a pledge was made to 'look sympathetically' at this problem. The complexities of computing the 'real' profits of companies have been extensively discussed, mainly as a result of the business liquidity crisis of 1974, and the related interest in 'inflation accounting'. We consider this issue further in Chapter 12. But the problems of measuring income when inflation is rapid are not confined to the business sector; the illusory nature of monetary returns from investment applies just as much to the income of individuals.

There is no difficulty in principle in adjusting the taxation of capital gains to take account of inflation. At present the taxable gain is the value on realization minus the original acquisition cost. To index the gain all we have to do is to increase the acquisition cost by the rate of inflation during the period between acquisition and realization. Each year the Government would publish a table of inflation factors showing the rate of inflation between any two dates, as measured by a suitable index. For example, suppose an individual bought an asset in 1971 for £1,000 and sold it in 1976 for £5,000. The table of inflation factors might show that between 1971 and 1976 the rate of inflation was 90%. We then increase the acquisition cost by 90% to obtain an indexed acquisition cost of £1,900. This gives a taxable gain of £3,100 as compared to a gain of £4,000 under the current tax system. If, on the other hand, the asset had cost £3,000, the notional acquisition cost would be £5,700, which exceeds the proceeds of the sale, and hence the result would be that many 'gains' would turn into losses. These calculations, although somewhat complex, are both simpler and more logical than alternative suggestions for 'tapering' the rate of tax according to the length of time for which an asset has been held.

But this is not the end of the story. As we have seen, it is not simply capital gains which are overstated when inflation occurs; and it would be wrong to index capital gains, but not other forms of unearned income, such as interest on bank and building society deposits, which generally accrue to less well-off individuals. The erosion of real capital values in inflationary times is no less true for the owners of small savings accounts than for the owners of ordinary shares. To index interest income we must distinguish between the *money* rate of return which an individual earns, and the *real* rate of return which is equal to that money rate of return minus the rate of inflation. For tax purposes this implies that taxable income is identified by multiplying actual cash receipts of interest income by the ratio of the real rate of interest to the money rate of interest. The Government would have to know not only the rate of inflation but also the interest rate which had been paid on each individual's savings, which can often change several times during a year (as during the rapid fall in interest rates during 1976–7).

But we must go on to look at the consequences for interest payments which are tax-deductible. For if we are to tax only real receipts of interest, only real interest payments can be allowed as a deduction. This would have some alarming implications for home-owners. Imagine a young couple who had just taken out a mortgage for £10,000 at an interest rate of 10%. As matters stand now they would receive a tax allowance of £1,000 a year for mortgage interest. But suppose indexation were introduced and only real interest was deductible. In the last few years the inflation rate has been around 15% which means that the real interest rate was *minus* 5%, and, according to the indexation formula, the couple would receive a tax allowance of minus £500! In other words, instead of receiving a tax allowance of £1,000 their allowances would actually be reduced by £500. A change of this magnitude would obviously bankrupt many home-owners unless other changes in the terms of the mortgage loan were made. For example, the repayments to the building society could themselves be indexed and would then start off at a low level and increase year by year in line with inflation. It is clear that indexation is an all-or-nothing affair. Once one starts it is impossible to stop until the whole tax system and the capital market has been changed. This is not to argue against indexation, on the contrary we think it is desirable in itself and an essential part of an equitable income tax, but to point out that indexation would involve substantial problems, of both a transitional and a long-run character.

We must now bring together this discussion with that of the preceding section. We have shown that the effective rates of tax on investment income are much lower than they purport to be; but we have also shown that the concept of investment income which is subject to tax described a tax base which, in inflationary conditions, is much higher than it ought to be. The net effect of the combination of these two factors depends on the nature of the portfolio an individual holds, the structure of interest rates, the rate of inflation, and many other factors. But in recent years there can be little doubt that the second of these distortions has been of greater quantitative significance than the first: that wealth-holders have been taxed on income which, in real terms, did not exist and that as a result the real value of the holdings of the representative individual in this category has declined. It is in many ways more appropriate, then, to regard the failure to index taxable investment income as a tax on wealth—it is certainly both a more serious and a more effective tax on wealth than the explicit one which has been proposed—and we develop this argument in Chapter 10.

It might be argued that a sort of rough justice operates in which the two anomalies described cancel out: that the excessive size of the tax base compensates for the ineffectiveness of the rates (or vice versa). That is not a view we can accept. It is not the case that unduly light taxation on one individual makes up for the unfairly heavy taxation of someone else. The effect of the present system of taxing investment income is that the tax payable on any particular component of *real* income can vary from zero to many times the amount of the income. Those rates are arbitrary and haphazard in their incidence: this is not only inequitable but also inefficient since there is no economic rationale to this pattern and any correlation between the social desirability of a particular transaction and the applicable effective tax rate is probably negative rather than positive. This has created major distortions in the capital market: but the ones created by the tax treatment of savings in the U.K. are much greater.

Taxation and savings

A major effect of the British tax system has been its effect on savings behaviour. Mill's dictum that 'no income tax is really just, from which savings are not exempted' (1865, p. 404), i.e. no income tax is just unless it is an expenditure tax, has not been generally accepted. But there are three forms of savings which do receive exemption or highly favourable tax treatment: investment in owner-occupied housing, pension funds, and life insurance. In consequence, these means of saving now account, in aggregate, for almost the *whole* of net personal saving in the U.K. (Table 4.2). We consider each of them in turn.

TABLE 4.2

Personal saving in the U.K. and U.S.A.

| | U.K.
(£ m.) | | | % | |
	1972	1974	1976	U.K. Average 1972–6	U.S.A. 1974
Total personal saving	2500	6713	9903	100·0	100·0
Investment in houses	1388	1656	2286	30·5	27·1
Superannuation funds	1421	2190	{5368}	39·6	20·8
Life insurance	1007	1057		18·8	8·9
Total, privileged saving	3816	4903	7654	88·9	56·0
National Savings	813	45	757		
Govt. stock, and local authority debt	−109	1273	1968	−1·9	27·2
Company securities and unit trusts	−1231	−1299	−1202		
Total, securities	−527	+19	+1523		
Building society deposits	2139	2017	3580		
less lending for house purchase	−2782	−2278	−3965		
Bank and finance house deposits	1740	2975	1323	14·1	9·0
less personal borrowing	−2308	−196	−995		
	−1211	2518	−37		
Other and unidentified	422	−727	763	−1·1	6·9

U.K. average is computed with figures adjusted to constant prices by C.P.I.

Sources: Based on data from: *Financial Statistics*; C.S.O., *National Income and Expenditure*; *Statistical Abstract of the U.S.*

Owner-occupied housing is given favourable tax treatment in several different ways. The income which is derived from it is not subject to tax. This concept of income from owner-occupation puzzles many people, who see their houses as items of expenditure, not of income. If individual X rents a house from individual Y, the rent which is paid is taxable income in the hands of Y. But if X and

Y happen to be the same person—i.e. if the owner of the house is also the occupier—no money actually changes hands and so the tax liability disappears. There is therefore a strong tax incentive for them to be the same person—a bias in favour of owner-occupation as against renting. At one time, tax was imposed on the notional 'income' from an owner-occupied house, under schedule A of income tax legislation. This tax was based on the rateable value of the house, a sum which was computed primarily for the purpose of levying local rates, and which purported to be the amount for which the property could have been rented in 1939. These figures became increasingly ludicrous, and when rateable values were revised in 1963 the Government was faced with the options of facing angry reactions to enormous increases in the amount of tax payable under schedule A or abolishing it altogether: they adopted the latter course. In addition to the exemption of this schedule A income the interest paid on loans of up to £25,000 for house purchase attracts tax relief. As we have noted, the anomaly here is not so much that this interest is deductible but that other interest payments are not. And finally, while capital gains in general are taxed those which are obtained on the taxpayer's principal residence are exempt.

It is the experience of most commentators on taxation that there is nothing more calculated to provoke a flood of apoplectic letters to the newspapers than the suggestion that the tax system is unduly favourable to owner-occupiers. Although the existence of the tax privileges we have described is incontrovertible, the writers of these letters have a point. What the tax system favours is owner-occupation, not owner-occupiers, and this distinction is not always made clear. It is not simply taxation which has led to the disappearance of private rented housing in this country—the existence of rent control and other legislation to protect tenants has probably been more important—but this has undoubtedly been a contributory factor. The result is that the only widely available forms of tenure in this country are now local authority housing and owner-occupation, and people who are not interested in or not eligible for the former have little alternative to the latter.

They are then faced with buying houses at prices which have been forced up by the tax-stimulated demand for them: prices which reflect the capitalized value of the tax concessions, as described in Chapter 1. Because mortgage finance for house-buyers is not unlimited, it is unlikely that these concessions have been fully capitalized, and housing is still probably the best investment available to private individuals even now, but it is certain that house prices are higher than they would otherwise be. Thus current house-buyers obtain relatively little benefit from the concessions. Indeed they may be worse off, since young married couples are forced to save for deposits towards house purchase or to repay associated mortgages at a time in their lives when incomes are low, outgoings high, and large compulsory savings of this kind inappropriate. In a better-organized world, many people in this category would rent property, at least for a time, and that is what they do in many other countries.

The principal losers from these features of the tax system have been people who might have preferred to rent property—people who find mortgage repayments a very serious burden, people who have or would like to have jobs which involve frequent movement around the country. The principal gainers have been those who have owned houses in the past—or rather their descendants, since capital gains on the house you are living in are virtually unrealizable. Perhaps if it had been understood that the main beneficiaries of the policy of tax concessions to owner-occupation were the dead the policy might have been adopted somewhat less enthusiastically. (Their descendants will also benefit, and we consider in Chapter 10 whether it might be possible to achieve rather greater equity and recoup some lost revenue by imposing taxes when owner-occupied houses are passed on to the next generation.) But this account demonstrates why tax capitalization is such a dangerous trap—although we believe it would be better if the system had never incorporated these concessions it does not seem that it would now be either equitable or desirable to withdraw them. The losses from so doing would be principally borne by those who are currently struggling to meet the initial mortgage repayments on a house—people who have derived little benefit from the concessions and who may actually have suffered from them.

The second favoured form of personal saving in the U.K. is life insurance. The most important tax concession given is that half of all premiums paid can be deducted from taxable income: eligible premiums may not exceed one-sixth of total income and relief is restricted to the basic rate. This amounts, at current rates, to a 17% subsidy on these premiums. The funds of life insurance companies are favourably taxed: although in principle they are subject to corporation tax at $37\frac{1}{2}\%$ (slightly above the basic rate of income tax), for a variety of complicated reasons, some of which are valid but several of which are not, very little tax is actually paid (Kay and Parkin, 1978). In 1975 some £120 m. was raised from the gross investment income of £1,590 m. of ordinary branch life insurance funds (Life Offices Association, 1976). Policies which qualify for these subsidies also exempt their holder from any liability for higher rate tax on the profits derived from them. Without these tax concessions, life insurance would be a thoroughly unattractive method of saving. Kay and Parkin examined the results of 61 companies for a 10-year endowment insurance policy with profits maturing in 1976. The median proceeds for a man aged 39 who had invested £10 per month were £1,593, an effective rate of return of $6\cdot1\%$. If he had simply deposited the money in a building society paying the standard interest rate recommended by the Building Societies Association, the same individual would have accumulated £1,621 over this period. He would also have been able to reduce, increase, or discontinue payments and to withdraw part or all of his savings at any time, so that it is likely that, given a free choice, he would have preferred to do so: and if he had saved regularly in this way almost all building societies would have paid him an enhanced rate of interest, increasing his proceeds by something between £50 and £100 and outperforming all but a handful of life insurance companies. The returns from 'without profit' policies were much worse: the median outcome from a sample of 46 companies was £1,306 (which should be compared with the £1,200 paid to the company over the period).

This picture is transformed by the tax subsidy: investment in a life insurance policy would have brought tax relief over the period totalling just under £200, while the building society could have offered nothing of the kind. The effect of this is to increase the number of insurance companies which 'beat' the building society from 19 out of 61 to 59 out of 61. (Even with this help, no non-profit policy gave an acceptable return.) It is very clear why life policies are an increasingly popular form of saving in the U.K., while in the U.S., where the tax advantages attached are very limited (see Goode, 1976), such contracts have steadily declined in importance: they comprised $11\cdot7\%$ of net personal financial assets in 1945 and $8\cdot9\%$ in 1970 (Bureau of the Census, 1976).

This discussion ignores the 'pure insurance' element of these contracts: the obligation on the company to pay a guaranteed sum in the event of the premature death of the policy-holder. However, the insurance content of the majority of contracts sold as life insurance policies is negligible. The actuarial value of the insurance element of the policies described above is about £8—less than 1% of the premiums paid and actually less than 5% of the tax relief obtained. Anyone substantially motivated to take out such a policy by insurance considerations was seriously misinformed—though in view of the selling efforts associated with the industry it is possible that some people were. This means that any justification of the present tax relief must relate to the desirability of contractual savings programmes, rather than life insurance as such—yet recent legislation has been explicitly aimed at denying relief to such plans unless they are disguised as life insurance policies.

The third form of privileged saving is through pension funds. Provided the fund meets a series of Inland Revenue criteria, pension contributions (whether made by employer or by employee) are excluded from income, and no tax is levied on the investment income of pension funds; but payments out of such a fund are taxable in full as earned income (except for the quarter which may be commuted as lump sum). In effect, savings of this kind are exempted from taxation while withdrawals are taxed, in just the manner which would be applied to all savings under an expenditure tax, which we discuss in Chapters 5 and 6. As a result, such schemes have been growing very rapidly. This growth is certain to continue, as social changes and legislation extend the coverage of occupational pension schemes to include manual as well as white-collar employees.

These factors have had very dramatic effects indeed on the structure and composition of personal wealth in the U.K. Over the twenty-year period for which data are available, the proportion of personal wealth which these three forms of privileged asset— houses, life insurance policies, and pension funds—comprise has risen from about 40% to almost 65%. The details are set out in Table 4.3, and comparative figures are provided for the U.S.A. Since the rise in importance of housing overshadows the increasing role of life insurance and superannuation schemes, it is worth emphasizing that as a proportion of financial assets alone these two comprise 39% (U.K., 1973); 26% (U.K., 1957); 21% (U.S.A., 1973).

TABLE 4.3

The composition of personal wealth

(%)

	U.K. 1957	U.K. 1973	U.S.A. 1973
Houses	26·6	49·9	35·6
(less mortgages)	(7·5)	(10·1)	(14·9)
Net housing	19·1	39·8	20·7
Life insurance	8·9	10·9	5·9
Pension funds	11·7	12·5	12·1
Equities	22·0	12·0	29·2
Govt. securities and bonds	23·4	13·9	10·1
Deposits	21·6	20·2	31·6
Other wealth less borrowing	(6·6)	(9·3)	(9·6)
Total wealth per head	100·0	100·0	100·0
(£, 1973 prices	1774	3431	4935)

Sources: Revell (1967); Diamond Commission (1977), Report No. 4; *Statistical Abstract of U.S.*; *I.M.F. Financial Statistics.*

These privileged assets all have certain characteristics in common. They are all what one might loosely describe as civil servants' assets rather than entrepreneurs' assets. They are all well suited to people who have conventional intentions and predictable career prospects, but not to those who have no settled plans, who wish to take risks, or who have uncertain incomes. They are all highly illiquid: none of them can readily be realized in an emergency, to tide over in the period between jobs, to start a business, or to buy or expand one. Two of them significantly reduce mobility between locations and between occupations. Indeed it is a notable feature that while it is normally part of the function of wealth to enhance economic freedom and personal security, these assets contribute very little to that. Each imposes contractual commitments which must be met even in adverse circumstances. Money in the bank increases an individual's ability to disagree with his employer: wealth which principally takes the form of accrued pension rights reduces it. (Although transferability of pension rights has been increased substantially, such rights are in almost all cases more valuable to those who remain with their present employer, and this is particularly true in the private sector.)

One result of this is that Britain now has the most attenuated small business sector of any country in the industrialized world. The Bolton Committee (1971) found that of thirteen countries it examined the proportion of manufacturing employment in small establishments (less than 200 employees) was lowest in the U.K. and was not much more than half that of the average of the other countries surveyed: and for very small firms the contrast is even more marked (Prais, 1976, p. 160). Technological factors are of course an element in the decline of small firms, but they can hardly account for the fact that while the number of small firms in the U.K. has halved in the last forty years it has almost doubled in the U.S.A. (Bolton, 1971, para. 6.9). Nor does such evidence as is available suggest that these trends result from the peculiar preferences of the British for large-scale organization. A recent international survey (*Vision*, 1977) showed that 61% of workers in Britain would prefer to work in firms with less than 500 employees. More significantly, Britain emerged as having much the highest proportion of the population who had thought about setting up their own business and the lowest percentage (after Holland) who had actually done so. And the finding that the median age of small firms in the U.K. is (at 22 years) three times what it is now in the U.S. and four times what it was in the late nineteenth century (Bolton, 1971, paras. 6.14–15) does not suggest that youthful vigour is characteristic of what remains.

The other side of this coin is the rapid growth in the size and significance of institutional investors. In the stock-market, personal shareholders have been persistent sellers of equities and financial institutions persistent buyers. In consequence, the distribution of holdings has been transformed as shown in Table 4.4. Not only are these institutional holdings large, but they are held in large units. Individual shareholdings of £100,000 or above represent almost 90% of the value of equities held by insurance companies (Erritt and Alexander, 1977). It is impossible to deal in quantities approaching this volume in the shares of any but a small number of large companies, and so the horizons of institutional investors are necessarily limited. Thus the growth of the institutional investor has not only channelled funds away from the smallest companies— in 1971 it was estimated that the total made available from these sources to companies with under 200 employees was about £7 m. (Merrett-Cyriax, 1971). It has also promoted concentration among very large companies, a process which has also gone beyond levels which have been achieved in other comparable countries or which are easy to justify on economic grounds (Hannah and Kay, 1977, Table 8.4 and *passim*).

TABLE 4.4

Ownership of shares by category of beneficial holder
(%)

Holder	1963	1969	1975
Personal sector	56·1	49·5	39·8
Financial companies and institutions	30·4	35·9	48·1
Other	13·6	14·6	12·2

Source: Erritt and Alexander (1977).

But the influence of the institutional investor has not been confined to the market in company securities. Life insurance companies, and to a lesser but still substantial extent pension funds, are committed to paying or guaranteeing fixed monetary amounts at dates rather far in the future. These guarantees are intrinsic to the concept of conventional life insurance contracts, though it is not obvious that they are of much value to investors, since the purchasing power of the amounts provided is quite unpredictable. The most successful recent developments in the life insurance industry have come from those who saw how the tax advantages of life policies could be obtained while this feature was abandoned (through 'unit-linked' life insurance). Nevertheless, it has been and remains true that insurance companies are anxious to invest a proportion of their funds in long-term fixed interest loans. Such loans are unattractive to most borrowers for much the same reason as they are unattractive to most lenders, but there are two main groups who are keen to borrow in this way—the Government, which can print money to finance repayment, and property developers, who were generally thought to be in a better position than industry generally to provide security of capital and income against such borrowings. In 1974 long-term loans financed 44% of the net assets of property companies; the corresponding figure for firms in manufacturing and distribution was 18%. (Business

Monitor M3, 1977). The prominence of life insurance companies as willing holders of Government stock has made funding operations a good deal easier throughout the post-war period, though with more benefit to taxpayers than to policy-holders as such stock has lost the major part of its value during the period. These possibilities have also made life easier—indeed possible—for property developers, and those who feel that this activity has been somewhat over-emphasized in post-war Britain should note the central role of the availability of long-term mortgage finance and the origins of this availability.

Taxation and distribution

Consider the career of an outstandingly successful manager in a British public company—the sort of man who might become chief executive of one of the hundred largest corporations. Starting his working life, in all probability, as a graduate trainee at the age of 23 or so, such an individual might quickly be picked out as a high-flier. Married at age 30, he might then expect to earn £8,000 p.a., and pulling sharply ahead of his contemporaries would certainly have doubled that income in the following ten years. In his mid-forties he is approaching board level and drawing an annual income of £20,000: and in his mid-fifties he becomes managing director with a salary of £35,000 which he draws for six or seven years before retiring in his early sixties. Few people are as successful as this: the number of company directors who matched his peak salary in 1973–4 was around a hundred, and there are perhaps twenty people starting work this year who can aspire to these heights.

Our hypothetical manager has fairly frugal tastes, and throughout his lifetime has reckoned to save around a quarter of his after-tax income. This means his maximum annual expenditure was around £8,000. On retirement, the accumulated wealth of such a man would approach £100,000. Feeling, with some justice, that he has been unusually fortunate in his career and unusually thrifty in his actions, he may be somewhat surprised to discover that there are in Britain at least 100,000 people richer than he is, and that they control well over 20% of all personal wealth. The example illustrates a central, but poorly realized effect of the British tax system —but one which is an inevitable consequences of a system in which high rates of tax on earned income are seen as the major redistributive device. There is a large number of very rich people in Britain, but the proportion of them who become rich as a result of personal savings from their own earnings is negligible.

Where then does their wealth come from? It is likely that some are in fact professional managers, since as we have noted above the impact of taxation on high earnings is not quite what it seems—but it is nearly what it seems, and it is not likely that many top wealth-holders are in this category. There are virtually no employees in other sectors who are as well paid as such a manager—a handful of lawyers, accountants, actors, and sportsmen. The main sources of wealth are necessarily inheritance and capital gains, and most fortunes are the product of some combination of the two. Thus Harbury and McMahon (1973) found that over half of those who died leaving over £100,000 had fathers who had done the same (after adjustment for price-level changes). And since capital gains generally require capital, it is not surprising that three-quarters had fathers with estates over £25,000. The unimportance of employment income as a source of major wealth is reflected in the fact that public administration—a sector which accounts for a major proportion of high income earners—was the occupation of only 3% of their sample. Of this small group, 88% had fathers at least as rich as them. Industrial occupational categories do not, unfortunately, distinguish proprietors from professional managers: but the industrial breakdown given by Rubenstein (1974) suggests strongly that it is primarily the former who are the business men represented among the top wealth-leavers.

Of course, to say that inheritance is close to being a necessary condition for wealth and that capital gains are the main route to increasing it is not to suggest that there is no relationship between wealth and personal exertion Small business men are generally in the position of being able to turn part of the earnings of setting up or expanding their firms into lightly taxed capital gains, although it is important to recognize that it is difficult to realize these gains without relinquishing partial or complete control of their operations. In the study by Harbury and McMahon the two sectors in which the influence of parental wealth on the fortunes of the son is smallest are engineering and finance: the former is the area of the industrial economy where small firms remain most prominent, while finance embraces those sectors in which earnings can be most readily and conveniently taken in the form of capital gain. That the expansion of a small engineering firm is a major route to self-made wealth is not something which causes us concern. The prominence of the financial sector here is rather more disturbing, since one does not have to take a wholly unsympathetic view of the activities of the City to believe that the correlation between private gain and social benefit is probably less strong in this area than it is in manufacturing industry and within the sector itself it is generally easier to defend the utility of those actions which generate high earnings than those which generate major capital profits.

The normal justification of inequalities of wealth derives from the need to sustain enterprise and effort. But it is difficult to survey the kind of evidence we have been describing without feeling that only a rather small proportion of major wealth inequality in the U.K. actually serves this function. Under the present U.K. tax system it is not too difficult to stay rich, but it is distinctly difficult to become rich—though these difficulties operate haphazardly, and with a degree of differentiation between sectors which seems, if anything, the opposite of that which consciously determined social priorities might dictate. It is not surprising to discover that the degree of concentration of wealth in Britain has been declining, though slowly (Table 4.5).

TABLE 4.5

Trends in the distribution of personal wealth in the U.K.

Group	Shares of different percentile groups in total wealth England and Wales, population over 25				Britain, over 18	
	1911–13	1924–30	1936–8	1960	1960	1974
Top 1%	69	62	56	42	38	25
Top 5%	87	84	79	75	64	50
Top 10%	92	91	88	83	77	66

Sources: Revell (1965); Diamond Commission (1977), Report No. 4.

But we attach importance not only to the concentration of wealth but to the mobility which underlies it. A concentrated structure is more acceptable if it is held by a changing group of people who are enjoying in their own generation the rewards of their own achievement than if it is owned by those whose families have always owned it—both because such a distribution should arouse less resentment and because such inequality is more likely to serve a function which is of benefit to the population as a whole. There is justice both in the left-wing criticism of the tax structure for its failure to shake concentrations of wealth and privilege, and in the right-wing criticism that it deprives people of the returns of effort and initiative. The present system gives us the worst of both worlds with maximal disincentive effect for minimal redistributive impact. It is not difficult to propose reforms which would lead to improvements on both counts, and these we will discuss in subsequent chapters.

5

THE CHOICE OF THE TAX BASE

IT should be clear from the previous chapter that many of the weaknesses of the U.K. tax system arise from the absence of a coherent view as to what should constitute an individual's 'taxable income'. We have illustrated this by pointing to several difficulties in the existing structure of the tax system which have become increasingly evident in recent years.

Firstly, there is a case for shifting part of the tax burden from earned income to some wider measure of an individual's wealth, to reflect his total resources or consumption over his lifetime. Secondly, the present taxation of capital income, especially in an inflationary era, is most unsatisfactory. Thirdly, whatever view one takes about the appropriate tax treatment of savings in general, it is clear that the discrimination among different forms of saving has some undesirable effects. These considerations lead us to believe that it is time to take a fresh look at the basis of our tax structure.

Suppose we go back to square one and ask the question, 'What principles should guide the choice of the tax system?' In the theory of taxation two different lines of thought may be detected.

One traditional approach is to say that since taxes are levied to finance collective expenditure on services which either cannot be provided by the market, or which the Government of the day chooses to supply from public funds, then the amount of tax paid by an individual should be related to the benefit which he derives from public expenditure. This school of thought has become known as the 'benefit theory' of taxation. But it is very difficult to measure these benefits because people can rarely be excluded from enjoying the benefits of many forms of public expenditure. Financing national defence or public television by voluntary subscription is usually found to be impracticable, and the tax authorities and detector vans are called in to help out the state.

The objection to the benefit theory of taxation is not, however, dased only on its impossible demands of human nature. We simply do not know the distribution of benefits of public expenditure, and there is little prospect of discovering it. How can we measure the benefits which any particular individual derives from defence, the police, or the Department of Industry? An alternative approach is to say that for a given level of public expenditure, the total cost of financing it should be divided among individuals according to their 'ability to pay'. The idea behind this is that an individual should make a contribution according to the 'sacrifice' which the tax burden imposes upon him, and that individuals should make equal sacrifices. This is not equivalent to saying that each individual should pay the same amount of tax because a rich man can pay much more tax than a poor man while being said to suffer the same 'sacrifice'. The evident difficulty of defining exactly what is meant by 'equal sacrifice' explains why the 'ability to pay' approach, like the benefit theory, has not contributed a great deal to the resolution of practical problems.

One reason for this is the confusion of two quite distinct issues. The first is the question of what is the best index of an individual's 'ability to pay'. Obvious candidates include income, wealth, and consumption. The second question arises once we have chosen a particular index, income for example. How should the tax burden be distributed among people with different incomes? In other words, how progressive should the income tax be? For the moment we shall consider these issues separately. In this chapter we examine the former, returning to the latter question in Chapter 13.

A natural way to measure an individual's ability to pay is his ability to earn. This, however, contravenes a basic criterion for a feasible index, which is that we must be able to *measure* it. What someone actually earns is not necessarily a good guide to what he could earn. A man who has the ability to produce a great deal but chooses to lie on a beach all year round will pay no tax. It would be difficult to prove that he had the ability to earn enormous sums, and impossible to measure at all accurately what he might have earned. Before this approach to the taxation of potential earnings is condemned as unjust and illiberal, we should recall the widely held belief that owners of property should pay full rates even if the property concerned is empty. The owner of an empty office-block is regarded as just as worthy an object of taxation as the owner of a building which is fully used.

Politicians and administrators charged with the responsibility for collecting taxes will be more interested in what measurable indices or tax bases they could use. At this stage we may distinguish three potential tax bases—wealth, income, and expenditure—the values of which measure how much an individual owns, earns, or spends respectively. Despite the fact that the idea of a tax on wealth is a relatively recent idea in the U.K. (as proposed by the Labour Government in a Green Paper in 1974, Cmnd. 5704), it has been used in many other European countries and was a favourite tax in times gone by. Representatives of the monarch rarely had the time to compute people's annual income or expenditure, and they would estimate an individual's visible wealth (acres of land of different types, number of servants and cattle), and levy a wealth tax at regular or irregular intervals depending on the Crown's needs. Such a tax is better described as a tax on assets rather than on wealth in its widest sense, because there are important components of wealth which cannot be measured, such as the right to a future income or pension, or an entitlement to continue living in a sub-sidized house. The most important component of wealth which cannot be measured is simply the present value of the future earn-ings which an individual may earn, sometimes described as 'human capital'. Apart from the special cases of slaves and football players there are no markets to enable us to put a precise monetary value on the stock of human capital. For this reason it is clear that wealth is not suitable as the index or base for the main source of tax revenue, a conclusion which is borne out by the current practice in all developed countries. Because of this we shall defer further dis-cussion of capital taxes until Chapter 10.

Income and expenditure as tax bases

In more recent times, as we have seen in Chapter 2, income was used as the index of ability to pay and this has become the norm in all countries. Nevertheless, there has always been a strong intel-lectual tradition ranging right across the political spectrum includ-ing such figures as Hobbes, Mill, Fisher, and, more recently, Kaldor, which has argued in favour of the use of expenditure as the measure of an individual's ability to pay. In this tradition two arguments have been deployed for the superiority of a tax based on expenditure over income tax.

The first justification for taxing an individual on his consump-tion is that it is more just to tax someone on the value of what he takes out of society in terms of the goods and services which he consumes, than on the value of what he contributes to society, whether in the form of earnings in return for labour services or interest in return for the supply of capital services. This argument is usually supported by reference to the famous question of Hobbes,

What reason is there, that he which laboureth much, and sparing the fruits of his labour, consumeth little, should be more charged, than he that liveth idly getteth little, and spendeth all he gets: Seeing the one hath no more protection from the commonwealth than the other? (Hobbes, *Leviathan*, Ch. xxx)

The answer to Hobbes is twofold. Firstly, there is no obvious reason to regard a tax on what an individual actually consumes as evidently more *just* than a tax on the total economic opportunities of the individual which measure his potential consumption. A one-legged unemployed man who manages to maintain a low level of consumption by begging is unlikely to be seen as just as suitable an object of taxation as a wealthy miser who chooses to spend very little and counts his money each night. A tax on potential consumption has as much claim for the title of a fair tax base as a tax on actual consumption. Secondly, Hobbes's example is very misleading. The injustice arises, so it would appear, because one individual enjoys a good deal of leisure ('living idly' while his neighbour 'laboureth much') and this is not taken account of when his tax bill is computed. This, however, has nothing to do with the distinction between income and consumption. If we consider Hobbes's example and look a year or two into the future, then the man who had worked hard, saved, and now wanted to enjoy the fruits of his work and saving in the form of consumption would, under Hobbes's regime of an expenditure-based tax, find himself facing a heavy tax liability. Both an income tax and an expenditure tax discriminate in favour of the 'idle', and unless we are prepared to tax people on the basis of what they *could* earn there is nothing we can do about it.

A more relevant distinction between an income tax and an expenditure tax is their treatment of saving, and this has been used as the second main argument for a tax on consumption. With an expenditure tax consumption incurs the same tax liability (for a given schedule of tax rates) regardless of the year in which the individual chooses to consume. There is no discrimination between those who prefer to spend while young and active, and those who prefer to spend in retirement. An income tax, on the other hand, is said to discriminate against saving because it gives rise to the 'double taxation of savings'. The reason for this is the following. Consider a world in which the only tax is an income tax, and two individuals who earn the same amount and hence pay the same tax. The first decides to spend everything this year and pays no more tax. The second decides to save up and spend the money next year. Because he saves he receives some interest on his savings, but under an income tax he is required to pay further tax on his interest income, and this has been described as double taxation. Although there is some force in this argument the position is more complicated than the simple label of 'double taxation' might imply. It should be obvious that what matters is not the number of times tax is paid (whether it be double, treble, or quadruple taxation), but the total tax burden. The important questions are whether taxing interest income discriminates between immediate consumption and deferred consumption, and whether this discrimination is a serious problem. On the first point, we have to decide whether the after-tax interest which the individual receives is less than the rate of return which the nation earns on investment which can be financed out of the individual's savings. In fact this is a complicated issue which depends on, among other things, the taxes and subsidies on investment by companies. Without delving further into these complications we may say that on average the U.K. income tax does provide an incentive to immediate consumption and hence a disincentive to saving by individuals (see King, 1977, Ch. 8).

Whether it is a first priority to remove this discrimination is another matter. There are certainly other distortions in the capital market which affect savings decisions. Access to opportunities for borrowing is not available to all, and in one important market, that for loans for housing, mortgages are rationed between those individuals who would like to borrow more at prevailing interest rates. But if we tried to calculate what would be the best way of taxing interest income, taking account of all the existing market imperfections, we would not only require an extensive and detailed knowledge of how these imperfections affected savings behaviour, but we would be most unlikely to come up with a system resembling the current tax treatment of saving. Hence there is a strong argument for not trying to introduce arbitrary elements of discrimination unless we are sure we are influencing decisions in the right direction. Although we believe that the 'double taxation of savings' implied by an income tax is an argument for an expenditure tax, it is not the only nor even the most important argument. Indeed, it is necessary to correct a common, but mistaken, impression that the main argument for an expenditure tax is that it would encourage savings. We know very little about the response of aggregate savings to changes in interest rates, and it is clear that, despite the large negative real rates of return on savings of recent years, people have gone on saving. It is unlikely that changes in the tax system would have a major effect on savings. The important thing is not to distort individual decisions more than is necessary, and the attraction of an expenditure tax is not so much that it would remove a disincentive to savings in general but that it offers a practicable way of eliminating the differential taxation of particular forms of saving and capital income.

Given that it is unrealistic to think of calculating a special tax rate for each form of saving and each type of income, and given the anomalies which have been introduced into the present system by 'special concessions', there is a powerful case for choosing as the tax base either income or expenditure, but not a mixture of the two. The arguments in principle for choosing between income and expenditure, which we have discussed above, do not seem to us to lean heavily in one direction or the other. Either base can be defended and the decisive arguments come from a consideration of what the respective tax bases imply in practice. So we shall now examine in more detail the implications of an income tax and in the next chapter we shall turn our attention to an expenditure tax.

The definition of income and the 'comprehensive income tax'

It may seem trite to observe that to operate an income tax it is necessary to have a clear definition of what constitutes 'income', but the sad truth is that no single definition of income commands universal assent. Those who either doubt, or are surprised by, this statement are referred to the voluminous literature on the subject (some of which has been brought together in the volume edited by Parker and Harcourt, 1969).

One of the most popular definitions of income remains that of J. R. Hicks (1939) who suggested that 'income is the maximum value which a man can consume during a week, and still expect to be as well off at the end of the week as he was at the beginning'

(p. 172). Unfortunately, it is not an operational definition, either for an accountant or a tax inspector. The difficulty lies in the word 'expect'. How can other people possibly determine what I expect? And what are they to do if my expectations are unreasonable? Accountants and revenue officers must work with verifiable facts, and hence they must look, not at what I could have *expected* to consume during a week or a tax year, but rather at what I could *in fact* have consumed while still remaining as well off at the end as at the beginning.

Unfortunately, these two concepts are not the same. If things always materialized as I expected, then there would be no divergence between them: but of course things never do. Consequently, if events go well for me in some particular year—I win the pools, my shares prosper, and my forgotten rich Australian uncle dies— my receipts in that year will be greater than I could have expected them to be, or can expect them to be next year. My 'income', defined in terms of what I could have consumed in that year, will be greater than my income in the Hicksian sense of what I could have expected to consume, and greater than my long-run spending capacity. Conversely, if I have an unexpectedly bad year, in which my shares collapse, I lose my job, and my wallet is stolen, my receipts fall below my permanent income; anyone who looks at my accounts will see a gloomy picture, but an unduly gloomy one, because these unexpected adversities are unlikely to happen again. An omniscient auditor or tax inspector would seek to remove from the published figures the influence of such events.

Of course, there is no practicable method of doing this; but in raising the problem we can see why the taxation of capital gains, and capital receipts generally, has posed such difficulties for the income and corporation taxes of this and other countries. The problem is that capital gains may arise for a variety of reasons and we would wish to differentiate between the components of capital gains, some of which are equivalent to other components of income and others of which are not. This is clearly impossible and in practice we can only adopt some rather crude categorization which is based on things we can actually measure; accountants have attached importance to the distinction between realized and unrealized gains, while the Sandilands Committee (see Ch. 11 below) distinguished 'holding' and 'operating' gains. The reader may find difficulty with the latter distinction, as did the Sandilands

Committee. These solutions are very unsatisfactory, and their proponents have compounded confusion by suggesting that their definitions gave the 'right' answer (for a further discussion of this see Kay, 1977). The distinction between the expected and the unexpected can never be observed, and after a careful consideration of the problems involved Hicks came to the following conclusion about concepts of income, including his own, 'They are bad tools, which break in our hands' (1939, p. 177).

British tax law initially took the view that all capital gains were windfalls and should not pay tax, unless they were obtained by traders in which case they were taxed as income. As we have seen in Chapter 4, it is rather easy to turn investment income into capital gains, and hence the view that capital gains are a different sort of animal from receipts of income has become more and more implausible. The result is the present unhappy compromise in which capital gains are taxed, although at lower rates than income.

Although similar procedures have been adopted in most other countries, there are advocates of the approach of treating all capital gains and most other windfall and capital receipts as income. This viewpoint has been especially popular in North America, but it also appeared in the Minority Report of the Royal Commission on the Taxation of Profits and Income in 1955. Its goal is to tax an individual on his 'comprehensive income', which is defined as the amount which an individual could consume without running down the value of his wealth. Simons has suggested that 'Personal income may be defined as the algebraic sum of (a) the market value of rights exercised in consumption and (b) the change in the value of the store of property rights between the beginning and end of the period in question' (1938, p. 50). It is this definition of personal income which has come to be known as comprehensive income and we can measure it by the value of what he does consume plus the change in the value of his wealth.

A comprehensive income tax (C.I.T.) would remove the present anomalies which arise from the differential treatment of capital gains, but only at the price of introducing substantial anomalies and administrative problems of its own. Capital gains under a C.I.T. would be taxed at full income tax rates, rather than the current concessionary rates, and, moreover, would be taxed each year as they accrued, unlike the present situation in which capital gains are taxed only when the asset concerned is sold. Such a proposal is clearly impracticable; firstly, it would require that all assets be valued every year; secondly, it would mean that people with illiquid assets (such as houses) would receive tax bills which they did not have the cash resources to meet. We are therefore thrown back on to the taxation of realized capital gains.[1] This is likely to increase the likelihood of 'lumpy' capital receipts which arise sporadically rather than smoothly over time, and increase the need for adequate averaging provisions. On the other hand, the taxpayer benefits because he can defer payment of tax until the date when he chooses to realize the gain.

It also raises the question of what to do about capital losess. One can hardly tax capital gains without allowing losses to be tax-deductible. Yet this might result in some of the less bright or less fortunate City 'financial operators' being the poorest people in Britain in a particular year (such as 1974 when the stock-market collapsed), according to Inland Revenue statistics, even though they were also still among the wealthiest members of society. They simply cut their losses and sold out. Presumably, individuals of this kind, with low or very probably negative comprehensive in-comes, would be helped by 'averaging provisions' so that their losses could be carried forward against future income. This, how-ever, would mean that for one, or perhaps several, years certain individuals who would be both wealthy and enjoying a high level of spending would pay no tax. The prospect of finding City finan-ciers who, on returning from a pleasant stay on a yacht on the French Riviera, were met at Heathrow by a chauffeur-driven Rolls Royce and a note from the Inland Revenue saying that their tax liability for this year had been waived, would send Fleet Street wild with excitement and M.P.s scurrying to put down awkward questions for the Chancellor. Comprehensive income is not an idea which it would be easy to put over at Question Time in the House of Commons.

On top of these problems there is the difficulty entailed in ad-justing the measurement of income for the effects of inflation. The adjustments required in the taxation of capital gains, investment income, and the treatment of mortgage interest were described in Chapter 4, and a comprehensive income tax would have to face these problems of indexation.

---

[1] The Meade Committee (1978) did, however, suggest a method, albeit com-plex, for approximating the taxation of accrued gains.

A comprehensive income tax would also seek to deal with the other problems we discussed in Chapter 4 when looking at why the present tax treatment of investment income is so haphazard. It is necessary to ensure that all investment income currently earned by institutions is attributed, by some means or another, to the individuals to whom it will ultimately accrue and is then taxed accordingly; only by this means can we reduce the large-scale avoidance of the present investment income tax and reverse the increasing institutionalization of savings. These procedures would have to be applied to trusts, to corporations, to pension funds, and to life insurance companies. This would mean that the income of a pension fund, for example, would be regarded as accruing to the individual who had rights in the fund, although most taxpayers would not appreciate a letter from the Inland Revenue demanding tax on income which they had never seen and which had been received by a distant pension fund. And how could we deal with unfunded schemes (such as that for Civil Servants) or inadequately funded schemes (such as virtually all U.K. occupational pension schemes)? The problems involved in 'unmasking' other institutions such as trusts are hardly less acute. In a rather similar way, but with equal difficulty, we could assess rich taxpayers on the 'income' which they derive from the durable goods which they presently buy in preference to more productive assets which yield taxable income; we might reimpose 'schedule A' on houses and extend it to other valuable items like pictures and jewellery.

It is true that what we have been describing is a rather idealized income tax, and that some of these difficulties could be avoided by not following the definition of 'comprehensive income' to the letter. After all, most of the countries which have a rather more successful record of economic management than Britain do manage to run an income tax, and it is clear that we could reduce some of the problems we have noted in Chapters 3 and 4 by moving in the direction of a comprehensive income tax even if that movement was only a partial one. But the pragmatic approach means that it is only too easy to lose sight of what it is that we are trying to tax, and to ignore the fundamental inter-relations between the different parts of the system or to be blind to their consequences. It is, after all, this pragmatism that has brought us to our present state, in which we are faced with high taxes on earned income which fail to tax spending out of inherited wealth, the almost random taxation of income from capital, the institutionalization of personal saving, and the gradual diminution in the tax base and corresponding increase in tax rates. But it may be inflation that provides the decisive argument. Britain's inflation rate is, and is likely to remain, higher than it has been in the past or in other comparable countries. Further *ad hoc* adjustments to deal with this are necessary, and we can expect that they will be made. But the full set of adjustments which are needed to deal satisfactorily with inflation are daunting, and it is this prospect which directs our attention most firmly to the expenditure base.

An expenditure tax

One advantage of choosing consumption expenditure as the tax base is that we require no valuations of an individual's wealth, and hence we avoid all the problems of measuring depreciation of assets (depreciation of consumer durables is less important and is discussed further in Chapter 6), of indexing for inflation, and of our inability to measure some important components of wealth, such as pension rights or human capital. It is no longer necessary to maintain what must inevitably be an arbitrary distinction between capital and income and this means that we can avoid the complexities involved in the indexation of capital gains and investment income, which, as we have seen, would involve major changes in the organization of capital markets as well as the tax system.

Problems of averaging are likely to be less severe also, because whereas an individual has little control over the timing of receipts of windfall gains he can choose when to spend his resources. Moreover, it seems likely that individuals prefer to maintain a relatively stable pattern of expenditure over a run of years, and not to enjoy a burst of spending in one year followed by relative deprivation in succeeding years. Averaging is achieved not by a set of provisions in the tax system, but by the individual's own voluntary decision on when to consume.

There are two important differences between a personal expenditure tax such as we have outlined, and existing taxes on expenditure often called 'indirect' taxes. A common objection to the imposition of indirect taxes is that they take no account of an individual's personal circumstances, and indeed are often, though not always, regressive. What progressivity does exist is achieved by taxing at higher rates of V.A.T. or excise duties those commodities which are consumed relatively more by the rich than by the poor. Since consumption patterns vary between individuals this is a rather arbitrary and haphazard method of redistribution, which is a blessing to the rich man who loves plain cooking and reading, and hard on the poor man who rejects conventional standards of attire and nutrition and adopts consumption patterns more usually associated with the rich by devoting himself to the consumption of whisky. It is important to realize that this objection cannot be levelled at an expenditure tax which is a tax on the total value of an individual's consumption expenditure during the course of a year. In itself it does not discriminate between consumption on different commodities, and can be as progressive as desired in exactly the same way as an income tax is progressive, that is by the existence of personal allowances and higher rates of tax. The degree of progression in the personal tax system is a quite separate issue from that of whether the tax base is to be income or expenditure.

The second difference between an expenditure tax and existing taxes on expenditure concerns the method of collection, and follows directly from the first. Because indirect taxes depend only on the total value of sales of a commodity and not on the identity and circumstances of those purchasing the commodity, they can be collected in the shops at the retail stage, or from the wholesalers (as was the case with the old purchase tax), or from the purchaser at the various stages of production (as occurs with V.A.T.). With an expenditure tax, however, the amount of tax depends upon the personal circumstances of the consumer, and the tax cannot be collected in the shops in the form of an addition to the bill.

How then can the tax authorities measure the value in any given year of an individual's expenditure? The first thing to say is that it does not require the taxman to follow housewives into the supermarket and surreptitiously observe the figures being rung up on the till. We can measure an individual's expenditure by observing what he does with the various cash receipts arising during the course of the year. He might receive amounts in the form of wages and salaries, tips, interest and dividend payments, gifts and bequests from other people, and he might receive cash from the sale of some of his assets (for example, shares or a house) or from borrowing money. Taken together these items form his total cash 'incomings'. We must also be careful to include items received not in the form of cash, but 'in kind', whether they be inherited goods (such as houses, paintings, or shares) or perks like free motor cars, lunches, and other fringe benefits. (These problems of identifying transactions and of policing the line between personal and business expenditures arise to the same extent and in just the same way with all taxes—income tax, expenditure tax, or V.A.T.) The total 'incomings' are matched by an equal total for 'outgoings' which describe what the individual does with his receipts. Some of these he may give away (to relatives or to charity), some he will use to meet the interest payments or repayments of the principal on loans taken out in the past, and some to save by placing his money in a building society account or by purchasing assets of various types (shares, for example). The remainder will be used to finance his personal consumption. In this way we can see that it is possible to calculate the value of an individual's expenditure by computing his various receipts and payments during the year, and we shall spell out in more detail how this would work in practice in Chapter 6.

It is also clear that some of the other problems associated with an income tax arise from the difficulty of defining an acceptable measure of an individual's *annual* income. In fact we shall now see that if we take a longer view and think of an individual's income over his lifetime, the difference between income and expenditure disappears. To see this let us consider an individual's lifetime accounts and imagine a very careful man who kept a complete record of all his receipts and all his expenditures. On the day after his death we enter his study and find in the left-hand drawer of his desk a complete record of all his receipts over his lifetime filed according to the year in which they were received. We will find his salary slips and notes of interest on bank deposits, perhaps some dividends, his pension while in retirement, and all the amounts which he inherited or received by way of gifts from others. In the right-hand drawer we find a similar set of notes, again filed by year, of all his expenditures and payments over the years, including gifts made by him to others. We also find a statement prepared immediately prior to his death of his net wealth (assets net of liabilities) which is to be bequeathed to his descendants. Into the left-hand drawer we then insert a file with the sale proceeds of the estate and into the right-hand drawer a file containing the same figure which is equal to the value of the estate passed on to his descendants.

Since in each year the items of 'outgoings' in the right-hand drawer must have been financed in one way or another from the 'incomings' in the left-hand drawer, the total of all the figures in the left-hand drawer equals the total of the entries in the right-hand drawer. We enter the world with nothing, and we leave the world with nothing. Our lifetime accounts must balance. The total of the entries in the right-hand drawer is simply the total value of the man's own consumption and gifts and bequests to others over his lifetime. The total in the left-hand drawer consists of his lifetime earnings, gifts received from others, investment income, and the sum of the net sales of assets over his lifetime including the value of his estate. Since we enter the world with nothing the value of net sales is equal to the capital gain the man has made on his assets over his lifetime. Hence the total in the left-hand drawer can be said to measure the man's total lifetime income, and is equal to the total of what he spends on consumption and gifts to others.

From this we can deduce that the effect of collecting a tax on consumption and gifts made on an annual basis is to impose a tax on lifetime income. We might propose an expenditure tax (including gifts in the tax base) as a superior form of income tax!

In effect, what this tax does is to tax an individual on his lifetime use of resources and for this reason we may describe it as a lifetime expenditure tax (L.E.T.).[1] The intellectual basis for the L.E.T. is different from that of the pure expenditure tax, although its operation is very similar. It is superior to a comprehensive income tax in that, although it can be described as a tax on lifetime income it avoids all the problems associated with an annual income tax which we discussed above, the unequal treatment of human and financial capital, the double taxation of savings, and the difficulty of measuring 'income' in times of inflation.

The arguments advanced in this chapter are the reverse of those normally associated with the debate over income versus expenditure. It is usual to argue that in principle expenditure has many conceptual attractions over income for the tax base, but that there are too many practical difficulties involved in measuring an individual's annual expenditure. We have argued that the choice in principle between income and expenditure is finely balanced, that we prefer lifetime income, but that to measure this the appropriate annual tax base is expenditure including gifts made, and that the compelling argument against a conventional income tax is the

---

[1] The tax has also been described by one of the authors elsewhere (King, 1978) as a comprehensive usufruition tax (C.U.T.).

administrative complexity of measuring an individual's annual income.

To see how the L.E.T. would operate in practice, we now turn to a discussion of how an expenditure tax might be implemented.

6

A LIFETIME EXPENDITURE TAX

In the preceding chapter we concluded that the most promising direction of reform of the U.K. personal tax system involved the transformation of the income tax into a direct tax on personal expenditure. Such proposals have been made before—we noted the distinguished intellectual pedigree of the concept—but it has been generally assumed that whatever the theoretical attractions of the expenditure tax the administrative problems of operating it were overwhelming.

Certainly the historical record is not encouraging. At present there is one country in the world that has a personal expenditure tax—Sri Lanka. The U.S. Treasury proposed such a tax in 1942, but the reception it received in Congress was so hostile that within a week the suggestion was withdrawn. N. Kaldor, distinguished dissentient member of the Radcliffe Committee of the early 1950s on the taxation of profits and income, invited consideration of the tax. The Committee consulted the then Chancellor of the Exchequer, and was doubtless relieved when he concluded that such a proposal was much too radical to fall within the terms of reference of a Royal Commission. Kaldor put forward his ideas subsequently (1955), but his work received more attention for its masterly analysis of concepts of income than its description of taxes on expenditure. Only in India were his arguments found persuasive, but the tax was never a serious one (the number of taxpayers never exceeded 1,000) and was withdrawn in 1966 (Chawla, 1972). But we believe an expenditure tax is a practical proposition, and this is no longer an eccentric minority view. Official reports in Sweden and the U.S.A. have shown how such proposals might be implemented in these countries (Lodin, 1976; U.S. Treasury, 1977) and the Meade Committee has analysed the possibilities and problems in the U.K. context.

We should stress that an expenditure tax does not operate by requiring an exhaustive listing of every purchase that has been made during the year of assessment. Many people will' be familiar with the rueful reckoning of their expenditure on a foreign holiday. It is certainly possible to try to relive your experiences, recording everything you spent—counting the drinks by the swimming-pool, the tip to the taxi-driver, and so on. If your recollections are sufficiently comprehensive, the resulting total will be a good estimate of your total expenditure. But there is a much easier way of reaching a more accurate answer. You simply measure how much foreign currency you took with you, add the amount of currency you bought while abroad, and subtract what was left when you got back. You measure, not the expenditure itself, but the sources of the expenditure, and can thus achieve a simple and reliable measure on the basis of a small number of recorded (and readily verifiable) transactions.

A personal expenditure tax would apply just the same principle. It taxes the sources of expenditure rather than the expenditure. All receipts—whatever their source or nature—are taxable; but any part of them which remains unspent can be deducted in computing liability. We can regard currency you buy as a taxable receipt: the currency you sell back attracts relief. But one problem remains. Some of the things you bring back from holiday have a value that extends beyond the period of the holiday itself. Your expenditure on a bottle of duty-free sherry, or on the bullfight poster that permanently adorns the wall, is attributable not so much to the holiday as to the subsequent days and years in which you drink the sherry and admire the poster. An accurate measure of holiday expenditure would require that you list and value every asset of enduring value which you purchased on holiday and subtract that valuation from the provisional estimate of your spending.

Clearly, this is a daunting administrative task, though a necessary one if an accurate measure of that particular period's expenditure is required. But the key to devising a feasible expenditure tax is the realization that it is not important, nor even particularly desirable, that this valuation be comprehensive. Suppose a few pesetas are left in your beach shorts until the following summer; then the allocation of expenditure to particular years is inaccurate but nevertheless expenditure over a period of years is correctly measured. And the same would be true if you kept a wallet full of foreign currency for next year's holiday (or purchased a Picasso etching or a bullfight poster). This year's expenditure would be overestimated, and hence a liability to expenditure tax so computed would be excessive; but all you would have done would have been to make a prepayment on account of your liability next year or in subsequent years, and there is no general reason why a tax authority should take exception to that. Normally people would not want to prepay tax in this way, and indeed you can always ensure that your holiday expenditure is accurately measured by returning your unspent notes to the bank (as exchange control regulations oblige you to do), so that the amount you did not spend is recorded. But there might be good reasons why taxpayers might choose to make prepayments. It might simply be convenient to do so—and in the case of durable goods (the poster or the Picasso) such prepayment when the purchase occurs is much the easiest way to collect the tax due. Or they might wish to prepay because they expect to pay tax at higher rates in future as their expenditure rises, and they would rather incur liability at their lower current rates. In all these cases, prepayment of tax would be acceptable—and indeed desirable, since it provides an opportunity for those with uneven patterns of expenditure to average their taxable expenditure. The objective of progressive taxation is to impose a higher average rate of tax on those with a higher average level of income (or expenditure). An incidental side-effect is that those whose average income (or expenditure) is no higher but is more variable also pay a higher average rate of tax. The possibility of prepayment diminishes this inequity.

An annual expenditure tax, which seeks to measure an individual's spending in each separate year of assessment, poses very serious administrative problems, because it requires that his assets be assessed annually. A lifetime expenditure tax, under which payments over the lifetime depend on spending during the lifetime but where payments in any particular year are not necessarily related to spending in that year, is a much more feasible proposition. It is also potentially a fairer tax than either an annual income tax or an annual expenditure tax, even in their idealized versions. We now consider more specifically how such a tax would operate.

The introduction of a lifetime expenditure tax would involve the creation of a class of 'registered assets'. These would include business assets and negotiable securities; some deposit accounts with banks, building societies, and other financial institutions would be registered, though we anticipate that current accounts with banks and balances held for day-to-day requirements and short-term savings would not normally be registered assets. The basic principle is that all receipts obtained during a year would be subject to tax, but after summing these receipts the taxpayer would deduct his net purchases of registered assets during the year. The resultant figure would be his taxable expenditure. The structure of the tax is illustrated in Fig. 6.1. Arrows indicate flows of receipts and payments. Transactions which cross unbroken lines are the subject of tax payments or deductions, and it is these transactions and these only that the tax collector monitors. Those that cross broken lines do not interest him. It is important to note that these criteria relate simply to cash flows, and that there is never any inquiry into or distinction between flows of capital and flows of income. The tax base is simply the sum of all net receipts which come across the unbroken lines; earnings and gifts, net surpluses from trading, and net receipts from dealings in registered assets. Since lifetime accounts balance, this is equal, over the lifetime, to the sum of all personal expenditures and gifts to others.[1]

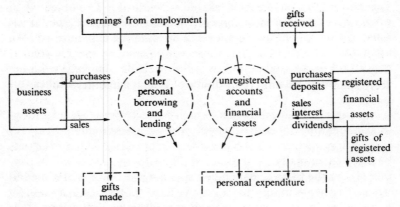

Fig. 6.1. The sources of personal expenditure

The easy questions on the present income tax form would go over to an expenditure tax form more or less unchanged. The first question would still be 'How much did your employer pay you

---

[1] If both registered and unregistered assets exist, and either (a) returns on unregistered assets are certain or (b) the tax is proportional, the lifetime expenditure tax is exactly equivalent to a lifetime income tax, as discussed in Chapter 5. If neither of these assumptions holds, there may be divergences.

during the year?', and people with incomes only from employment and negligible savings or dissavings would notice no real difference. It is the treatment of savings and investment income that is drastically altered, and the changes mostly represent simplifications. At present, the taxpayer must record the proceeds of sales of securities during the year of assessment, and obtain from his records the corresponding acquisition costs at various different dates in the past: additionally, he must declare his purchases during the year so that these can be recorded and related to his subsequent disposals. The gains thus computed are then taxed on a separate basis with a number of available optional treatments and complications. Under an expenditure tax he would simply write down the gross figures for sales and purchases during the year and the net proceeds would be added to his other receipts. The questions would relate to this year's transactions alone.

Similarly, the tax treatment of his trading activities would be much simplified. Tax would be based on the cash accounts of the business, and the proprietor would simply pay tax on the net amount which he withdrew from the business during the year. Life insurance policies would generally be registered assets, so that the whole of any premiums paid would be deductible against tax, but all receipts from policies would be taxable. This would seem to impose a heavy liability when a policy matured, and if the proceeds were spent there would (and should) be such a liability. But if they were not all dissipated immediately tax could be deferred until they were used for expenditure by depositing them in registered accounts, and life insurance companies would no doubt be quick to facilitate such arrangements. Figure 6.2. gives some impression of what an expenditure tax return might be like.

There would be two new sets of questions. One would ask for details of gifts received during the year, including gifts of valuable assets, subject of course to some exemption limit. Receipts would no longer escape tax simply because they had not been earned. Details of accrued interest would not be requested (so those with forgotten bank accounts would no longer be embarrassed when they or the Revenue remembered). Instead, institutions authorized to operate registered accounts would at the end of each tax year notify both taxpayer and revenue of the amount of net additions or withdrawals, and the form would ask for this information.

The simplifications involved in moving from an income base to

Fig.6.2.

Expenditure Tax: Assessment Year 1988

Receipts

1. *Employments* Enter here the total of all payments from
   your employer (attach form E2)

   Taxable benefits in kind: see note X
2. *Businesses*   Enter here the gross sales proceeds of all
   businesses owned or operated by you (list
   details on form B1)
3. *Partnerships* If you are a partner in any business, enter
   here the total of all distributions to you.
4. *Gifts*   Enter the total of all gifts and inheritances
   received. You may neglect the first £100
   from any person. (list details on form G1)
5. *Pensions, social security and national insurance benefits.* See
   note 5.
6. *Securities*   Enter the total sales proceeds of securities
   sold during the year.
   Enter here the total of all dividends and interest payments received
   (list details on form S1)
7. *Registered accounts* Total of net withdrawals from each
   account (list on form R1 and attach forms
   R2)
8. *Life insurance policies* Total of maturities (attach forms
   L2)

9. *All other receipts* See Notes

10. *TOTAL RECEIPTS* (Total of lines 1–9)

Payments

11. *Employments* All admissible expenses connected with
    your work (see note Y) (list on form E1
    unless you claim the standard deduction)
12. *Businesses*   Total admissible expenses of businesses
    owned or operated by you (give details on
    form B1)

13. *Securities*   Total acquisition cost of securities pur-
        chased (list on form S1) ☐

14. *Registered accounts* Total net deposits in registered ac-
        counts (list on form R1 and attach forms
        R3) ☐

15. *Life insurance policies* Total premiums paid in the year (if
        the policy is a new one, attach form L3) ☐

16. *Other payments* See notes. Give details on form P1 ☐

17. *TOTAL PAYMENTS* (total of lines 11–16) ☐

18. *NET TAXABLE EXPENDITURE* (Subtract line 17
        from line 10) ☐

Extracts from notes to taxpayers

4. Gifts of registered assets which you have received must be listed on
   form G1 but need not be included in the total.
5. If you received a pension or social security or national insurance
   benefits in 1988, you should have received form SS1 at the end of
   the year. If so, enter the total from it in line 5. If you have not
   received SS1, contact your local tax or social security office.
6. Gifts of registered assets which you have made count as disposals
   for this purpose.
9. You must list here all other receipts in 1988 unless (i) they are
   returns of or on money you have yourself already paid and (ii) you
   have not claimed tax relief on that payment in this or any previous
   year. (e.g. tips and bonuses must be entered; receipts of principal or
   interest on loans need not be included *unless* you claimed tax relief
   when you made them).
11. You may claim a standard deduction of £50. If you wish to claim
    more you must provide full details on form E1.

Notes to reader

Forms B1, G1, S1, P1 etc. are supplementary statements which need
be completed only by those who have items in these categories: the total
is then brought forward to the main form.

Forms E2, R2, SS2 etc., are supplied by the institutions involved, and
the taxpayer need only transfer the total figure to his tax return.

an expenditure base arise principally from the shift from an accruals base to a cash flow base. It does not matter whether a receipt is an item of capital or income. It is unnecessary to determine the date of the *transaction* to which any particular item relates; the issue is simply when and whether a particular cash payment occurred. Every question on the expenditure tax form asks only about actual cash payments which took place during the year of assessment. The result is that for taxpayers with simple affairs, the procedures involved in completing an E.T. form would differ very little from those which are required at present; and for those with more complex circumstances, people who participate in businesses and have substantial investment incomes, the return in Fig. 6.2 would be easier to complete.

Nevertheless, the form raises difficulties through its unfamiliarity, and this is not a negligible consideration. Unsatisfactory though the present income tax system is, a few individuals and most accountants have experience and understanding of its operation. No such expertise is presently available for an expenditure tax system. Taken too seriously, of course, this argument would imply that no change in the tax system could ever be made, however miraculous the expected improvement. But it does highlight the central administrative difficulty raised by the expenditure tax. This is not the traditional 'How would it work?'—the answer to that is 'better than at present, at any rate'—but 'How do we get there from where we are now?'

A radical transition to an expenditure tax

This transitional problem is a serious one. We have described how an expenditure tax could be operated by simply monitoring those transactions which cross the solid lines of Fig. 6.1, and once the new tax system was fully functioning this would indeed be true. Expenditure could only be financed out of sources which were either the subject of a tax charge now, or which had been the subject of such a charge at some date in the past; present or past employment income, trading surplus or gifts, or withdrawals from registered assets. But this would not be true on the day when the expenditure tax was introduced. On that day there would exist a substantial stock of assets which could, unless some procedure were devised for recording its existence and monitoring its subsequent disposition, be used for subsequent consumption, and which could be spent without involving its holder in any liability to expenditure tax at any time. Indeed the whole of existing personal wealth would potentially be available for this purpose.

Although the owners of this wealth would not have paid expenditure tax on it, they might in accumulating it have paid income tax: and it would be fair and consistent with the spirit of the tax that this should be regarded as prepayment of expenditure tax. If savings have been derived from taxed income, it is unjust that expenditure from them should be taxed also. As we saw in Chapter 4, however, the proportion of personal wealth in the U.K. which has been accumulated from taxed income is probably rather small. Nevertheless, some of it has been: and the smaller the total amount of the wealth, the larger the proportion of it which is likely to have been subject to income tax at some time. But there are no rules by which we can hope to distinguish between wealth which was saved out of earnings and wealth which originated from capital gains or from ancestors who picked the right side in the Wars of the Roses. It is possible that one could attempt, as the Meade Committee (1978) did, to devise some very crude rules for separating 'life-cycle' and other components of wealth: capital up to some rather arbitrary figure, perhaps related to age, could be deemed to have been derived from earnings, and amounts in excess of that a proper object of taxation, so that a credit of that amount would be given against future expenditure. But the rough justice which would be done would be extremely rough.

Combined with this problem of equity is a straightforward problem of enforcement. Wealth which is concealed on the appointed day for the transition can be spent thereafter without involving its owner in a liability to expenditure tax, and indeed can even be a source of tax relief if it is subsequently converted into registered assets: wealth which attracts the attention of the tax inspector would be substantially less valuable. Thus there would be a strong temptation as the transition approached to convert assets into inconspicuous forms: jewellery, gold coins, banknotes stuffed under the mattress. Kaldor (1955) was prepared to deal with the last problem by calling in the currency on the appointed day, noting that if the threat were believed it would be unnecessary to carry it out. But devices of this kind are very far fetched.

Moreover, the problems of equity and enforcement are by no means unrelated. If measures are thought to be fair, then they will be less widely evaded and there will be general support for effective action against those who try to get around them. There seems to us no possibility of devising transitional arrangements which would not be grossly inequitable in many particular cases, and which would not be seen to be inequitable in many particular cases. This is not only a serious objection in itself, but one which more or less precludes effective action to enforce whatever transitional rules might be devised. It would be a remarkably selfless opposition political party which, faced with the manifest injustices of the transition, did not promise to abandon the tax or to undermine whatever specific transitional arrangements were proposed. If this is the only route by which an expenditure tax can be reached, then however alluring the prospect at the end may be, we shall never go down it. We therefore devote the remainder of this chapter to an analysis of evolutionary proposals by which, in time, the present tax system might be transformed into an expenditure tax.

The first stage: administrative reforms

If progress is to be made in simplifying and improving the structure of direct taxation in the U.K., it is essential to start with some administrative reforms. The most important of these are the abolition of the schedular system—by which the year of assessment and date of payment do not necessarily correspond and differ for different kinds of income—and a shift from a cumulative to a non-cumulative system of P.A.Y.E. This means that tax liability in any year would depend on total income in that year, and not on a hotchpotch of different years. It would also mean that the amount of tax deducted from a worker's wage in any particular week would depend only on his earnings in that week and not on his earnings in other weeks of the year. We described the meaning and operation of cumulative and non-cumulative P.A.Y.E. in Chapter 2.

It may seem surprising that we should attach such importance to what seem rather technical administrative changes, which do no more than bring British practice into line with that of almost all other countries. But their practical consequences can hardly be overestimated. Consider such diverse problems as: How can we reform local authority finance? How can we achieve a sensible relationship between the tax and social security systems? How can we establish independent sources of finance for devolved assemblies in Scotland and Wales? How can we make progress towards an expenditure-based system of direct taxation? All these are either difficult or impossible to resolve within the present administrative structure. With these changes, the possibilities open to us on all these fronts are transformed, as we show in this and subsequent chapters. Schedular taxation and cumulative P.A.Y.E. are apparently innocuous in themselves, but by making it necessary to design other aspects of the system around them they have imposed constraints which are responsible for many of the deficiencies and complexities of the U.K. tax structure.

It is inconceivable that anyone would propose adopting the schedular system if it did not already exist: it dates from the nineteenth century, when income tax was a tax on kinds of income rather than on the individuals who received it. It probably creates more bewilderment and misunderstanding than any other aspect of taxation, and the only thing to be said in its favour is that there are some (minor) transitional difficulties involved in its abolition. The sooner these are faced and taxation is based on a single statement of total income in a particular year, presented at the end of the year, the better. Some payment on account by businesses whose precise liability could only be assessed in arrears would be required, and this might well be based on the earnings of the previous year: so the practical consequences might not be very different, but at last people would begin to understand why things happened that way.

Under a non-cumulative P.A.Y.E. system, an individual would be credited each week with $\frac{1}{52}$ of his annual allowances, so that an individual with a single personal allowance of £945 would be allowed to earn £18·20 per week tax-free, and would pay tax on the excess. Thus with a basic rate of tax of 34% and earnings of £40 he would pay tax of 34% of £21·80, or £7·42. If income accrues evenly throughout the year, he will pay just the right amount of tax. With a progressive tax system, however, a worker whose earnings fluctuate from week to week may pay too much tax. If his 'good' weeks push him into a higher tax bracket, the rate at which he pays extra tax on his extra earnings will be greater than the rate at which his liability falls in the 'bad' weeks, and hence he would be due a refund of overpaid tax at the end of the year. Surprisingly, in countries where this operates this 'over-withholding' and consequential refund is generally rather popular with taxpayers (Barr *et al.*, 1977, p.143). But the advantage of the cumulative system is that such overpayments are avoided: most people pay more or less the right amount of tax in the course of the year. As we saw in Chapter 3, however, the administrative burden this imposes on both Inland Revenue and employer is considerable.

Britain (and Ireland) are the only developed countries in which a cumulative P.A.Y.E. system operates. Britain is also, as it happens, the country which has least need of one. The reason is the extremely wide range of incomes which are taxed at the basic rate. In a non-cumulative system, overpayment arises only if earnings fluctuate sufficiently to move the taxpayer to an income level at which he is liable to a different marginal rate of tax. But in the U.K., anyone whose weekly earnings average between (approximately) £30 and £140 is paying tax at the basic rate, and hence under a non-cumulative system everyone whose weekly earnings remain within this range would pay the right amount of tax. These limits cover most of the taxpaying population. The principal group who fall outside it are those who suffer periods of sickness or unemployment during the year. Their income does not often fall below the exemption limit (or does so only marginally) but their taxable income may well fall to zero because sickness and unemployment benefits are exempt from tax. This is because of the administrative difficulty of taxing them under a cumulative P.A.Y.E. system, which would require that the tax records of everyone who gained or lost entitlement to benefit be transferred to or from the Government department paying the benefit. When these benefits were introduced in their present form in 1948, they were taxable, but this principle was quickly abandoned because of the paperwork involved. So the main reason we need a cumulative rather than a non-cumulative system of P.A.Y.E. is that sickness and unemployment benefits are untaxed, and the reason they are untaxed is that we have a cumulative rather than a non-cumulative system of P.A.Y.E. We sympathize with the reader who finds this difficult to believe.

The abandonment of cumulation does not make it essential that all taxpayers should complete an annual tax return. It would be possible to continue the present system under which the Inland Revenue collates information from various employers, checks liabilities, and issues refunds or claims automatically at the end of each tax year: and while there would be a marginal increase in the frequency of refunds this would not in itself require a change to universal annual returns. But there are substantial arguments for requiring this. It promotes understanding of the system by the taxpayer. It increases the probability that allowances due will be claimed and taxable income will be reported (although recipients of casual income are legally obliged to notify the Revenue even if they do not receive a return, it is unlikely that many people do and indeed it is widely assumed by many of those who are not required to make annual returns that such income is in principle, as it is in practice, tax-free). But most importantly, a system which relies on the taxpayer to report transactions, with selective checking and deterrent penalties for evasion, is cheaper to administer, more flexible, and probably more comprehensive than one which attempts to rely on the Revenue securing independent knowledge of all taxable items.

These changes would involve a substantial movement towards a 'self-assessed' income tax, under which the taxpayer computes his own liability and posts a cheque or claims a refund accordingly. Such a system operates in the U.S.A. and in many other countries and has been recommended for the U.K. by Barr *et al.* (1977). But if an environment is created in which it is at least possible for the taxpayer to calculate his tax bill for himself if he wants to, it is of rather little importance whether he is actually asked to add up the figures or whether the Revenue will do it for him. We believe it self-evident that it should at least be *possible* for taxpayers to check their liabilities for themselves.

Towards an expenditure tax

Administrative reforms on these lines would be desirable whether or not any other changes are made in the structure of income tax. They would certainly be desirable and probably necessary if progress were to be made towards an expenditure tax, since only by means of an annual return would it be possible to be confident that individuals obtained the reliefs to which they were entitled and paid the tax to which they were liable. We assume that such changes would be accompanied by extensive computerization of U.K. income tax administration, which has already occurred in most comparable countries and is slowly being introduced in Britain (although the schedular system makes the process more difficult).

At the same time, we would like to see progress in the following directions: firstly, in acknowledging that expenditure is the most appropriate base for the main direct personal tax; secondly, in assimilating the existing unsystematic reliefs for saving to the expenditure tax arrangements; and thirdly, in extending these arrangements to other forms of saving. We have described the three main forms of 'privileged' saving in the present U.K. tax system: life insurance, pensions, and housing. As we move to an expenditure tax, new life insurance policies would obtain full tax relief on premiums paid, and proceeds of the policy, whether by surrender or maturity, would be taxable in full. As we noted on page 91, this would probably lead to some changes in the institutional arrangements made by companies to deal with policy maturities, so that the whole sum due need not be drawn from the policy proceeds immediately it matured. Unfortunately, it would be necessary to continue the present very complicated rules for existing policies, at least for some years, since otherwise current policy-holders would suffer the disadvantage of the new procedures (the tax on proceeds) without having received the benefits (relief on premiums and accumulation).

We have also described housing as a 'privileged asset'. The Meade Committee has discussed in detail the most logical treatment under various tax arrangements. But it is not clear that tinkering with the tax treatment of housing would improve the efficiency of the much-distorted housing market, and because tax concessions in this area have been largely capitalized, as we noted in Chapter 3, any change in the *status quo* would be likely to involve major inequities and hardships to particular individuals. If we were to describe what might be done about the U.K. housing market we should need to write a book, and this is not it. The U.K. is by accident or design committed to an outcome in which those who can buy their own homes and those who cannot are housed by local authorities, and no foreseeable tax changes will alter that situation.

Pension funds are already taxed on L.E.T. principles—contributions are exempt but the proceeds are taxed—and therefore no change in these arrangements would be required. But there are at present substantial restrictions on the benefits which can be provided from schemes that qualify for Inland Revenue approval: these restrictions could be abandoned and the associated administrative machinery abolished, since if people can save in this way for themselves there is no need to limit the amount they save in this way via a pension fund. Equally, once people have the opportunity to save in this way for themselves there is little reason to compel them to make such provision through a pension fund. Under an expenditure tax, it is very much easier for people to make 'life-cycle savings' to ensure that part of their income is available to them after their retirement. So we expect that there would be less demand for extensive occupational pension schemes, and people who were offered good schemes of this kind would no longer be at a great advantage relative to those who were not. We expect that state and private schemes would continue to provide basic pensions to ensure against poverty in old age: but would envisage that more elaborate provisions might become voluntary. If this happened, the present extreme complexity of pension fund administration could be reduced, and the proportion of personal wealth which was held in pension funds would diminish while that held directly by individuals would rise.

In addition to these changes, it would be essential to bring other types of savings into the expenditure tax framework. The procedure for dealing with land and negotiable securities would be as follows. After some appointed day, A day, the new rules would be applied. Purchase costs would be deductible and proceeds would be taxable. Any seller of securities subsequent to the appointed day would therefore be liable to tax on the whole of his receipts from the sale, unless they were reinvested in other securities or registered assets. If he had purchased his securities after A day, he would obtain no relief against this liability, since he could already have claimed their cost as a tax deduction: but if he could show that they represented a pre-A-day acquisition, he might be allowed to deduct the purchase price from the proceeds. This means that for securities which he had purchased under the previous income tax regime, he would be taxed on the capital gain as at present, but at income tax rates. This means that in spite of the relatively conservative nature of the transition to an expenditure tax involved in these proposals, many people spending out of accumulated wealth would pay more tax than they do under the present tax structure right from the start.

Changes would also be needed in the taxation of unincorporated businesses. The base for taxation would be shifted from the profit of the business to the net amount withdrawn from the business during the year by the proprietor, since all sales proceeds would be taxable (whether capital or current in nature) and all expenses would be deductible (whether capital or current in nature). The small business man would pay only on that part of his profit which he chose to withdraw for his own consumption, and would be fully relieved of liability on what he reinvested in the future growth of his firm. He would therefore obtain the twin benefit of a system vastly more conducive to the expansion of small business (aided by an increase in the importance of personal saving relative to that of institutions) and a substantial reduction in the administrative burdens involved in preparing tax accounts. There are opportunities to make similar simplifications in the taxation of incorporated businesses: we discuss these further in Chapter 12.

The other major category of personal saving is deposits in accounts with banks, building societies, and other financial institutions. In general, it seems to us undesirable that current accounts and balances used for transactions purposes should be registered assets: monitoring the balances on accounts which are the subject of frequent small transactions would be a nuisance for the taxpayer, the financial institution, and the Revenue alike. But both the logic of the tax and the desirability of allowing as much freedom of choice as possible in savings behaviour suggest that taxpayers should have the opportunity to make deposits in registered accounts. All payments into such accounts would attract relief: all withdrawals would be taxed. But these accounts would mainly be intended for long-term and contractual savings, not for day-to-day purposes. These objectives can be achieved by requiring that basic rate tax be withheld from withdrawals from registered accounts, with provision for rapid refunds from the Revenue in cases of hardship. This would have the effects of making it inconvenient to operate frequently on registered accounts, and of ensuring that people who did so did not end up with tax liabilities which they could not pay because they had already spent the full amount which they had withdrawn. In due course it would be desirable to assimilate unregistered accounts fully to the expenditure tax system by abolishing tax on the interest derived from them: registered accounts would then fall within the right-hand box of Fig. 6.1, unregistered accounts into the central circle.

Once all these changes had been made, the British income tax would have been transformed into a direct tax on personal expenditure. It is interesting to note that, with two exceptions (the more extensive monitoring of gifts and the treatment of registered deposit accounts), every change involved is a simplification. The taxation of life insurance policies and companies is much more straight-forward. Most of the burdensome aspects of pension fund adminis-tration disappear. The tax treatment of capital gains and of small businesses, which are the most difficult parts of the present income tax system to understand and to administer, is greatly simplified. Why do so many people believe, as we used to believe, that an expenditure tax might be fine in theory but could not work in practice, when in reality it is likely to be rather easier to operate than the existing income tax? We think there are two reasons. One is that the expenditure tax has not been explicitly compared with the present tax structure, but rather with some idealized income tax system which was not too precisely defined but which was assumed to be working smoothly and efficiently. We had simply forgotten how complicated and unsatisfactory the system was at the moment.

The other reason is that it is common to view any proposed change to the tax system in isolation. If we take for granted that every other aspect of the tax structure is to be operated more or less as it is now, then it is almost inevitable that any change will seem difficult and expensive to make. But if we take a broader view of the system as a whole and look at sets of interrelated changes, a much wider range of possibilities is feasible. The case of P.A.Y.E. cumulation and the taxation of sickness and unemployment bene-fits is a good, if limited, example of how changes can be costly on their own but yield cost savings if taken together. This is one reason why it is essential, even for an understanding of the adminis-tration of taxation policy, to be aware of the underlying principles of taxation involved, since only then is it possible to see these inter-relationships and the effects of the system as a whole. It is also for this reason that a tax system which is to be fair, simple, and efficient in administration must stick closely to a well-defined set of under-lying principles. When we depart from these—for good or bad reasons—we begin to generate anomalies and loopholes: these demand *ad hoc* solutions which give rise to further anomalies and loopholes: and so on down a path of ever-increasing complexity. A principal merit of an expenditure tax is that it really can be operated in a way which is close to such basic principles, while as we saw in Chapter 5 a comprehensive income tax presents many more problems; spending is easier to measure than income, and cash flows are easier to recognize than accruals. A satisfactory annual income tax would be difficult to operate even in a perfect world, which is why it does not work very well in the U.K.

7

SOCIAL SECURITY AND TAXATION

A T the beginning of the twentieth century the system of help for the poor, based on the Poor Law and the institution of the workhouse, was under great strain. In 1908 a non-contributory means-tested old age pension was introduced, and in 1911 the National Insurance Act brought in unemployment and sickness benefits which were financed out of employers' and employees' contributions. The principle of earning benefits by paying contributions remains the aim of the present system.

The path for development of social security after the Second World War was mapped out by the famous Beveridge Report of 1942 (Cmd. 6404). Beveridge recommended a comprehensive system of social insurance against sickness, unemployment, and retirement, with flat-rate benefits above subsistence level financed by flat-rate contributions. Families were to be helped by a new system of family allowances. Those whose needs were not met by the national insurance scheme (whose numbers were expected to be small) would receive means-tested 'national assistance'. But in practice the levels at which national insurance benefits were set were sufficiently low that anyone with no other income would normally be eligible for national assistance; so that the latter scheme did in fact become the normal means of support for large numbers of people who were retired, sick, or unemployed. This feature remains true today. In 1966 national assistance was renamed supplementary benefit (S.B.).

The present system

'Insurance' implies a clear relationship between contributions and receipts, and this was central to Beveridge's conception. But the insurance element of the present system is now almost wholly illusory. 'Contributions' are entirely earnings-related, and additional contributions produce no additional benefits, although there are earnings-related supplements to sickness and unemployment benefits. To claim benefit at all, however, some record of contributions is necessary; although people who have not paid contributions are eligible for supplementary benefit. The main practical effect of what is left of the contribution principle is to deny unemployment benefit to jobless school-leavers and the unsuccessful self-employed (who must apply for supplementary benefit instead). It is doubtful whether this result is desirable at all, and it is certainly not one for which it is worth maintaining the administrative machinery of contribution records. National insurance contributions are more appropriately regarded as part of the income tax system and could advantageously be incorporated with it.

The basic national insurance benefits are unemployment benefit, sickness benefit, and the retirement pension. For the first two there are earnings-related supplements in addition to the basic benefit, and unemployment and sickness benefits (as well as supplementary benefits) are tax-free whereas pensions are taxed. The value of these benefits is shown in Table 7.1. Other benefits paid are widows' pensions, maternity benefits, and payments for those made redundant, the value of which depend on length of service.

TABLE 7.1

Principal social security benefits, November 1977
(£ per week)

	Single householder	Married couple (no children)
Retirement pension	17·50	28·00
Unemployment and sickness benefit	14·70	23·80
Long-term supplementary benefit	27·90	28·35
(including rent)	(22·90)	(35·35)
Short-term supplementary benefit	14·50	23·55
(including rent)	(19·50)	(30·55)

Notes: (1) The long-term rate is paid to pensioners and those who have been continuous claimants for two years; no allowance has been made in the above figures for discretionary payments for items such as heating.
(2) The figures for rent have been taken as £5 for a single householder and £7 for a married couple. The figure for the average rent addition actually paid in 1975 was £4·93 for all households (Supplementary Benefits Commission, Annual Report, 1976, Table 15).

Despite these benefits there will be families whose incomes are inadequate to meet their needs and supplementary benefits exist to help such families. The scale of these benefits is shown in Table 7.1. In addition to basic scale benefits an allowance is paid for the whole family's rent and rates (provided these are not judged to be unreasonable). This is the minimum income to which a family is held to be entitled. There is one important caveat, however, which is that families can apply for supplementary benefit only if the head of household is not in full-time employment. Those families where the head of household works but has very low earnings cannot obtain the basic entitlement to subsistence income. We shall return to this problem later. For all others, supplementary benefit makes up their income to the prescribed level. They are therefore subject to a means test, which takes account of the family's total resources including its capital assets on which a rate of return is imputed.

It is clear from Table 7.1 that the main national insurance benefits are below supplementary benefit levels because the latter are topped up by provision for rent and rates. This means that in themselves they are inadequate to prevent individuals or families from falling below the official subsistence levels and we shall look below at the consequences of this.

There are numerous other means-tested benefits. The most important of these are rent and rate rebates. Each family applying for rebate is assigned a 'needs allowance' (which depends on the size of the family) and receives a subsidy of 60% of its rent and rates plus or minus a certain fraction of the amount by which its income is less or more than its needs allowance. The value of this fraction constitutes an extra marginal tax rate on the family's income and can vary between 6% and 33%.

Other means-tested benefits include reduced dental, optical, and prescription charges, free school meals, and many others. The National Consumer Council (1977) identified 45 different national and local benefits, and since then a special grant for heating costs has been introduced. Each benefit may have its own rules for eligibility and its own set of forms to complete, although the introduction of the 'passport' system, under which eligibility for one benefit automatically carries over to other benefits, has led to some rationalization.

We described on page 26 how the system of family allowances and tax allowances for children is in the process of being combined into a single child benefit scheme. Although households where the head is in work are ineligible for supplementary benefit, families in this position can receive family income supplement. Under this scheme a family receives 50% of the shortfall between its income and a 'prescribed amount' which depends upon the size of the family. There is an upper limit to the supplement which can be paid; in 1977 this was £9·50 a week for one child plus £1 a week for each additional child. In 1975, 64,000 families (half of them one-parent families) were receiving family income supplement at an average weekly rate of over £4 (*Social Trends*, 1976, Table 5.26).

Failings of the present system

It will be apparent from the above description that one of the present difficulties is the sheer complexity of the system. The number of benefits and the intricate formulas for computing the amount of benefit, involving 'needs allowances' and 'prescribed amounts', are enough to confuse the dispassionate student and must seem bewildering to potential claimants. It is worth bearing in mind that one reason the poor are poor is that they are not qualified as chartered accountants. So one of the questions we shall look at below is whether there is not a simpler comprehensive scheme which would achieve the objectives of the current system without its complexities.

The broad objective of social security is to provide financial help to individuals and families who face distress and difficulty in a variety of circumstances, when the bread-winner is sick or un-employed, or the family is left without a bread-winner because of death or breakup of the family. One objective is to ensure that an adequate minimum income is guaranteed to all; another is to pre-vent families who are not necessarily poor from suffering unduly when income falls through some misfortune.

But a first question is to ask how many people do not receive the 'minimum income' and are thus let down by the system. To measure the numbers in poverty we have to define poverty, and there is no unique way of doing this. Two broad approaches may be distinguished. The first is to lay down an *absolute* level of income below which a family is defined to be in poverty. The second is to change the standard of poverty each year in line with some measure related to the living standards of the rest of the community. This represents a way of measuring *relative* poverty. We might examine this by looking at the number of people whose incomes fall below some specified fraction of the average. This level would change over the years and so there is a difference between the numbers of those in absolute poverty and the numbers in relative poverty. Most people's conception of poverty contains both a relative and an absolute component. We are more likely to contribute to a collection on behalf of the poor of Bangladesh than the poor of Sweden; but we might also regard inability to afford a television set as a mark of poverty, a view which would have been surprising in 1958 and incredible in 1938.

Table 7.2. shows the numbers of people in various years living

TABLE 7.2

Numbers in poverty in Britain, 1953–1973

	Standard of 1953		Standard of 1971	
	% of population	Number (m.)	% of population	Number (m.)
1953	4·8	2·4	21·0	10·6
1963	1·4	0·8	9·4	5·0
1973	0·2	0·1	2·3	1·3

Source: Fiegehen, Lansley, and Smith (1977), Table 3.4.

in households with income below the poverty line according to two standards of absolute poverty, the first defined as the national assistance scale in 1953 and the second the same scale (which had become the supplementary benefit scale) in 1971. It can be seen that there has been a dramatic decline in the number of people living in poverty during the post-war period. This mainly reflects the substantial rise in living standards, resulting from economic growth. The benefits of this growth have been shared by most sections of the community including the poor. In 1953, 21% of the population (over 10 million people) were living in poverty as defined by the 1971 standard: by 1977 this figure had fallen to 2·3% of the population. Nevertheless, it is remarkable that, again to judge by the 1971 standard, as many as 1·3 million individuals were living in poverty in 1973.

An alternative measure of the extent of poverty is the number of individuals living in poverty in any year according to the standard of poverty used to determine supplementary benefit scales in that year. Some estimates of numbers on this basis are shown in Table 7.3. This is not a measure of 'absolute' poverty because the real

TABLE 7.3

Numbers in poverty in Britain according to current standards,
1953–1973

	% of population	Number (m.)
1953	4·8	2·4
1963	5·5	3·0
1973	3·0	1·7

Source: Fiegehen, Lansley, and Smith (1977), Table 3.6.

value of supplementary benefits has risen over the years, but it may be thought to represent some general conception of a minimum. It has weaknesses, however, and a more generous Government which raised the level of benefits would increase the number living in poverty according to this criterion! But it is a measure of how far the present system has failed to achieve its objectives. By this standard around 2 million people are living in poverty in Britain, despite the panoply of measures designed to assist them.

Who are the poor?

The fact that so many people slip through the net of the welfare state in an affluent society is a serious deficiency in the system of income maintenance. To see why the system has failed we need to know who the poor are. It is instructive to note that even if 'the poor are always with us', at different times in history they have included very different groups of people. When Rowntree studied poverty in York at the end of the nineteenth century, low earnings were clearly its principal cause. In the 1930s most of those in poverty were the unemployed and their dependants; but in the 1970s, most of those who are poor are poor because they are old.

A study of poverty based on an analysis of the income and expenditure of over 7,000 families in 1971 was carried out by the National Institute of Economic and Social Research (Fiegehen,

Lansley, and Smith, 1977). It examined two questions. The first was to find out which characteristics seemed to account for most of the families in poverty (defined as income falling below the supplementary benefit level). The second was to find out which groups were subject to a particularly high risk of poverty. Both aspects of poverty are important. The former tells us about the relative importance of different causes of poverty and the latter which groups are especially in need. In the sample studied over half the poor were retired people, and between one-fifth and one-quarter of the retired were in poverty. Moreover, the survey excluded those living in institutions. Adequate provision for old age is clearly a major problem. The other groups vulnerable to poverty were found to be one-parent families and, to a lesser extent, the unemployed (it is still true that unemployment is a high risk category—one in five of the unemployed in the sample was in poverty). The major surprise was that poverty was not associated with having children to support, with the exception of single-parent families. This is a significant change from earlier periods, when it was thought that the burden of supporting a family was an important cause of poverty. The risk of poverty is significant only for families with large numbers of children; it exceeded 10% in the study only for families with five or more children and such families were only about 1% of the total number of households in the sample.

TABLE 7.4

Recipients of supplementary benefits, U.K.

('000s)

	1961	1975
Pensioners	1323	1739
Unemployed	142	556
Sick and disabled	280	255
One-parent families[1]	78	281
Others	78	59
Total	1901	2890

[1] Figure for 1961 is for families headed by a woman.
Source: Social Trends (1976) H.M.S.O, Table 5.23.

These conclusions are reinforced by the statistics of those receiving supplementary benefits shown in Table 7.4. The majority of recipients are pensioners, and the old clearly form the core of those in need. The remaining important groups of recipients are the unemployed, the sick and disabled, and one-parent families. This last group has grown in importance between 1961 and 1975. Supplementary benefits were originally conceived as a final line of help for those who had fallen through the net of social insurance, but this is hardly true today and in 1975 there were almost 3 million recipients of supplementary benefits. One of the grave disadvantages of this is that by no means all of the people who are entitled to benefits actually claim them. There may be several reasons for this; the wish to avoid the stigma of 'going on national assistance', a reluctance to go through the detailed questioning involved in claiming for means-tested benefits, and the sheer cost in terms of time and effort involved in claiming for a number of different benefits, some of which may be quite small. Inadequate 'take-up' is a major problem of means-tested benefits and the fact is that we do not really know why the take-up is so low and why it varies so much between benefits. Reviewing a number of local surveys of take-up rates the National Consumer Council (1977) concluded that not only were the rates surprisingly low but that the official national estimates (based primarily on the Family Expenditure Survey) were much higher than those found in local surveys. Moreover, take-up rates varied markedly for different benefits. For supplementary benefits, the official estimate of take-up for 1975 is 75% (*Annual Report of the S.B.C.*, 1975, Tables 10.1 and 10.2), whereas for rent allowances for tenants of privately owned property the rate seems to be often no more than 10%. The official estimate of the take-up of F.I.S. is 75%, but some local surveys put the figure much lower. A publicity drive has probably increased the rates in these areas to something more like the official figure, but ignorance of many of the means-tested benefits, especially in the housing field, seems at least partly responsible for low take-up.

Tax and social security

The relationship between the tax system and the social security system has recently been a subject of increasing concern. One difficulty is that the threshold at which income tax is payable has been for some households less than subsistence income as defined by the supplementary benefit level. There is certainly an element of paradox in an outcome in which the taxman collects revenue from groups whose earnings are below the level of basic social support provided for those who have no resources of their own. Unfortunately, the problem is rather more complex than many of those who have commented on this situation have recognized. It is very costly to raise the tax threshold and this is because the level of the threshold affects the liabilities of every single taxpayer, and not simply of those with low earnings. The effect of this is that the present outcome is by no means as irrational as it at first appears.

To see this, suppose that the tax threshold and benefit level were the same, so that we are more or less equally concerned to redistribute income to those on the verge of paying tax and to those in receipt of social benefits. To increase the incomes of the second group by £1 per week simply requires that benefits be increased by that amount. To give a similar benefit to the potential taxpayer requires that the tax threshold be raised by £3 per week (since 34% of £3 is approximately £1). But the effect of this is to give £1 per week to every taxpayer (and more to higher rate taxpayers since they receive relief at their marginal rate). This is much more costly, and the revenue can only be recouped by raising very sharply the marginal tax rate faced by those at and a little above the threshold so that the gains made by those with incomes higher than this are clawed back. Because marginal rates cannot exceed 100%, this can only be done roughly; and it can only be done at all by accepting very high marginal rates of tax, with corresponding disincentive effects, on those with low incomes. Thus a situation in which resources for those with low incomes have been deployed in raising the supplementary benefit level rather than the tax threshold is not necessarily irrational, but a possibly appropriate response to the difficult trade-offs between equity, efficiency, and incentives which are part of the problem of formulating satisfactory tax schedules. The people who suffer, of course, are those in full-time employment with low earnings. It is worth noting that the U.K. tax threshold is quite high by international standards, although the marginal rate paid by those who cross it is outstandingly high.

This argument supposes that working taxpayers and recipients of supplementary benefit can be treated as separate groups. In principle this is true, since those in work are ineligible for benefit and those who obtain supplementary benefit but are able to work are required to register for employment and accept a suitable job, if offered. But such provisions can only be limited in effectiveness; and there has been recent concern that the interaction of the tax and benefit systems makes voluntary unemployment as attractive as even reasonably well remunerated work.

TABLE 7.5

Annual income of a married man with two children

(£)

In work throughout year		In work for 6 months, S.B. for rest		S.B. for whole year	
Earnings	3770	Earnings	1885	Earnings	0
Child benefit	130	Child benefit	130	Child benefit	130
Tax	−639	Supplementary		Supplementary	
National		benefit	1080	benefit	2160
insurance	−217	Tax	0	Tax	0
		National		National	
		insurance	−108	insurance	0
	3044		2987		2290

The table shows equivalent annual figures for the same family as in Table 7.6.
Source: Own calculations.

In Table 7.5 and at subsequent points in this chapter we illustrate the circumstances of a household containing a husband, wife (who does not work), and two children aged 12 and 14. When in work, the husband earns £72·50 per week. This was approximately the average earnings of male manual workers in manufacturing in 1977. Table 7.5 shows the net income of such a household for the tax year 1977–8 if the husband was in work throughout the year. If he were not in full-time work, the family would be entitled to supplementary benefit at the rate of £37·05 per week, plus rent and rates, made up as shown in Table 7.6. We assume that rent is £5 and rates £2 per week: the family receives £2·50 per week in child benefit so that their supplementary benefit would be £41·55 per week.

It appears that such a family is substantially better off in work than if it receives supplementary benefit, and comparison of the first and third column of Table 7.5 suggests that this is true: the net income provided by supplementary benefit is only 75% of that obtained when the head of the household is in work. But the middle column of Table 7.5 shows what would happen if the husband worked for six months of the year and received supplementary benefit for the rest. In this case there is virtually no difference between his net earnings under these assumptions and what he would receive in work. How does this come about? The reason is that while he is in work he pays only national insurance contributions because his earnings over the year as a whole do not quite reach the tax threshold. If he did substantially more work during the year, however, he would pay tax at 39¾% on these earnings. When he receives supplementary benefit, he pays no tax at all: and since the S.B. rate is about 60% of his gross earnings this tax liability almost exactly eliminates the differential.

TABLE 7.6

Net weekly household income of a married couple with two children,
January 1978
(£)

In work		Unemployment benefit		Supplementary benefit	
Earnings	72·50	Benefit	23·80	Benefit	23·55
Child benefit	2·50	Child (1)	3·50	Child (1)	6·40
Tax	−12·29	Child (2)	3·00	Child (2)	4·60
National		Child benefit	2·50	Child benefit	2·50
insurance	−4·17	Rent rebate	4·00	Rent and rates	7·00
		Rate rebate	1·52	Tax rebate	12·37
		Earnings-related			
		benefit[1]	10·00		
		Tax rebate	12·37		
	58·54		60·69		56·42

Notes: Rent and rates are assumed to be £7·00. The children are assumed to be aged 12 and 14.

[1] This is the figure received on the assumption that the man received average earnings in the 1976–7 fiscal year of £59 per week. The supplement due on average earnings of £72·50 was £12·05.

Source: Own calculations.

We have used annual data because it clearly illustrates the principle, but people in this position probably rarely think about their income in this way (and in grossing up S.B. rates to annual figures we have ignored the fact that they are changed in the course of each tax year). What happens on a weekly basis depends on whether unemployment occurs at the beginning of the tax year or at the end. If it happens towards the end of the year, his weekly budget will be made up as in Table 7.6. He receives a tax rebate of £12·37 per week (though he will not necessarily receive this promptly or on a weekly basis), and the effect of the rebate is to make him more or less as well off on S.B. as in work. If he is unemployed at the beginning of the tax year, then he will receive no rebate and may think he is worse off. But if he succeeds in getting a job later in the year, his tax payments will then be lower than they would have been if he were in work throughout, and the net effect over the year as a whole will be just the same.

If he were in work for part of the year, it is likely that this household would be eligible for unemployment benefit, and we show in Table 7.6 what it might receive in this case. After some weeks it would be entitled to rent and rate rebates (which would be awarded for a period of six months). The tax position is just the same as with supplementary benefit, and hence the net weekly receipts of the household would, as shown in Table 7.6, be greater than if the head of household were in work. We have ignored in this discussion other benefits such as free school meals and prescriptions which increase the financial returns from unemployment still further. The net effect is that although national insurance and supplementary benefits are set at levels well below average earnings, even people with substantial earnings would find it financially advantageous to be unemployed for part of the year. Permanent unemployment is less attractive. There is nothing special about our example, and much more spectacular results can be obtained by postulating larger families.

It is important to note that raising the tax threshold would not mitigate the problem facing this particular household in any way. It would simply reduce the tax liability on the man's earnings over that part of the year for which the man was employed. An increase in the tax threshold would therefore increase both the net of tax income of the man continuing in work, and the tax rebate to the man who was unemployed for the remainder of the year by exactly the same amount. Raising the threshold would, however, reduce the number of people affected in this way because fewer households would be liable to tax.

The difficulty arises simply because the additional earnings of someone whose taxable income is sufficient to exhaust his tax allowances are taxed in full at $39\frac{3}{4}\%$ (34% income tax$+5\frac{3}{4}\%$ national insurance contributions), while national insurance and supplementary benefits are not taxed at all. It can only be alleviated by taxing these benefits in the same way as other income.

There is little evidence to suggest that the results of these anomalies are particularly serious, in the sense that much voluntary unemployment does in fact ensue. But it is clear that the picture which our calculations have presented is intuitively perceived by many people and justifiably resented, and that this impression that 'it is not worth while to work' brings both tax and social security systems into disrepute. The anomalies which arises from the non-taxable nature of sickness benefit are even more surprising. Many employers, including Government departments, now supplement a sick employee's national insurance benefit to a level which reflects his normal earnings. But since the benefit component is not taxed while the whole of earnings is, people in this position are necessarily better off when sick than when in work; in many instances by a substantial amount. Table 7.7. shows how the family we have been considering is better off when the bread-winner is sick and away from work, to the tune of £15·70 a week.

TABLE 7.7

Net household income when (a) in work (b) sick, December 1977
(£ per week)

In work		Sick	
Earnings	72·50	Sickness benefit	23·00
Child benefit	2·50	Child (1)	3·50
Tax	−12·29	Child (2)	3·00
National insurance	−4·17	Child benefit	2·50
		Supplement from employer	33·00
		Earnings-related benefit	10·00
		Tax rebate	1·14
		National insurance	−1·90
	58·54		74·24

See notes to Table 7.6.
Source: Own calculations.

Such difficulties are bound to arise when benefits which are paid as a substitute for earnings are taxed differently from earnings. When the net weekly receipts of a man who is sick or unemployed can vary by as much as £10–£20 on the basis of wholly capricious factors—such as the time of the year when this sickness or unemployment occurs—it is inevitable that the benefit system will prove too generous in some cases and too mean in others. The only reason why these characteristics are not more widely disliked and exploited than at present is that the system is so complex that they are very poorly understood. But there is a general feeling of unease at the interrelationship of tax and benefit system, and that unease is fully justified.

A further problem with this interrelationship is the 'poverty trap'; the disincentive effects of the high marginal rates of tax which result from the interaction of the tax system with the implicit tax rates which result from the withdrawal of means-tested benefits as income increases. It is possible to face simultaneously an income tax rate of $39\frac{3}{4}\%$, an implicit tax rate from F.I.S. of 50%, and rates of 6%–33% from losing rate and rent rebates, so that marginal tax rates can in some cases exceed 100%. To calculate the implicit marginal rate is a complex matter. The rates are not simply additive because of the interaction between the different benefits. In Table 7.8 we show how a poor household earning £30 per week cannot significantly increase its net income, and may actually reduce it, by increasing its earnings by any sum less than £20 per week.

These implicit marginal tax rates are very complicated to work out, not least for the individual concerned. Means-tested benefits are not awarded at the same time as tax is collected, and the periods over which they are calculated differ from the fiscal year. Some benefits (for example, F.I.S. and free school meals) run for up to twelve months once eligibility has been determined. Consequently, an increase in wages does not necessarily affect benefits received for several months, and a temporary increase might not affect them at all, or alternatively might affect them for a very lengthy period. This complexity conceals the poverty trap which many families face. In December 1975, 50,000 families were facing effective marginal tax rates in excess of 100% (Hansard, 22 November 1976, written answer by D.H.S.S.). It is doubtful whether any Government would openly advocate marginal tax rates of over 100% and this suggests some rationalization of the tax and benefit system. Equally, this very complexity makes it possible that a number of people are quite unaware that their marginal tax rates are so high, and so the disincentive effects are reduced. Whether a system which works only because people do not understand it is desirable is another matter.

TABLE 7.8

Net weekly household income at various earnings levels, December 1977 (£)

Earnings	30·00	35·00	40·00	45·00	50·00	55·00
Tax	0	0	1·23	2·93	4·63	6·33
National insurance	1·73	2·01	2·30	2·59	2·88	3·16
Take-home pay	28·27	32·99	36·47	39·48	42·49	45·51
Child benefit	2·50	2·50	2·50	2.50	2·50	2·50
Family income supplement	8·90	6·40	3·90	1·40	0	0
Rate rebate	1·76	1·56	1·36	1·17	0·96	0·66
Rent rebate	4·76	4·14	3·51	2·92	2·31	1·46
Net income	46·19	47·59	47·74	47·47	48·26	50·13

Household consists of a married man with non-working wife and two children aged 12 and 14 and pays rent of £5 per week and rates of £2 per week.
Source: Own calculations.

The final drawback to the present system that we may distinguish is the administrative complexity and cost of the system which is entailed by running so many different kinds of benefits at the same time. This is particularly true of means-tested benefits. Each case has to be investigated individually and some attempt made to verify the statements made by the claimant. Inevitably the costs are high not just for the administrators but for the claimants themselves. They have to be aware of the existence of a large number of schemes and each one involves both time and effort on the part of the claimant as well as the need to complete a number of quite challenging forms. Indeed, it is hard to see how someone in full-time employment would have the time to claim for all the benefits to which he or she might be entitled. The costs of paying national insurance benefits are about 4% of the benefits paid out, and costs are as high as 10%–15% of benefits for many of the means-tested

benefits (Meade Committee Report, 1978, App. XIII.3). It is obvious that a reduction in the number of means-tested benefits could
bring both greater simplicity and savings in costs.

Fundamental reforms

The complexity of the present system and its failure to eliminate
poverty suggest that it might be better to abandon the system and
instead adopt a single comprehensive scheme of income maintenance. One such proposal (originally put forward by Lady Rhys
Williams during the last war) is to scrap *all* existing social security
benefits and replace them by a single payment to households, the
amount of which would depend on the size and composition of the
household. This payment would be a kind of 'social dividend'. It
would be paid automatically to all households regardless of circumstances, and would be tax-free, thus representing a guaranteed
minimum income for each household. All personal tax allowances
would disappear and income tax would be imposed on all income
other than the social dividend. The operation of a social dividend
scheme is illustrated in Fig. 7.1. This shows how a family's income
after tax depends on its income before tax and the social dividend.
If there were no tax or benefit system at all each family would find
itself on the dashed 'no-tax line' on which income before tax
equals income after tax. With the social dividend scheme a family
receives the guaranteed minimum, shown by the distance OA in
the figure. As its earnings rise part of the increase is taxed away and
so net income rises less fast than gross income—the slope of the
line AD is less than the slope of the no-tax line. At some level of
income, shown by OC in the figure, the amount of tax paid equals
the social dividend received. This is the break-even level of income.
Below this level of income families are net recipients and above it
they are net contributors to the public purse.

A universal tax credit scheme would have just the same effect.
The idea of a tax credit is that instead of receiving a personal
allowance for income tax of, say, £945, an individual would be
given a weekly tax credit of £6·18 (£945×34%÷52). All his income would be taxable, but he could offset this credit against his
liability: so that if his income for the week was £50 he would pay
£10·82 (£50×34%−£6·18). For someone who earned as much as
this the system would work just as it does at present; the difference
is that those with low incomes could reclaim the credit, so that a

man with an income of £15 and a tax liability of £5·10 would receive a refund of £1·08. If the scheme is extended to the whole population, then it is exactly equivalent to a social dividend for everyone of £6·18. (The proposals of the 1972 Green Paper on tax credits would have covered only those in employment.)

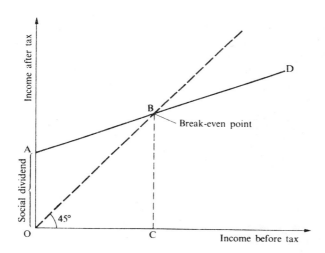

Fig. 7.1. A social dividend scheme

An alternative approach, but one which is again the same in its effects, is a negative income tax. The basic idea of a negative income tax is to extend the tax system to cover people whose incomes are below the current tax threshold. At present such households pay no tax and receive no benefits from the tax authorities. Under negative income tax households with incomes above the threshold would continue, as at present, to pay tax to the Government, and households below the threshold would receive money from the Government, just as they do under a tax credit system. The amount received would be the tax rate multiplied by the shortfall

of the family's income below the threshold. To see the equivalence
of a negative income tax and a social dividend scheme we may look
at Fig. 7.1. The tax threshold is the point at which no net tax is
paid, and is therefore equivalent to the break-even point of the
social dividend scheme. This is the income OC. Above this point
tax is paid and net income increases along the line BD. Below the
threshold a family receives negative tax payments which help to
offset the fall in its earnings, and it moves down the line AB. A
family with no income receives a guaranteed minimum of OA
which is equal to the tax rate multiplied by the value of the tax
threshold.

These systems appear simple, easy to understand, and capable
of providing a minimum income for all. Their drawback is their
cost. It is clear that a social dividend of £6·18 per week, which is
what could be financed from the existing personal tax allowance, is
quite inadequate for subsistence of any kind. In order to finance
the payment of a social dividend adequate to provide for those with
no other source of income, the tax rate has to be very high because
the social dividend is paid to everybody. Hence we need a high tax
rate to 'claw back' the dividend from the majority of families who
are not in need. To see how high the tax rate would have to be let
us assume that all other income is taxed at a single standard rate of
income tax (we have commented elsewhere on how little revenue is
raised by the higher rates of tax so this is a not unreasonable
assumption). Suppose that the social dividend (averaged over
different household types) is set at one-third of average incomes.
This is the same order of magnitude as current supplementary
benefit levels. The tax system must raise enough revenue to finance
both the social dividend and Government expenditure on goods
and services. The latter is around 25% of national income, and so
the required standard rate of tax would be approximately one-
third plus one-quarter, or somewhere between 55% and 60% Of
course this is a very rough calculation but it is clear that a social
dividend scheme of the kind we have outlined would require a very
high standard rate of tax, almost certainly in excess of 50%, and
this is unlikely to be judged acceptable.

So both social dividend and negative income tax schemes require
either unacceptably low guaranteed levels of social support or unacceptably high marginal rates of tax. It is possible to alter the
pattern of marginal tax rates by having, for example, a much higher

marginal tax rate on low incomes, but the basic conflict remains. It is worth noting that it is principally in the U.S. that schemes of this kind have been seriously discussed, and this is possible because the minimum income projected there is so low; thus the proposals put

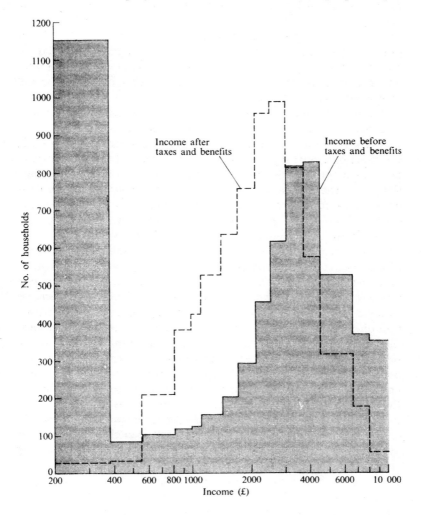

Fig. 7.2. Distribution of income in the U.K.
      (distribution is that of households sampled for *Family Expenditure Survey*, 1975)

forward in Senator McGovern's 1972 election campaign (which were considered wildly extravagant) would have given a married couple $2,000 per year, a figure little in excess of the U.K. supplementary benefit level at the time although per capita incomes in the U.S. were around twice as great. We can see why these proposals are ruled out in a European context by examining Fig. 7.2, which shows the distribution of household income in the U.K. before and after all taxes and benefits. The income distribution before taxes and benefits has two peaks, one between £3,000 and £5,000 and one close to zero, and these correspond to the typical incomes of households whose heads respectively are and are not in full-time work. The distribution of final income, by contrast, is more compressed and single-peaked.

Any scheme which distributes taxes or benefits by reference to income alone must operate by shifting the whole pre-tax distribution to the right, and hence preserves its initial shape. To ensure that adequate resources are provided for those with very low original incomes, it is necessary to move everyone to the right by the full amount of the subsistence income, and then keep the results within what aggregate national resources permit by compressing the resulting distribution with very high marginal rates of tax. All feasible social security systems operate by providing social support on a much more generous basis to those who are not in work than to those who are, thus shifting the left-hand peak in Fig. 7.2 well to the right and producing the single-peaked distribution of final income illustrated there. This reduces their cost very substantially; the disadvantage is that they do not deal satisfactorily with those who find themselves in the valley between the two peaks; those who have low earnings from full-time work, and heads of households who find it difficult, because of disability or the need to look after young children, to work full time.

Any attempt to solve the problem of poverty by a single comprehensive system of income maintenance, whether this is dressed up as a social dividend or a tax credit system, founders on the question of cost. It is necessary to pay more to poor people who are out of work than to those who are in work, and more to those who have been sick or unemployed for a prolonged period than to those who have recently suffered a loss of earnings in this way. In addition people's needs vary. There are substantial individual variations in housing costs, dietary requirements, disability, and so on. To pay everybody a social dividend equal to the requirements of the most needy individual would clearly be prohibitively expensive. Selectivity is essential. This is not to say that benefits must necessarily be means-tested. They may be paid according to certain characteristics of the recipient other than income, such as sickness, one-parent family status, disablement, old age.

The problems encountered by the present system and the sheer cost of alternative income maintenance schemes reflect the very real difficulty in finding a trade-off between conflicting aims and objectives. We have discovered no blueprint for reform which appears to offer a solution to the problems described above. This does not mean, however, that the present system cannot be improved, and a number of general issues have emerged from the discussion of this chapter.

Firstly, one effect of taxing sickness and unemployment benefit would be to remove some of the anomalies we described earlier. Secondly, if we refer back to the composition of those in poverty we find that the single largest group is the old. One reason for this is that the basic national insurance retirement pension is inadequate to prevent many people falling below supplementary benefit levels, and for various reasons they do not claim means-tested supplementary benefits. In the long run there is reason to hope that the reform of pensions initiated by the Social Security Pensions Act 1975 and the growth of occupational pensions will mean that pensions will be sufficient to prevent recourse to supplementary benefit on anything like the current scale.

But the main problem is that the new pensions scheme will not provide adequate pensions for twenty years or more. In the meantime the problem of the elderly will remain. The alternatives are either to increase state pensions to supplementary benefit levels, an expensive operation with $8\frac{1}{2}$ million pensioners, or to continue as we are with 22% of pensioners having to apply for supplementary benefit (this is in the figure for 1975 taken from *Social Trends*, 1976, Table 5.22) and many more not claiming benefits for which they are eligible. Neither of these alternatives is attractive and the problem of how to provide for the elderly over the period of the next twenty years or so is perhaps the most difficult problem in the field of social security.

In addition to the cost, there is a further problem in raising pensions which applies equally to the idea of raising other national insurance benefits, such as unemployment and sickness benefits, to 'subsistence' levels. At first sight there is a great attraction in the Beveridge idea of setting all national insurance benefits at subsistence level and using means-tested supplementary benefits as a genuine source of help for those with special needs. This would greatly reduce the numbers relying on supplementary benefits (in addition to the pensioners, 23% of those receiving unemployment benefit in 1975 also received supplementary benefit—*Social Trends*, 1976, Table 5.22) which in turn would help to reduce administrative costs. Unfortunately, the major reason for the shortfall of national insurance benefits is that supplementary benefits contain an allowance for rent or mortgage payments and rates, although rent and rate rebates help to reduce the gap. If there were a competitive housing market, national insurance benefits could be raised by some average price of housing services of a certain minimum standard, and the Beveridge principle adopted. But the housing market is in such a mess that any average allowance for housing costs would, on the one hand, leave many families with inadequate resources to meet their actual housing costs, and, on the other hand, be much too generous to many families living in heavily subsidized accommodation. The only real solution is reform of the housing market, but in the absence of this those responsible for running the social security system have to carry on as best they can, and one can only sympathize with them.

Whatever reforms are carried out there will always be a need for some form of help of last resort to cater for special or temporary need. It is very likely, and this was part of the Beveridge plan, that this help would be provided by means-tested benefits. As we have seen, one of the problems of means-tested benefits is that they experience low take-up rates. To overcome this greater advertising would help, but it is difficult to mount an effective campaign to advertise as many as 46 different benefits. Moreover, take-up is likely to remain low as long as claimants are expected to be aware of and understand both the existence and the rules for eligibility of so many benefits. Some rationalization is called for. This is easier said than done, but it should be possible to make some progress. Increases in national insurance benefits might make it possible to abolish some of the means-tested benefits altogether. Others could be merged; for example, some progress has been made in rationalizing the different benefits for housing into a single housing benefit.

The costs of applying for benefit could be reduced by extending the 'passport' system. Nevertheless, there will remain a need for a number of means-tested benefits to help those with special needs.

So far we have considered those not in full-time employment. But there remains the question of how to help those households where the head is in full-time employment and whose income is inadequate. At present such people cannot claim supplementary benefit even if their incomes fall below benefit levels. Wage-earners in this position would be better off financially if they were unemployed. This has been true since 1975 when the 'wage-stop' was abolished, under which an unemployed man could not claim more unemployment benefit than his previous take-home pay even if this was well below supplementary benefit level. To help those with low earnings a number of measures are possible, although they each have their own drawbacks. The first would be to raise the tax threshold to at least supplementary benefit level to increase the take-home pay of the lower-paid. A second measure would be to allow those in employment to claim supplementary benefits. This would be equivalent to a tax rate of 100% on earnings below benefit levels, and might provide employers with an incentive to offer low wages or even to reduce them. A third measure would be to introduce minimum wage legislation to ensure that those in employment receive adequate net incomes. This proposal has often been argued against on the grounds that setting statutory minimum wages would result in greater unemployment amongst those who were previously poorly paid. This is true in principle, although we have very little evidence as to what the quantitative effects of such legislation would be and how much unemployment would be created. Its advantages are that those in employment would receive adequate incomes, and those made redundant would be taken care of by unemployment and supplementary benefit. Without further information on the likely effects of minimum wage legislation it is difficult to be more definite, but such a proposal should not be ruled out simply because it has one undesirable consequence. In this area there are no ideal solutions.

The final set of benefits to consider are those relating to children. As we saw earlier, the fact of having children to support is becoming less important as a cause of poverty. Moreover, the shift from tax allowances to child benefits paid in cash to the mother is widely accepted as the best way for the system to evolve. The crucial question is how large should child benefits be? The answer to this question depends upon social attitudes to the encouragement of child-bearing, the effects of financial incentives on such decisions, and the cost of bringing up children. On the latter points we are very short of empirical evidence, and without it we hesitate to form a judgement about the appropriate level of child benefit.

There is one change, however, which we would recommend. The present system is excessively generous to working couples without children. Such a couple may claim both a married allowance and an additional personal allowance against the wife's earnings. The only justification for this can be to help couples with children, and this would be much more effectively achieved by a straight increase in child benefit. Hence we believe there is a strong case for abolishing the married man's allowance and using at least part of the proceeds to increase child benefits. We discuss this further in Chapter 13.

8

INDIRECT TAXES

Direct and indirect taxes

THE *Oxford English Dictionary* defines an indirect tax as one which is 'not levied directly upon the person on whom it ultimately falls, but charged in some other way, especially upon the production or importation of articles of use or consumption, the price of which is thereby augmented to the consumer, who thus pays the tax in the form of increased price'. We argued in Chapter 1 that the economic analysis contained in this definition is shaky, and in general such a distinction cannot be made. We mean by indirect taxes only what is usually meant by them (listing the most important in Table 8.1 on p. 136) and attach no special significance, and particularly no economic significance, to the classification.

Nevertheless, many people do. Indeed, it has almost become part of the conventional political wisdom of the U.K. that the tax structure relies too much on direct taxation—especially income tax —and too little on indirect taxes. We have already seen in Chapter 3 how a substantial change in the relative importance of these taxes has come about. In a period of inflation, a progressive income tax takes an ever-increasing proportion of real incomes while the real yield of indirect taxes (which are in many cases levied as fixed monetary amounts) declines. This shift has not been intended, and it reinforces the case for indexation, which is the only way in which inflation can be prevented from accidentally bringing about changes which no one wants to bring about by design. So it is not surprising that the balance of direct and indirect taxation should now be a subject of attention.

But some of the reasons which people have for believing that the present balance of direct and indirect taxation is wrong are bad ones. One is that it is thought that the disincentive effects of high rates of direct taxation can be reduced or avoided by a shift to in-direct taxes. This argument is quite simply false. Let us ignore for

the moment the role of savings, since it is the incentive to work
rather than the incentive to save which is at the centre of this concern: we have dealt with savings incentives at greater length in
Chapter 5. Then anyone considering whether to work longer hours
or assume more responsibility will weigh the obvious costs against
the benefits in terms of increased consumption which he (or she)
would derive: the additional effort would, we shall assume, generate additional earnings of £10 per week. Now compare a 50% tax
on all income with a 100% tax on all expenditure—since that is the
rate which is needed to maintain the same revenue. Then our
worker would discover that the extra £10 per week was reduced to
a net £5 per week by the income tax: with taxes on expenditure, it
would remain £10 but would only buy the same bundle of goods,
the additional £5 being absorbed by the indirect taxes. The reality
of the final outcome is exactly the same in both cases. It is possible
that for a time people might be misled into working harder to earn
larger monetary amounts before they noticed the reduced purchasing power of what they were receiving; but it is improbable
that this irrationality would persist for long. If it did, then inflation
—which puts larger quantities of less valuable money into wage-
packets in just the same way—would have precisely the same beneficial effect on incentives to work, and few people would find this
easy to believe.

The hope that the disincentive effects of high marginal rates of
taxation can be reduced by recasting direct taxes as indirect ones
is therefore quite chimerical. We should note also that the view
that shifting from income tax to a pay-roll tax (like employers'
national insurance contributions) would confer benefits, or even
make a significant difference in anything but the short run, is
erroneous in just the same way and for just the same reasons. A
pay-roll tax on all forms of employment will lead partly to employers being unable to pay the same money wage as before—and
hence to lower earnings than would otherwise have occurred—and
partly to an increase in labour costs which will be reflected in
higher prices for all goods and services. It is not easy to say which
of these effects will be predominant, but this determines only
whether we have (in the first case) slightly lower wages and lower
prices or (in the second case) somewhat higher wages and higher
prices, and the disincentive effects will be the same regardless of
whether its incidence resembles more that of an income tax or a

general commodity tax. One cannot remove the disincentive effects of taxes by disguising them under a different name, and those who look at our E.E.C. neighbours and are attracted by the combination of lower rates of income tax and higher pay-roll taxes are guilty of an error which is certainly not made by Continental managers and trade-unionists. What matters is the relationship between take-home pay and prices in the shops and this seems to be understood much better by the ordinary person than by many tax experts.

There are, however, two possible grains of truth in these arguments. One is that people may be more resentful of the fact that over half of the product of their extra effort goes in tax if this fact is intimated to them on their pay-slip than if the same money is extracted by their shopkeeper in a slightly more roundabout way, and that this resentment itself leads them to do less work—that people are willing to deprive themselves if they can also see that they are simultaneously depriving the taxman. (Musgrave (1959) describes this as the 'spite effect'.) Some people may have this psychological make-up, but the Social Survey (Radcliffe, 1954) found more people cited high prices than high taxes as an adverse influence on their incentive to work, and it is a weak argument for a particular tax structure that it would help to conceal the realities of the tax system from people who have pathological views about it.

The second point is that indirect taxes are generally less progressive than direct taxes—mainly, though not entirely, because there is a threshold of income which is exempt from income tax while all expenditure, however small, is vulnerable to commodity taxation: we pay commodity taxes on every penny of expenditure but not on the first £945 of income. This means that the marginal rate of income tax is generally substantially above the average rate, while for commodity taxes there is little difference between the two. Thus indirect taxes can yield the same revenue from lower marginal rates, and hence disincentive effects (which depend on these marginal rates) would be reduced if this were done. This argument is perfectly valid, but it rests on the reduction in progressivity, not on the shift in the structure of taxation, and this reduction could be equally well—and more honestly—achieved by altering the rates of direct tax than by changes to different kinds of tax.

The second bad argument for preferring indirect to direct taxes suggests that the former are voluntary in a sense in which the latter are not: this notion is reflected in an older terminology which distinguishes 'escapable' and 'inescapable' taxes. It is true that any particular indirect tax can be avoided by any particular individual who chooses not to consume the taxed good. But it is also true, given that a certain amount of revenue is required, that taxes in general cannot be avoided by individuals in general. So an 'escapable' tax leaves the person who escapes it worse off—since he would have preferred, in happier circumstances, to have consumed the good which is taxed—and it makes everyone else worse off too, since it requires a higher rate of tax on those who continue to consume the good. Thus the tax structure to which this argument would lead is the worst possible in terms of economic efficiency—it maximizes the welfare loss which is additional to the basic and inescapable burden of the tax.

Principles of indirect taxation

What then would an efficient system of commodity taxes be like? A first principle is that there should be no taxes on intermediate goods—on items like sheet steel or turbo-generators which are sold to other producers rather than to final customers. Taxes on things must of course ultimately be paid by people, so that levies on producers must finally be borne by taxpayers generally in one capacity or another, as consumers, workers, or owners of firms. Hence the imposition of taxes on producer goods does not reduce the tax burden in any way; in fact it will actually increase it by inducing producers to make different and (from a social viewpoint) less efficient choices of inputs. Essentially, the principal objectives for indirect taxes—raising revenue, achieving some distributional aims, or encouraging or discouraging particular consumption patterns— can all be more efficiently achieved by the imposition of taxes on final goods alone (Diamond and Mirrlees, 1971).

The burden of commodity taxation should therefore be confined to final goods: how should it be distributed among them? Economic efficiency requires that indirect taxes should be cast so as to minimize the distortion of consumer choice involved—that as far as possible, the revenue should be raised without diverting tax-payers into less preferred patterns of consumption in their (collectively unsuccessful) attempts to avoid tax. At first sight, it might appear that this implies that all commodities should be taxed at the same rate and this has often been assumed; but there are at least two reasons why such an argument is false. First, while a uniform tax on all commodities will minimize distortion of the consumer's choice between different commodities, it will nevertheless have disincentive effects on his choice between leisure and work. So if a heavier tax is levied on commodities for which demand is inelastic —goods which the consumer will buy in any case—a lower rate of tax can be imposed on other goods and the disincentive to work reduced with little consequential distortion of choice of commodities. And if heavier taxes go on goods which are in some respects substitutes for work—like camping, sport, and yachts— and lighter ones on complementary activities—like overalls, travel to work, and this book—then this too will tend to ameliorate the disincentive effects of commodity taxation. These considerations underlie the 'Ramsey rules' (Ramsey, 1928; Baumol and Bradford, 1970) which say, very roughly, that commodity taxes should have the effect of reducing demand for all commodities in the same proportion.[1]

But these rules ignore the second weakness of the case for uniform commodity taxation—that it ignores the distributional impact of such taxes. This is a basic objection not only to uniform taxation, but to the Ramsey rules themselves. These are the answer to the question, 'If we are not concerned about the source of tax revenue, but simply aim to raise a given amount of revenue with minimal disincentive effect, what commodity taxes should we impose?' But if we are really not concerned about the source of our tax revenue, we should not impose commodity taxes at all; we can simply divide public revenue requirements equally among the whole population and raise them by means of a universal poll tax which avoids distortion altogether. Of course, the distributional consequences of this would be unacceptable, and that is why we adopt income and commodity taxes instead. But this means we cannot choose rates for these taxes independently of our view of distribution, so that commodity taxes must be chosen according to principles which take account of the distributional characteristics of goods as well as their demand elasticities.

Since the commodity composition of expenditure changes as income rises, indirect taxes can be used to influence distribution by imposing higher taxes on goods which attract a higher proportion

---

[1] The rules take this precise form only for small tax revenue and compensated changes in demand.

of the expenditure of the rich. It need hardly be said that this too cannot be accomplished without disincentive effects—if managing directors spend a larger fraction of their income on caviar than their deputies then a heavy tax on it will discourage the latter group from aspiring to the positions of the former. And further analysis suggests that there may not be much advantage in using commodity taxes in this way. Adjustments to income tax can achieve similar effects more sensitively, and without diverting rich and poor alike into celebrating festive occasions with cider and fish paste rather than champagne and caviar. We might still, however, see some case for taxing 'prestige goods', such as Rolls Royces, whose attraction is derived not so much from their intrinsic utility but from the prestige which their limited availability confers on the owners.

Differential commodity taxation does not look a promising method of redistributing income, but there is a further possibility we could consider. We saw in Chapter 5 that an ideal tax system might be one which avoided disincentive effects entirely by taxing not earnings but the ability to earn. If we look at the kinds of goods which are consumed in relatively large quantities by the affluent, we might try to distinguish two categories. There are goods like large houses, expensive motor cars, and yachts, which most people would like to buy if they could afford to. But there may also be other goods which are consumed only or mainly by people with high earning ability. Books and opera tickets might come into this category. We have seen that it is impossible to levy taxes on the first kind of good without disincentive effects; but it is possible to avoid them by taxing the second. Taxes of this kind represent a method —the only method—of relating tax liability to earning capacity as distinct from earnings. For example, if certain social groups send their children to public schools and if appointment to lucrative jobs in the City is made from this group, then we would wish to impose a heavy tax on public school fees. We might also redistribute by subsidizing goods which people with high earnings potential tend not to buy at any price—such as bingo sessions and certain Sunday newspapers. The difficulty with such a policy is immediately evident. We are confident that readers of this book have above-average earning capacity. But are they reading it because this is the kind of book which people of superior intellect and ability like to read: or is it that they have acquired their superior intellect and ability as a result of their taste for reading books like this one? Probably both are true; but in the former case we should wish to tax the book heavily and in the latter case to subsidize it heavily.

Whatever category readers actually do comprise, they may by now share our scepticism as to whether there are in fact large gains to be obtained by departures from a general principle of uniformity in commodity taxation. The administrative arguments against doing so are substantial. In order to exploit differences in the distributional characteristics of goods, it will be necessary to adopt a rather fine commodity classification—to distinguish not only cheese from other dairy products but Cheddar from Camembert and White Stilton from Blue. (The 1974 cheese subsidy scheme attempted just that.) Such distinctions are likely to lead to administrative nonsense and to large and pointless distortions of consumer choice. It is not easy to believe that the information required to devise an optimal scheme is likely to be available, or likely to be used to good effect if it is.

There remain some arguments for taxes or subsidies on particular commodities. One is simple paternalism—I, as Chancellor of the Exchequer, think that people (presumably other people) drink too little milk or too much beer and seek to remedy the situation by fiscal incentives. Another justification for these corrective taxes can arise if they allow prices to be adjusted so as to ameliorate the effect of inefficiencies elsewhere—if electricity for space-heating is too cheap, then one way to stop excessive use of such electricity is to impose a tax on space-heaters. As the example suggests, it is usually preferable (though not always possible) to tackle such problems directly rather than to adopt 'second-best' policies of this kind. A slightly different argument concerns goods whose production or consumption imposes costs or benefits on those who are not themselves directly involved in buying and selling them— goods which are made in smoky factories, transported in juggernaut lorries, or grown in attractive orchards. The 'external effects' of these goods are not fully accounted for by the person or organization who provides them. Hence they will tend to be over- or under-supplied—there will be too many juggernauts and too few orchards. Economists have long argued (with rather little practical effect) that these problems might more appropriately be dealt with by means of taxes and subsidies on the products concerned than by administrative regulation.

A further reason for indirect taxes may be to act as a tariff; to improve the balance of payments by discouraging imports and to give advantages to British producers of competitive goods. An effect of E.E.C. membership has been that duties which were formerly wholly or partly tariffs have been recast as indirect taxes. This is not a substantive change, since domestic production of tobacco and wine (from English grapes) is insignificant. The relative prices of (foreign) wine and (domestic) beer are unaffected. This consideration may also have been one motive for the so-called 'luxury' rate of V.A.T. (p. 139 below), which falls heavily on imported goods.

Indirect taxes in Britain

If we examine the structure of commodity taxes in the U.K., we find one general sales tax—V.A.T.—and heavy duties on three products—tobacco, alcoholic drinks, and petrol. Table 8.1 shows their relative contributions to revenue in 1975. We consider these major indirect taxes in turn.

TABLE 8.1

Revenue from indirect taxes, 1975

		(£ m.)	(%)
V.A.T.		3502	35
Tobacco		1583	16
Hydrocarbon oils		1521	15
Beer	616 ⎫	1476	15
Wines and spirits	860 ⎭		
Vehicle licence duties		705 ⎫	
Tariffs		540 ⎪	
Stamp duties		266 ⎪	19
Betting duties		258 ⎬	
Car tax		169 ⎪	
Other		11 ⎭	
		10 031	100

Source: C.S.O., *National Income and Expenditure* (1976).

The basic principle of V.A.T. is that it is a sales tax chargeable to the sellers of all output, with the proviso that in computing their liability firms may deduct any V.A.T. which has been levied on inputs into their products. We can see how this works by considering a simple example with a standard rate of V.A.T. of 10%. Suppose a man discovers a block of iron which with the aid of a magic wand (provided free of charge) he turns into steel worth £100. Adding V.A.T. at 10% he sells this to a motor-car firm for £110. The firm buys additional components which cost £500 to make and on which it is charged £50 V.A.T., and employs labour at a cost of £400. It sells the car for £1,300, charging 10% V.A.T., to make up a total price to the purchaser of £1,430 and secure a profit of £300. The firm now assembles its accounts for this set of transactions, which are

Revenues			Costs	
£			£	
	V.A.T.			V.A.T.
Car	1,300	130	Steel	100	10
			Components	500	50
			Labour	400	
			Profit	300	
				1300	60

It must now account to the Customs and Excise for the difference between the V.A.T. levied on its outputs (£130) and the V.A.T. charged on its inputs (£60) so that it makes a payment of £70. This amounts to 10% of the £700 of *value added* in the car factory: the difference between the values of inputs and outputs, made up of £400 of labour costs plus £300 profit, and indeed it would be possible to compute the tax in this way. (This would be an *accounts* basis for the tax, in contrast to the *invoice* basis which is what we are describing and which is used in the U.K. and in the E.E.C.) At the same time as the V.A.T. man receives the car firm's cheque for £70, he also gets £50 from the component manufacturer and £10 from the steel producer, so that in aggregate £130 (10% of the value of the final output) is levied on the sequence of transactions involved in the production of the car. It is easy to check that this amount would remain the same however few or many transactions are involved in the chain of production.

Thus the main advantage of V.A.T. is that it is a method of

levying a tax on all commodities that enter consumption while effectively exempting all intermediate goods—those who buy goods for further processing receive a refund of the tax which they have been charged, and only those who are the final consumers of the goods actually pay it. Thus it seems an ideal tax judged by the first of the principles of indirect taxation described above—the taxation of producer goods is systematically avoided. The price paid for this is a high one, however. As will be clear from the exposition above, the tax is complex and, as is inevitable if a charge is levied on every transaction in the economy and refunded on most of them, it is very expensive to administer. We noted in Chapter 3 the increase in Inland Revenue costs over the period 1966–7 to 1975–6: the rise in Customs and Excise costs over the same period is much greater, from £33 m. to £174 m., and V.A.T. is a major culprit. It is estimated that it costs about twice as much to collect per £ of revenue as did the purchase tax which it replaced (cf. Customs and Excise, 1976: and estimates of Richardson Report, 1964.) But the administrative burden is much greater than this. V.A.T. is a self-assessed tax—forms must be completed and tax paid or refunds claimed by the taxpayer himself, subject to random checks by control officials. Compliance costs incurred by taxpayers will certainly exceed direct costs by a substantial margin. Although we do not know how large these costs are, the number of taxpayers increased from 74,000 in the last year of purchase tax to 1·2 million under V.A.T.: and the number of collectors rose from 2,000 to over 13,000 (Parr and Day, 1977). While V.A.T. is relatively easily manageable for large organizations with sophisticated accounting systems, a survey of a limited group of small retailers put compliance costs at 78% of the revenue obtained (Godwin, 1976).

The Richardson Committee concluded in 1964 that V.A.T. had no merits sufficient to compensate for these acknowledged administrative problems, and proposals to introduce it were rejected at that time. Two developments led to its implementation in the U.K. The first was the adoption of the French V.A.T. by West Germany and subsequently by other members of the E.E.C. In both France and Germany, V.A.T. replaced unsatisfactory turnover taxes, levied cumulatively at each stage of production, which were both expensive to run and inefficient in economic effects (the rate of tax depended only on the number of stages in the production process). In Britain, however, purchase tax, a single-stage, broadly based commodity tax levied on wholesalers, had developed into a relatively cheap and simple fiscal instrument. But the adoption of V.A.T. became part of the process of harmonization to E.E.C. institutions. Such harmonization would have substance as well as form only if two further conditions were fulfilled; first, if there was similarity between countries in tax base and rate structure, and second, if they ceased to refund tax on their exports and levy it on imports, as at present (i.e. if the tax had an 'origin' rather than a 'destination' basis). The second development was the failure of an attempt to tax services (purchase tax was levied only on physical commodities). S.E.T. (selective employment tax) was a weekly tax per employee, chargeable to firms in service industries, and administered by levying it on all employees and refunding it to manufacturers. The case for S.E.T. was poorly presented (mainly in terms of a desire to transfer labour from service to manufacturing industry), the definition of the borderline between the two sectors gave rise to constant anomalies, and the tax proved wildly unpopular. V.A.T. offered a mechanism by which the taxation of services could be integrated into a general system of commodity taxes, and when it was introduced in 1973 S.E.T. disappeared, unlamented. If a more acceptable method of imposing a general tax on services could have been devised—and possibly S.E.T. might have developed into such a tax if the base had been shifted to payroll, as was proposed, and the anomalies had been ironed out—then the administrative advantages of a purchase tax/services tax system, especially for small firms, would suggest that arrangements of this kind might be superior to the present V.A.T.

As V.A.T. is currently operated, there are three rates of tax: zero—which includes food, books, and children's clothing—the standard rate, currently 8%; and the 'luxury' rate of $12\frac{1}{2}\%$, levied on such diverse items as vacuum cleaners, fur coats, and boats. Additionally, some products—such as financial services, education, and funerals—are exempt. Exemption is not the same as zero rating, since while the exempt trader need pay no tax on his outputs his zero-rated colleague can reclaim the tax paid on his inputs as well: so it is always better to be zero rated than exempt, and (if the value of output sold to final consumers is less than the value of taxed inputs) it may even be more beneficial to be standard-rated than exempt. Consumption of food does not rise in proportion to income (Fig. 14.1, p. 245) and because it is both zero-rated and a

substantial part of the budgets of poorer families the distributional
impact of V.A.T. is slightly progressive.

TABLE 8.2

Rates of V.A.T.

Zero	8%	12½%	Exempt
Food	All other	Electrical goods	Land
Water	commodities	(not cookers,	Insurance
Books		heaters)	Postal services
Fuel and power		Radio and	Betting
Construction[1]		television sets	Finance
Exports		Boats	Education
Transport		Aircraft	Health services
Children's		Small caravans	Burial and
clothing		Cameras and	cremation
Protective		projectors	
clothing		Binoculars	
Large caravans		Furs	
		Jewellery	
		Petrol	

[1] New construction is zero-rated. 'Improvement' is zero-rated, but 'repair'
standard-rated: the distinction is obviously unenforceable.

V.A.T. is the only major tax in the U.K. for which inflation
poses no problems. The base is simply the value of current transactions and the tax is proportional, so receipts rise automatically
with, and no faster than, prices in general. But inflation has had
substantial effects on the other major indirect taxes. The taxes on
tobacco, alcohol, and petrol are fixed monetary amounts; unless
they are regularly increased in inflationary periods their real value
and the real cost of the relevant products will steadily decline. This
is precisely what has happened, as Table 8.3 shows. In this table,
we show not only the actual rates of tax which were levied at the time
but also what these rates would be if adjusted to 1977 price levels.
If these taxes had kept pace with inflation between 1966 and 1977
cigarettes would be dearer by 6p per packet, whisky by £2 per
bottle, beer by 2½p per pint, and petrol by 13p per gallon. Since
1974, however, increases in these taxes have amounted to *de facto*

indexation and justifications offered for these increases suggest that this is more or less a conscious policy.

TABLE 8.3

Indirect taxes, 1966–1977

Year	Actual rates				At 1977 prices			
	cigarettes	whisky	beer	petrol	cigarettes	whisky	beer	petrol
1966	16	1·88	4·3	18	46	5·43	12·3	52
1969	18	2·20	4·7	23	46	5·59	11·9	57
1972	18	2·20	4·7	23	37	4·58	9·8	47
1975	29	2·80	7·5	37	39	3·77	10·0	50
1976	31	3·16	8·7	39	36	3·63	10·0	45
Tax, 1977					40	3·45	9·7	39
Retail price, 1977					53	4·15	28·0	82

Cigarettes: pence per packet of 20 standard tipped.
Whisky: £ per bottle blended whisky.
Petrol: pence per gallon 4 star.
Beer: pence per pint.
All figures include V.A.T. where applicable. Figures relate to August in each year.
Sources: Reports of Customs and Excise; own estimates.

As Table 8.3 shows, the difference between the rates of tax imposed by V.A.T. on the major part of consumers' expenditure and the rates on these selected items is very great: tax accounts for the major part of the price of cigarettes and whisky, and the effective rates on beer and petrol, though lower, still mean that the prices of these commodities relative to others are wildly different from what they would be if the structure of indirect taxation were non-discriminatory. The taxes on alcohol and tobacco are not, of course, imposed for reasons which are recognizably economic in character. There is some talk of the inelastic demand for these commodities (demand for tobacco is inelastic—a 10% price rise might reduce consumption by 1½%—and the same may be true for beer, but consumption of wines and spirits is rather sensitive to price: see Deaton, 1975). The unpleasant consequences which their consumption has for others may also be cited (although smokers make reduced demands on public services by dying prematurely and alcohol as social lubricant has beneficial as well as adverse external effects). But the real reason these taxes exist is that it is rather easy to induce feelings of guilt about these forms of consumption: and as a result it is more acceptable to raise revenue in this way than in others. Taxes on alcohol were raised very sharply during and immediately after the First World War, and those on tobacco during and just after the Second World War, in periods when such moralistic sentiments were particularly easily aroused.

The adverse consequences of smoking on health have drawn attention to the tobacco tax. A common view is that the Government 'cannot afford' to discourage smoking because of the loss of tax revenue which would result. A reduction in smoking would affect the Government budget in a rather wide range of ways. The most immediate secondary consequence would be a reduction in medical costs and in claims for sickness benefit. These savings would grow, but over time a number of other factors would become important. Because reduced consumption of cigarettes would significantly increase life expectancy, there would be a rise in revenue from income tax, but an increase also in the cost of retirement pensions and medical treatment for larger numbers of elderly people, partly offset by a reduction in widow's pensions and benefits. Atkinson and Townsend (1977) have quantified a number of these items, which are substantial, and the effects on revenue from tobacco duties are not the only, or necessarily the dominant, element in the calculation of the effects of changes in smoking habits on the Government budget.

But as this discussion should make clear, to evaluate these factors simply from the standpoint of their effect on Government revenue and expenditure is to take an extremely—indeed offensively—narrow viewpoint. What is required is a much wider cost-benefit analysis, and the framework of this has been set out by Atkinson and Meade (1974). Recent work by Atkinson and Townsend (1977) leaves little doubt that an increase in the tax on tobacco would yield an increase in both Government revenue and social welfare. But the force of these arguments has not influenced policy sufficiently to prevent a substantial cut being made in the real burden of the tax. On the (low) estimate of demand elasticity cited above, simple indexation of the tobacco tax over the period in which the relationship between smoking and lung cancer has been known would have reduced deaths from this cause by between 500 and 1,000 per year.

The major change which has been made in tobacco tax has been to shift the tax on cigarettes from one based on weight of tobacco to one in which tax is levied at 30% of the retail price and 0·9p per cigarette. This change had made cigarettes with coupons less attractive (since the value of the gifts is, in effect, subject to this 30% tax); has favoured the sale of king-size cigarettes (since the 0·9p is independent of the length of the cigarette); and has reduced the incentive for manufacturers to economize on the tobacco content of cigarettes. These moves have been made in response to E.E.C. harmonization proposals. Doubtless, there is some advantage to them, but we have been unable to discover what it is. Tobacco substitutes are taxed on the same basis as other tobacco products.

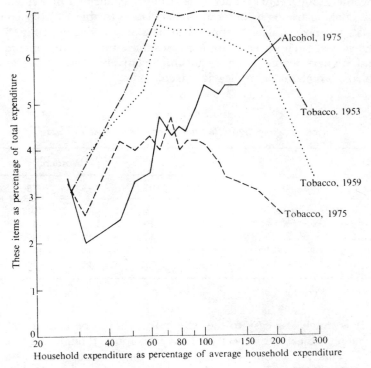

Fig. 8.1. Spending on alcohol and tobacco related to household expenditure

One result of the embarrassment which people feel about their consumption of alcohol and tobacco is that information about the incidence of these duties is unreliable. When asked by the Family Expenditure Survey to record their expenditure on drink and cigarettes, people do not tell the truth, and it is believed that such spending is substantially under-reported (in the case of alcohol, by about 40%; *Family Expenditure Survey*, 1975). Figure 8.1 shows the available data, but it is necessary to bear in mind that the incidence of deception (and self-deception) may be related to income level. But it seems that the tobacco tax is regressive (it takes a higher fraction of income from the poor than from the rich) and there is some indication that this regressivity is increasing, since tobacco consumption seems to have fallen more among high-income groups. This tendency is strongly confirmed by evidence on smoking trends in different social classes (Table 8.4). By contrast, the tax on alcohol appears to be a progressive one; Fig. 8.1 shows that such expenditure increases more rapidly than income, and higher-income groups consume relatively more wines and spirits, which are more heavily taxed.

TABLE 8.4

Percentage of cigarette smokers by sex and social class

		Men		Women	
Social class		1958	1975	1958	1975
I	Professional	54	29	43	29
II	Intermediate	58	43	43	38
III	Skilled	60	47	42	45
IV	Partly skilled	54	48	42	41
V	Unskilled	61	57	42	48

Source: Lee (1976).

It is much less easy to see why petrol should be considered a suitable subject for especially heavy taxation, though there are arguments for a somewhat higher tax than that on other commodities. Some rationale can be derived from the second-best and external effects arguments described above. Motorists impose disutility on each other and on the population at large: and since road space is costly to provide but can be used free of charge, provision will be excessive if all demands at a zero price are met. To the extent that the case for petrol tax rests on these arguments, the usual objections to the taxation of intermediate goods do not apply: the demands of industry for road transport are clearly not less offensive or less pressing than those of private motorists. But it is difficult to decide what levels of tax would be justified by these considerations. Taxes on vehicles and on petrol amount to more than 150% of related public expenditures, but in the light of the arguments above it is not clear that this figure is too high.

We have already noted that the structure of indirect taxation occasions much less criticism than do the present direct taxes, and we share this view. But we do not consider that the weaknesses of the present direct tax system would be significantly alleviated by a shift from direct to indirect taxes, and we think that the proper balance between the two is actually one of the less important questions facing current British tax policy. The prominence of this issue in current debate is, we suspect, the product of a failure to understand fully the implications of one of the basic principles of public finance which we described in Chapter 1—the irrelevance of the formal incidence of a tax to its effective incidence. It follows from this that one cannot make major improvements, or indeed large changes, simply by changing the identity of the payer of a tax. Nevertheless, there are reasons for supposing that the U.K. would do better to rely rather more on indirect taxes than it does at present. The most important of these is the problem of enforcement. Any tax is subject to difficulties of defining the base, of policing, of preventing avoidance and evasion. These problems increase more than proportionately with the rates of any particular tax, and indeed we have seen how at very high rates of tax they become overwhelming. If this is so, then if we are to have two broadly based taxes it is better to have two 'medium' taxes rather than one high and one low tax, and some narrowing of the gap between the 8% standard rate of V.A.T. and the 34% basic rate of income tax would be advantageous. For this purpose, it is desirable to have a more broadly based set of indirect taxes than at present—in practice, this means levying V.A.T. on food, as we shall discuss in Chapter 14.

9

LOCAL TAXATION

Rates and local authority finance

LOCAL authorities levy rates on immovable property—houses, shops, offices, factories (though not farms)—within their area of jurisdiction. The basis of the tax is the 'net annual value' of the property. This figure is assessed from time to time and is intended to be the amount for which the property might be let if the tenant were responsible for all repairs. The rate is then fixed as a poundage, so that with a rate of 70p in the £ the owner of a property assessed at an annual value of £500 would pay £350 each year in rates. Although in general there is more than one local authority exercising functions in any area, a system of 'precepting' means that the lower tier authority is responsible for all rate collection.

We distinguish domestic rates—levied on houses—from industrial and commercial rates. Domestic rates are a tax on housing, and a heavy one. The yield of domestic rates in 1976–7 was about £1,800 m. The C.S.O. estimated consumers' expenditure on housing in 1976 at £10,900 m. (including rates); this is a rather arbitrary and unreliable figure, but it suggests an effective tax rate on housing of 20%, and it is clear that housing is taxed much more heavily than the bulk of consumers' expenditure (the average rate is 10·8%, see p. 25). Such heavy taxation would normally severely discourage consumption of a good, but this probably does not apply to housing. This is not for the obvious reason that people need houses: they do, but they do not need houses of a particular size or quality and can and do economize on these things. Rather the disincentive effect of rates is offset by the existence of specific subsidies to all major forms of tenure—tax concessions to owner-occupation, subsidies to local authority tenants, and rent controls in the private sector—and the net effect of all these factors on the over-all demand for housing is unclear.

Since no free market in rented housing has existed for many

years, it is difficult to measure satisfactorily the rental values which are supposed to be the basis of the tax. Two post-war revaluations have been conducted (in 1963 and 1973). In these, assessed values for house property have in practice been determined in relation to other assessed values, and it is obscure how the process ever got started: it has now been proposed that any future domestic revaluations will be based on the capital value, rather than the rental value, of the house, and a divisor will be specified to produce comparability between domestic and non-domestic valuations. Revaluations change, often rather radically, the relative tax burden on different ratepayers; and both revaluations have led to extensive discontent with the rating system and the establishment of Committees of Inquiry. The Allen Committee, reporting in 1965, identified the regressive impact of the rating system. This arises at the lower end of the distribution largely because many people (especially pensioners) live in houses which reflect their past, rather than their current, income; while at the upper end rateable values increase less rapidly than either the capital value of houses or the incomes of those who live in them. As a result of the Allen Report, a system of rate rebates was instituted. It was much extended in 1974 and in 1974–5 rebates were paid to 2·2 million claimants. Additionally, rates are paid for recipients of supplementary benefit. These measures would largely have eliminated the problem of the rate burden on low-income households were it not that the number claiming is thought to represent only 60%–70% of those eligible for rebate (National Consumer Council, 1977). The Layfield Committee, which reported in 1976 (Cmnd. 6453), had a broader brief which enabled it to investigate local government finance as a whole. Its major recommendation was for a much clearer demarcation of the functions of central and local government, either by a tightening of central control or a strengthening of local autonomy (the latter was clearly preferred). This second change would, the Committee considered, have required the introduction of a local income tax, in part to supplement and in part to replace the present rating system. These recommendations were rejected by the Government in Cmnd. 6813, 1977 (the Green Paper).

Many people think of rates only as domestic rates, and it is not widely realized that domestic rates are not the most important component of the total rate burden nor rates the most important source of finance for local authorities. Industrial and commercial

TABLE 9.1

Sources of local authority finance

	1966–7		1976–7	
	£ m.	%	£ m.	%
Government grants	1457	51	7200	63
Non-domestic rates	804	28	2500	22
Domestic rates	611	21	1700	15
	2872		11 400	

Sources: Cmnd. 6813 (H.M.S.O., 1977); C.I.P.F.A., *Return of Rates*; Layfield Report, Tables 26, 27 (H.M.S.O., 1976).

rates are not paid by the buildings themselves, though this impression is sometimes given; thus one commentator on local government finance has written 'industry and business will have to pay more. This is right and proper; such hereditaments can obviously afford to contribute more to the public purse' (Ilersic, 1973, p. 104). The formal incidence of rates falls on the occupiers of property, the businesses which make use of it; the effective incidence is divided, in very uncertain proportions, between the owners of the business, their employees, the people who buy its products, and the owners of the actual property. Rates are borne by the owners of commercial and industrial property to the extent that they are capitalized, i.e. reflected in a lower capital value for the rated property (see Ch. 1). Where land prices are a principal element in property values, this is likely to be the case: thus if the rates were removed from Central London office property, competition could be expected to bid rents up to very nearly the present level set by rent and rates together and the main effect would be an increase in property prices. This will be partly true for commercial property in other city centres. Outside these areas, however, rates primarily represent an addition to the cost of one factor of production—buildings. The result of this will be that offices and factories will tend to be more cramped, less well fitted, and less well located than they would otherwise be, and since the tax is an extremely heavy one (in 1976–7 it averaged 72·5% of 1973 rental values) this effect is likely to be substantial. The incidence of the tax will largely fall on final consumers, in these cases, but since they will not be willing to pay more for goods produced in highly rated areas deviations from the over-all average level of rates will be reflected in different local levels of profits, earnings, and employment opportunities. Industrial and commercial rates are a worse tax, not a better one, for being a poorly perceived and understood tax on intermediate goods.

'Site-value rating', which would be based on land values alone, would seem much more attractive, since it would fall entirely on landowners and have no distortionary economic effects. But although it operates in some countries (Australia and New Zealand) there are some practical difficulties in its application to the U.K. (there is no comprehensive register of land ownership), and it could not plausibly be expected to yield revenue on the scale of the existing rating system.

In general we have been able to consider tax policy quite independently of public expenditure decisions, and that reflects the structure of decision-making in the U.K. This is not possible in examining local government finance, since local authorities are autonomous units with a requirement to balance their budgets and to raise from rates or charges that part of expenditure which is not financed from Government grants. The theory of central-local government financial relations distinguishes three main reasons for central government support of local authorities. 'Spill-overs' are benefits of local expenditure which arise outside the area of the authority which undertakes the expenditure. Local governments which are principally concerned for their constituents will not undertake enough of such activities, and those which do extend them will impose an 'unfair' burden on local residents. This problem can be dealt with by specific central government subsidies to certain activities, and in the U.K. Government grants to local authorities originated in this way with payments towards the cost of 'national services' such as main roads and education which were thought to generate 'spill-overs'.

Other features of the relationship between central and local government have recently received more emphasis. A second function of grants is to redistribute revenue among local authorities. We might ask why it is necessary or desirable to redistribute among governments rather than directly to persons. The rationale is that without this, if a man lives in a poor area with a relatively low local tax base or in one in which local authority services are particularly expensive (perhaps because there is a high proportion of children or old people), he will have to pay higher taxes to secure the same level of services than someone with the same income who is more favourably located. This is not only horizontally inequitable, but likely to lead to movements between local authority areas which exacerbate the initial problem (as may have happened in the U.S.A.).

The third function of central grants is to alleviate 'fiscal imbalance'. If taxes are raised by that level of government which is able to levy them most efficiently, while expenditures are determined at the level of government which is able to administer *them* most effectively, there is no reason to suppose that the resources and needs of any particular tier of government will match. It is the experience of the U.K. and of most other countries, that tax collection has become more centralized than expenditure decisions, and there is therefore a need for offsetting grants from the centre to local units (revenue-sharing).

Less attention is now given to 'spill-overs' than to redistribution and fiscal imbalance. One reflection of this has been a movement away from reliance on specific grants for particular services and towards a single Rate Support Grant which local authorities are, in principle, free to allocate between services as they wish (an 'unhypothecated' grant). The grant contains a 'resources' element and a 'needs' element. The *resources element* brings local authorities whose rateable value per head is below a specified figure up to that standard. The taxpayer stands in as ratepayer for the missing amount, just as if he owned a building in the area with the required rateable value. Thus in the extreme case of Rhondda a penny rate brings in £34,560 from local residents and £112,186 from the central government (1976–7). The criterion of rateable value per head is not necessarily a good measure of the affluence (or otherwise) of a particular area; no explicit account is taken of the fact that the price of property, relative to other goods, varies over the country. The rateable value in an area may be low because housing is cheap rather than incomes low. Rateable values tend to be high in London and the South-East, where housing is expensive, so these areas gain little, and rural areas too much, from the resources element in the grant. Layfield proposed to relieve this by relating redistribution to income per head rather than rateable value per head: the authors of the Green Paper reject this, in terms which imply that they do not understand the problem. They do, however, note that the resources element falls short of a full equalization system because it redistributes only by supplementing those below the standard, without taxing those above. A 'unitary grant' system combining both resources and needs elements, and enabling all authorities to provide a specified volume of services at the same rate poundage, is proposed to remedy this.

The *needs element* is based on statistical analysis of past local authority expenditure patterns and is designed to reflect the additional costs which are imposed on authorities by the age structure of their population or the physical characteristics of their areas. (Since the choice of which variables to include is politically determined, the objectivity of the procedure is not as great as it might appear.) The method also assumes that observed expenditure differences reflect differing needs rather than differing resources, service standards, or efficiencies. The remainder of the rate support grant is distributed on a *per capita* basis, except for a proportion earmarked specifically for the subsidy of domestic ratepayers. As a result of the louder volume of protest which greets increases in domestic rates, every domestic ratepayer finds the rate he pays reduced by a fixed poundage (18½p in 1977–8).

TABLE 9.2

Local authority expenditure, 1965–1975

	1965 (£ m.)	1975 (£ m.)	% increase
Local authority current expenditure (on goods and services)	2188	9806	348
Central government current expenditure (on goods and services)	3852	13 101	240
Gross domestic product	31 221	93 146	198

Source: C.S.O., *National Income and Expenditure* (1976).

Local authority expenditure has risen much more rapidly than public expenditure generally, national income, or the local tax base (Table 9.2). An analysis of this for the Layfield Committee (App. 6) attributed slightly more than half of this increase to growth in the output of local authority services and the rest to a 'relative price effect' by which the price of these items rises more rapidly than prices generally. This 'relative price effect' has been extensively discussed (see Institute for Fiscal Studies, 1973) but arises entirely from *an assumption* that there is no change in the productivity of local government services (a similar assumption is made for central government activities), while there is an increase in productivity in the economy in general. While this may be true, there is no evidence for it; and if it is true then it is a matter for inquiry rather than a fact of life. (It is quite possible that the productivity of local government services has fallen, or, less probably, risen; we simply do not have, and badly need, measures, of output from local government as well as inputs into it.) Whatever the cause of increasing local government expenditure, the result has been an increase in 'fiscal imbalance'. The proportion of expenditure financed centrally has risen from 51% in 1966–7 to 63% in 1976–7 (Table 9.1), but this has not prevented the rating system coming under increasing strain.

In addition, it has become clear that there is a problem in relations between central and local government, though it is not so clear what the problem is. The Layfield Committee diagnosed a lack of 'accountability'—by which it meant that the decision to spend and the decision to raise the revenue for the expenditure should be taken by the same unit of government. But, as Cripps and Godley (1976) have argued, accountability of this kind is a marginal concept. If, as is the case with unhypothecated grants, authorities which spend more on some particular service must spend less on another or raise the rates by the amount of the additional expenditure, then accountability is achieved. Authorities must determine their priorities in a way which reacts directly on their constituents.

The expense-account lunch is a familiar instance of the problems which arise when the spending authority and the financing authority are different. Unless claims are subject to rather detailed monitoring—for 'reasonableness' as well as for accuracy (Layfield's centralist solution)—such lunches are likely to prove more expensive than those which people would buy for themselves. An alternative (Layfield's system of local responsibility) is to leave people to pay for their lunch from their own pockets. But accountability is also achieved by saying 'here is £5, go and buy your own lunch', and this is accountability which is effective because it operates at, though only at, the margin: every extravagance does actually have to be paid for by the person who eats it, while every economy benefits him.

This is how a system of block grants should work. But it is fatally undermined if there are grounds for believing that if today's lunch is expensive tomorrow's allowance will be increased. If this is so, a rapid escalation in the cost of lunch is almost inevitable, and expenditure may soon be greater than under either alternative system. Repeated modification of the basis of allocation of the rate support grant has meant that changes in rates have become substantially unrelated to changes in expenditures. The Layfield Committee contrasted the experience of Ealing and Liverpool (Table 9.3) and though the example is extreme, the difficulty is obvious. If changes in grants have a larger effect on the financial outcome than changes in expenditure, it is hardly surprising if local authorities devote more attention to lobbying for the former than controlling the latter.

Thus while it is true that accountability could be reconciled with an extensive system of grant finance if these grants were based on an objective and stable formula, the readiness of the Green Paper to acknowledge that even a unitary grant based on resources and needs might be modified to reflect actual past expenditures indicates clearly how improbable such an outcome is in practice. This forces us back to Layfield's conclusion that accountability and effective financial control require either greater centralization or greater local autonomy. This means a reduction in fiscal imbalance; either decision-making rises to where taxes are levied, or powers of taxation are devolved to where decisions are made.

The Layfield Committee saw the institution of a local income tax (L.I.T.) as the key to an increase in local autonomy. The Green Paper rejects this. This derives partly from opposition by central government to local autonomy; the first objective of central-local relations is stated to be 'to ensure that the local services reflect national priorities and national policies and are provided at broadly comparable standards' (para. 2.2) and the Paper is pervaded by sentiments of this kind. The second difficulty is the administrative problem of operating a local income tax. The Committee conceded that a local income tax would require an additional 12,000–14,000 Inland Revenue staff, and an annual expenditure (private and public) of £100 m. per annum (at 1975 price levels, and presumably 1975 manning levels also). The Revenue evidence to the

TABLE 9.3

Rates in Ealing and Liverpool, 1974–1976 (pence per £ rateable value)

	Year	Expenditure	Change in annual balances	County precept	Rate support grant	Domestic rate subsidy	Domestic rate
Ealing	1974–5	66·1	−7·7	+13·9	−22·6	−13·0	36·6
	1975–6	95·9	−0·9	+22·6	−38·1	−18·5	60·9
% increase		+45%					+66%
Liverpool	1974–5	82·4	+3·7	+19·9	−41·4	−13·0	51·6
	1975–6	116·4	−7·4	+27·0	−67·0	−18·5	50·6
% increase		+41%					−2%

Source: C.I.P.F.A., Return of Rates (1974–5 and 1975–6).

Committee is a dreary list of difficulties which might arise; since, as was noted, such taxes are in operation in Belgium, Canada, Denmark, Finland, Italy, Japan, Norway, Sweden, Switzerland, and the U.S.A., it seems reasonable to infer that most of these problems are not insuperable and we can confine attention to those which are peculiar to the U.K.

There is in fact no doubt that it would be difficult and costly to integrate a local income tax into the present U.K. income tax system. It would require that each taxpayer make an annual declaration of residence; the information given would then be processed and employers would be notified which local authority's tax table should be used in conjunction with the ordinary P.A.Y.E. procedures for each employee. The employer would then be responsible for collecting the local income tax which was due to the appropriate authority. Even with these elaborate procedures, the Inland Revenue argued, and the Committee agreed, that this could only be operated if the present system of tax allowances were simplified. It was also argued that it would be impractical to bring investment income fully within the scope of the tax.

These problems are real, and are probably such as to exclude a local income tax in the U.K. They arise because under the U.K. administrative arrangements there is no single annual return and assessment of the taxpayer's income from all sources. If there is such a return, there is absolutely no difficulty about incorporating a residence declaration and the L.I.T. due can readily be computed either by the taxpayer himself or by the Revenue. That is how the tax works in other countries, and the additional costs involved there are small. The Layfield Committee was assured that there was no intention of adopting such a system in the U.K., and it was beyond its terms of reference to ask why not. It is not beyond ours, and we argued in Chapter 6 that such changes would be desirable anyway.

Devolution

We can deal with this topic rather briefly, since although as we write it is not clear whether there will be devolved assemblies in Scotland or Wales, it is stated that if there are they will not have separate powers of taxation. It is contended (Cmnd. 6890, 1977) that although it is desirable that such powers should exist it is administratively impracticable to provide them. The claim is surprising. Scotland is a larger administrative unit than many independent countries (including three members of the E.E.C.) and has a conveniently short land frontier. Powers of taxation are exercised, without apparent difficulty, by Denmark, Eire, Luxemburg, and indeed Monaco, Andorra, and the Vale of the White Horse District Council.

The problem in the U.K. is that the two major broadly based taxes—V.A.T. and income tax—are so administratively unwieldy that it is difficult to adapt them in this, or indeed any other, direction. This complexity is intrinsic to an invoice-based system (see p. 137) of V.A.T., and it is unavoidable that differences in rates between Scotland (or Wales) and the rest of the U.K. would either have to be small or accompanied by a system of refunds on exports and levies on imports. While this is not impossible it is not an attractive option. A regional income tax is a more appealing possibility. For reason we have described above, this can be done easily if, and only if, we move away from the present administrative arrangement towards a system of non-cumulative P.A.Y.E. with annual returns.

Even without this, it would of course be possible to have a separately administered regional income tax, to have differential rates of pay-roll tax or petrol tax, or to operate a simple general sales tax. (Differential pay-roll taxes have in fact been used to promote regional employment.) While these latter taxes are not particularly satisfactory ones, American experience indicates that even within quite small areas it is feasible to have widely differing local tax systems so long as the rates are not too high. The real obstacle to devising appropriate arrangements is not the intrinsic difficulty of the task but an absence of genuine will to so do.

CAPITAL TAXATION

As yet we have not considered a group of taxes which can best be described as capital taxes. These include taxes on the value of property owned or transferred to another individual, but it is both difficult and misleading to attempt a clear-cut distinction between taxes on income and taxes on capital in just the same way that we have argued against making a rigid distinction between income and capital. For example, we have already examined capital gains tax when discussing the taxation of unearned income, and rates (a tax on the value of property) when looking at the structure of indirect taxes. There is one group of taxes, however, which would immediately be recognized as constituting an example of capital taxation, and that is taxes levied on inheritance, gifts, and the transfer of wealth from one generation to another. Another example of a capital tax is an annual wealth tax.

Taxes on capital have a longer history than taxes on income. This may seem surprising to those people who regard the idea of a wealth tax as a recent left-wing idea, but rulers found it easier to measure their subjects' wealth than to perform the more sophisticated calculations necessary to compute their income. The idea of death duties goes back many centuries. Modern legislation dates from the introduction of probate duty in 1694 which lasted until the famous budget of Sir William Harcourt in 1894 which brought in estate duty. In the eighteenth and nineteenth centuries two other taxes on transfers at death were enacted, legacy duty and succession duty, and these survived until 1949. These two latter duties embodied the principle that the tax paid should reflect the circumstances of the recipient, or donee, rather than the size of the estate. Estate duty related the tax paid on transfers of wealth only to the circumstances of the donor. There have been many suggestions for replacing estate duty with a tax on the receipts of beneficiaries. Such a tax is often called an accessions tax and in 1972 the Government published a Green Paper (Cmnd. 4930) to stimulate discussion on the idea of moving towards inheritance taxation. But when estate duty was finally overhauled in 1974 it was transformed into capital transfer tax which continued to relate tax liability to the size of the estate.

Capital transfer tax did, however, bring one very important change to the system of taxing transfers of wealth in Britain. For the first time it extended the taxation of estates to cover gifts. Under the old estate duty the principle was not to tax gifts at all, but in order to prevent gifts made 'in contemplation of death' avoiding tax altogether it was necessary to include gifts made just before death in the taxable estate.[1] If the only loophole were death-bed gifts then a rule including gifts made within a few weeks of death would be sufficient. But wealthy individuals and their wealthy advisers are sufficiently ingenious to plan to give away at least part of the estate well before the expected date of death, and by so doing they were able to avoid tax altogether. The Government responded by extending the length of the period before death within which gifts made were taxable from nothing to three months, then to a year, three years, five years . . .! Before it was replaced, estate duty covered gifts made within seven years of death. Clearly, the taxman favoured the healthy, wealthy, and well advised.

The addition of gifts to the base of the transfer tax was a logical and necessary step, although since the introduction of capital transfer tax the Government has seen fit to reduce the tax rate on gifts to considerably less than the rate applying to transfers on death, except for the very largest transfers. Allegedly this was to help ease the problems of the transfer of small private businesses, but it increases the possibility of tax avoidance and reintroduces the creation of rules to prevent deathbed gifts which are now defined to be those made less than three years before death. Another change which followed the inclusion of gifts is that the tax is based on the *cumulative* lifetime total of gifts and bequests made. It is not an annual tax. There is a lifetime exemption of £25,000 which may be given away tax-free, and an annual exemption of £2,000 (in 1977–8).

The move to replace estate duty by capital transfer tax was inspired by the evident failings of estate duty. Avoidance of estate duty became so easy that it was sometimes described as a 'voluntary

---

[1] The technical phrase '*Inter vivos* gifts' is used to describe gifts made before the date when they would become taxable as transfers on death.

tax'. There have been so many changes to the detailed tax legislation, all designed to stop up the loopholes, that the tax avoidance
industry has grown as rapidly as any. Yet despite these efforts the
tax has done little to bring about a more equal distribution of
wealth, and seems relatively unimportant in comparison with the
effects of high rates of inflation which we discuss later. The easiest
way of avoiding estate duty was simply to hand on wealth to the
next generation and hope that you lived for another seven years.
That way you would never pay tax at all. In a study of the importance of tax avoidance by *inter vivos* gifts Horsman (1975) found
that in the late 1960s the value of gifts made upon which duty was
never charged was probably of the order of £330 m. a year. The
amount of tax avoided was estimated by Horsman to have been
£177 m. in 1968 compared to actual receipts of death duties in that
year of £382 m. Given the importance of avoidance by this means
it is strange that the Government gave way to pressure and introduced lower rates of tax on *inter vivos* gifts under capital transfer
tax.

Gifts were not the only method by which it was possible to avoid
paying estate duty. Lower rates of duty were charged on agricultural land and property, assets of private business, growing
timber, and works of art. No doubt a good case was made out for
the special treatment of each of these classes of assets in turn, but
these arguments almost always overlook the basic principle of the
capitalization of taxes of which we have given several examples in
this book. If a concession is made to the taxation of growing timber
then wealthy individuals will switch at least part of their wealth
from other assets into growing timber. This extra demand will bid
up the price of timber until there is no net advantage in passing on
wealth in one form rather than another. Tax revenue falls, and
those who gain are the people who happened to own the timber
when the concession was announced. It is hard to see what is
achieved by this, and in the case of farming it can have perverse
results. The reason for giving concessions to agriculture is to help
farmers continue in the profession. But all that happens is that
farms become much more valuable than would otherwise have
been the case (thus making farmers even more concerned at the
prospect of paying tax) and it becomes even more difficult for the
genuine small farmer to borrow enough to purchase his own farm.
On top of this, many farmers become millionaires, a fact which

they find puzzling because there is no change in their standard of living. The only way in which they can enjoy the benefit of their good fortune is to abandon farming, at which we hope they were skilled, sell out, and go and live in the South of France. We suspect many farmers would be happier on their farms than in the casino in Monte Carlo.

We would have hoped that the introduction of capital transfer tax would have seen the end of these anomalies. Not a bit of it; reduced rates apply to gifts *inter vivos*. Although this concession was given to reduce the 'threat' to small businesses, it applies to transfers of *any* kind of asset. We shall return to the subject of small businesses later in the chapter. Agriculture too receives special treatment. It is zero-rated for V.A.T., exempt from rates, receives concessions for capital gains tax, and the value of agricultural property is reduced by 50% for the purposes of capital transfer tax. There are restrictions on those who may benefit from agricultural relief but the definition of 'working farmer' is not too difficult to satisfy. There is also special relief for gifts made to charity and for works of art and historic buildings.

Another method of avoiding tax has been for the wealthy to set up trusts, the trustees of which could distribute the income and capital of the trust in any way they wished to individuals on a list of potential beneficiaries. This sort of trust, called a discretionary trust, could (provided it satisfied certain minimal conditions) escape estate duty altogether and hence was an attractive way of handing on family wealth down the generations without paying tax. It was clearly important to stop up this loophole. Some steps were taken in 1969 and the switch to capital transfer tax also brought with it changes in the tax treatment of trusts. It may be that in due course these changes will be seen to have stopped up some of the more serious loopholes—provided, of course, that the relevant provisions have not been repealed by a different Government. But the rewards for successful ingenuity in this area are great, and the use of trusts, many of which are set up for the sole purpose of tax avoidance, seems likely to remain a vehicle for the rich to hand on their wealth. Indeed, a leading authority on the subject has written, 'in Great Britain it is probably true to say that 95% of all discretionary and accumulation trusts are created solely for tax-saving reasons' (Wheatcroft, 1965, p. 136).

Although there are high nominal tax rates at the top end of the scale, the numerous possibilities for avoidance mean the system raises little revenue and average tax rates are rather low. As Atkinson has commented, 'Where those with good tax advisers—and perhaps few scruples—can pay little tax while others pay tax at rates up to 80%, there can be little respect for the equity of taxation' (Atkinson, 1972, p. 129).

It is possible for individuals who are obviously far from being paupers to die leaving estates for tax purposes which bear little relation to their real wealth. It is generally believed that the largest sum ever paid in death duties, by a considerable margin, was the £11 m. paid on an estate estimated at between £40 and £60 m. on the death of the third Duke of Westminster in 1953. When the fourth Duke died in 1967, his estate amounted to a little over £4 m. (duty paid not disclosed). It is not thought that this change resulted entirely from dissipation of the ducal assets, since the family was still understood to possess some 300 acres of central London, including a large part of Mayfair, as well as substantial estates elsewhere (*The Times*, 27 Feb. 1967 and 24 May 1972).

TABLE 10.1
Rates of Capital transfer tax, 1977–1978

Value of total estate (£)	Marginal rate (%)	Average rate (%)
25 000	10	0
50 000	30	10
100 000	45	24
250 000	60	48
1 000 000	65	58

These rates apply to transfers on or within three years before death. Lower rates apply to *inter vivos* gifts.

Another major cause of the failure of death duties to produce revenue is the rate structure. At first sight this may seem surprising because the 'enormously high' rates of up to 8% imposed by Harcourt in his 1894 Budget have steadily risen and the top marginal rate today is 75%. But to pay an average tax rate of even 30% requires the transfer of an estate of £133,000 and that is before taking any account of the special concessions to gifts or particular assets described above. If the money is handed on as a gift (provided it is made more than three years before death) an average tax rate of 30% would need a gift of £266,500 and if the gift consisted of a small business it would have to be worth £1,113,707. In 1977–8 a single person on average earnings pays income tax (including national insurance contributions) at an average rate which exceeds 30%. We should also note that transfers between husband and wife (whether during life or on death) are completely exempt from tax.

The reason for this disparity between high marginal and low average rates on capital transfer is the very high exemption level below which no tax at all is paid, £25,000, and the slow build-up of marginal rates (see Table 10.1). With good advice few people need pay much capital transfer tax. The exemption level may remove the 'average' family from the tax net but it also reduces the effective tax rate charged on the larger estates. In real terms the exemption level is much higher now than it was in 1894. Moreover, the effective lifetime exemption level can be very much higher than the apparent value of £25,000. This is because each year any individual may give away £2,000 tax free. A married couple can therefore pass on to their children £4,000 each year without incurring tax at all. This is obviously much easier for the wealthy family which can transfer the ownership of stocks and shares, than for the more typical family whose main assets are in the form of an owner-occupied house the ownership of which is difficult to transfer bit by bit. Over a twenty-year period a couple could pass on more than £100,000 without paying a penny in tax! On top of this there is a tax-free allowance of £5,000 for gifts made in 'consideration of marriage'. There cannot be many married couples who anticipate returning from honeymoon to a cheque for £5,000.

The combination of very high exemption levels at the bottom and high marginal rates at the top has not been very effective in redistributing wealth. Redistribution is about average tax rates and raising revenue, and capital taxes in their present form are not major revenue raisers. In 1975–6 estate duty and capital transfer tax raised £380 m., which is equivalent to less than one percentage point on the standard rate of income tax and compares with total Inland Revenue receipts of £18,144 m. (which of course exclude V.A.T. and other indirect taxes which are collected by the Customs and Excise). It is natural to ask whether this low yield is inevitable, or whether it can be substantially raised. We shall return to this question later.

Inflation as a capital tax

There is, however, another tax on capital and that is inflation. The reason for saying that inflation acts as a tax is the following. Suppose that we are in a world of stable prices in which the interest rate is 10% a year and there is a proportional income tax of 50%. The after-tax rate of return to both lenders and borrowers is 5%. Now suppose there is an inflation of 10% per annum, that prices are expected to go on going up at that rate indefinitely, and that the economy has adjusted to this perpetual inflation so that all 'real' economic decisions are unchanged. In particular borrowers and lenders again face a real rate of return of 5% per annum. In order to abstract from the interaction between inflation and taxation let us assume that the tax system is indexed so that tax is charged only on real interest income, and only real interest payments are deductible. The equilibrium money rate of interest will rise from 10% to 20%. The real rate will be 10% (20% minus an inflation rate of 10%), and half of this will be taken in tax leaving a real after-tax rate of 5% once more. Inflation causes few problems in the sort of world we have just described.

But the crucial point in this example is that investors accurately foresee that inflation will be 10%, and hence they can adjust the terms on which loans are made accordingly. But if inflation is un-anticipated the situation is very different. Suppose that in our example nobody foresaw the beginning of the inflation, and went on believing in stable prices. Then the money interest rate of 10% would only just cover the fall in the value of money resulting in a zero real interest rate. With an indexed tax system no tax would be charged but lenders would find that they had received no real return on their savings at all, whereas they were prepared to lend the amounts they did only because they believed they would get a real return of 5%. If, on the other hand, the tax system were not indexed, and of course in reality it is not, the situation is much worse. Of the money rate of interest of 10% half is taken in tax, and with an inflation rate of 10% savers are left with a real rate of return of minus 5% (for a discussion of the effects of inflation under the present tax system see Ch. 4). That is, their capital has effectively been taxed at a rate of 5%. With a real income before tax of zero it is not unreasonable for them to argue that they have in fact paid a capital tax of 5% on their wealth. For borrowers, of course, the opposite is true. The burden of their debt has fallen in real terms, and if they can deduct all their money interest payments against tax this can be seen as a 5% subsidy to debt. A tax on assets and a subsidy on liabilities imposed at a rate which has nothing to do with the circumstances of the individual taxpayer, but which depends solely on the rate of inflation, is a very odd state of affairs and does not appear to correspond with the platform of any political party.

This effect of inflation occurs only when inflation is unanticipated. In practice some inflation will be anticipated and some not. But the point remains that the outcome is arbitrary (unless individuals make indexed contracts), and if unanticipated inflation can act as a capital tax it is perverse that the Government exacerbates the problem by refusing to index the taxation of property income. Of course, indexation does involve serious problems, as we pointed out in Chapter 5, and we would prefer to move the tax system in the direction of a lifetime expenditure tax.

A wealth tax

It is clear that there are major weaknesses in the existing taxation of capital in Britain. There are two directions, not necessarily incompatible, in which efforts to reform the system could be made. The first would be to overhaul the methods of taxing transfers (gifts and bequests), and the second would be to adopt an annual tax on wealth. The Government feels that the introduction of capital transfer tax meets the first approach, and recent debate has been centred on proposals for an annual wealth tax. These were published for public discussion in the form of a Green Paper (Cmnd. 5704) and were examined in detail in a report of a Select Committee of the House of Commons (published in 1975: H.C. 696—1). The Committee was, however, unable to agree upon a Report, and the published document contains several minority Reports.

The motive for putting forward the idea of a tax on wealth largely derives from a feeling that the distribution of wealth is too unequal. Table 10.2 shows some of the available evidence on the distribution of wealth in Britain. These figures have been produced by the Royal Commission on the Distribution of Income and

TABLE 10.2

Distribution of personal wealth in Britain, 1974
(%)

	Excluding pension rights	Including pension rights
Top 1%	25·0	13·8
Top 5%	47·4	30·0
Top 10%	61·5	41·1

The series excluding pension rights is the Series C produced by the Royal Commission, and that including pension rights includes both occupational and state pensions.
Source: Royal Commission on the Distribution of Income and Wealth, Report No. 4, Cmnd. 6626, H.M.S.O., 1977, Tables 35 and 37.

Wealth, although they are subject to both error and difficulties of interpretation. (For a careful analysis of the evidence on wealth distribution see the study of Atkinson and Harrison, 1978.) It is clear from the table that there is substantial inequality in the distribution of wealth, although it is difficult to know what standards of comparison we should use when making value judgements about the distribution of wealth. Another feature is that rich people choose to hold their wealth in very different forms from those of less rich people. Table 10.3 shows how two groups of individuals, those

TABLE 10.3

Asset composition of personal wealth in Britain, 1974

Asset	Range of wealth (£)		
	500–10 000	Over 200 000	Average
Dwellings	58·5	11·6	42·7
Land	0·5	21·6	4·5
Company securities	1·7	42·1	10·8
Life policies	19·1	2·5	14·9
Building society deposits	7·0	1·2	7·5
Cash and bank deposits	5·9	7·4	7·2
Other	7·3	13·6	12·4
Net wealth	100·0	100·0	100·0

Source: Royal Commission on the Distribution of Income and Wealth, Report No. 4, Cmnd. 6626, H.M.S.O., 1977, Table 24.

with net wealth in the range £5,000–£10,000 and those with wealth over £200,000, divide their holdings between different assets. The first group holds more than half in the form of owner-occupied houses and another quarter in savings with life assurance companies and building societies. Holdings of shares and other company securities are negligible. For the richest individuals the picture is very different. Company securities comprise not far short of one-half of the wealth of this group and land over 20%.

The figures shown in Table 10.3 do not include wealth held in the form of rights to future pensions. Yet it is clear from Table 10.2 that the estimates of the inequality of wealth-holding depend quite sensitively on whether or not we include the value of pension rights (both occupational and state) in the value of an individual's wealth. An individual cannot sell these rights, and he must live at least to retirement age for them to be of any value. But they have an actuarial value and most people would be very upset if their pension rights were taken away. Estimates by the Government Actuary form the basis of the figures in Table 10.2. To value a pension right to a particular individual we have to estimate his chance of survival until the year when the pension will be paid, the pension which will be paid in future years, the tax rate which will be paid on the pension, and the rate at which the future pension should be discounted. The value of the pension will probably be uncertain, especially if it is 'index-linked', and may therefore depend upon future rates of inflation. The valuation of pension rights involves making forecasts of all these factors over a considerable time period and is a difficult exercise.

It would not matter so much if the final result was not very sensitive to the assumptions made but, unfortunately, this is not the case. The value to a 40-year-old male of a pension scheme which begins at age 60 and pays the maximum approved benefits is shown in Table 10.4 under various assumptions about the growth of his earnings and the rate of inflation. It is easy to see that the value of his pension rights is extremely sensitive to the assumptions made about his earnings prospects, the future rate of inflation, and upon whether or not his pension is indexed. With variations of the magnitude shown in the table it would be impossible to include pension rights in an individual's taxable wealth without provoking bitter dispute about the assumptions made in valuing this right. It would also be impossible to value pension rights in cases where

TABLE 10.4
Value of pension rights of man aged 40
(£)

		With indexation inflation rate			Without indexation inflation rate		
		2½%	7½%	12½%	2½%	7½%	12½%
Real growth	0%	6200	21 000	105 000	4300	11 500	32 000
of earnings	2%	7700	31 500	156 000	6500	17 500	47 500
	5%	14 000	57 500	284 000	11 700	32 000	86 500

Assumptions: (i) Earnings of £5,000 per year at age 40—20 years service in scheme paying maximum I.R. approved benefits based on final salary—retirement at 60;
   (ii) no benefit on death before retirement;
   (iii) an interest rate of 7½%;
   (iv) 'with indexation' assumes pension indexed after retirement; 'without indexation' assumes no subsequent increase.
Source: Own calculations based on English Life Table 12.

there was no contractual arrangement to provide a pension. For example, a director of a small company may have no formal right to a pension but a very high expectation of a good pension, not least becasue the directors could decide to award him a pension. In these cases no valuation could reasonably be made and if formal pension rights were taxed informal schemes would proliferate. But if pension rights were not regarded as taxable wealth there would be inequities between those with occupational pension rights and those, such as the self-employed, who had to provide their own pension, and, equally important, inequities between those in generous pension schemes and those in poor schemes. Again this would be unimportant if the numbers were small. But they are not. The total value of occupational and state pension rights is of the same order of magnitude as all the other forms of personal wealth put together, about £200,000 m. each (Royal Commission on the Distribution of Income and Wealth Report No. 4). And, as we have seen, for an individual pension rights can be enormous. At the rates of interest and inflation prevailing in 1975, the value in that year of an inflation-proofed pension of £8,500 a year for a senior male Civil Servant was almost £300,000 (written answer in Hansard,

20 May 1975). Pension rights pose a very serious problem for a wealth tax.

The other form of wealth which it is quite impossible to measure is 'human capital', the value of future earnings, which we discussed in Chapter 5. Since this form of wealth would not be subject to tax, it seems preferable to regard a 'wealth tax' as proposed as an annual assets tax, charged on assets which can be easily identified and valued, which somewhat diminishes its theoretical attractions. In addition to concern with the distribution of wealth, there is the argument that wealth gives rise to 'taxable capacity' in its own right. Thus Kaldor, when discussing tax reform in India, cited the example of a beggar and a man who hoarded gold, both of whom received no current monetary income (1956). But it is clear that in some ill-defined sense the man with great wealth has a greater taxable capacity. If by this is meant that the wealthy man can enjoy a high standard of living then, although this is obviously true, it is an argument for a tax on expenditure rather than a wealth tax as such. Of course, it may be argued that wealth gives power, influence, and security as well as monetary benefits, and this is no doubt true. But it is difficult to relate these non-pecuniary benefits to any monetary valuation of wealth, and power also derives from sources other than wealth. Nevertheless, it suggests the idea that a tax on wealth could be used to tax *all* the benefits of wealth-holding, both pecuniary and non-pecuniary. With this idea a wealth tax would replace all existing taxes on the holding (though not the transfer) of wealth and the income which derives from it. Taxes on unearned income and on capital gains would be replaced by an annual tax on wealth.

Such a proposal has been put forward by Flemming and Little (1974), and we must say that it has evident attractions in principle. But in order to work it would have to be applied to everybody, and this would entail the daunting task of valuing the wealth of each individual every year. Of course, conventions would be adopted, but these would be open to political pressure and in no time concessions and loopholes for the rich would have been opened up, leaving the rest to pay the tax. Valuation problems have always been considered the biggest obstacle to the introduction of a wealth tax, even for a tax applying only to the top 1% of the wealth distribution. These problems would become enormous if extended to the rest of the population, and in those European countries which use a wealth tax very generous valuations are made, especially for owner-occupiers and no attempt is made to tax pension rights. To exclude the latter from the tax base would be inequitable in the context of a wealth tax which would replace the existing methods of taxing investment income, and to attempt to include them would be impracticable. The idea of a comprehensive wealth tax, although appealing in theory, founders on the problems of what to do about pension rights and of valuation.

An alternative version of a wealth tax is one that applies only to those at the very top of the wealth distribution. This was the basis of the proposals in the Green Paper on Wealth Tax which envisaged a threshold of £100,000. This would mean that the tax applied to only the top 0·6% of wealth-holders. This is such a small proportion of the total distribution that, combined with the concessions proposed for pensions, the 'national heritage', and business assets, the tax would have achieved little by way of real distribution of wealth, and would have been more of an irritant than a comprehensive tax. To adopt a very high threshold for a wealth tax is to throw away one of the attractions of such a tax, namely its relative simplicity as a means of taxing unearned income compared to the current taxation of property income.

In our introduction we discussed what was meant by 'practicable' tax reforms. In these terms, a wealth tax is simply impracticable, although in principle it seems an attractive tax. By this we do not mean that it would be impossible to run something which could be described as a wealth tax, and indeed this is done in other countries though there is none in which it raises substantial revenue. But the simple fact is that the only assets which could be brought fully within the tax would be quoted securities and bank accounts; these amount to a small proportion of all assets and one which would get smaller. The list of those which would or could be dealt with in only a limited or arbitrary way is much longer; private companies, agricultural assets, houses and other durable goods, 'national heritage' items, trusts, life insurance policies, pension rights, and so on. The result is that the base of a wealth tax would be so deficient that it could not, without intolerable administrative strain and complexity, bear the strain of other than very low rates; would inevitably impose extensive anomalies and distortions in operation; and would not raise significant revenue or effect any noticeable redistribution of wealth.

Gifts under a lifetime expenditure tax

There is another way of looking at the distribution of wealth, and that is not to focus on the share of any percentile group, but to look at the continuity of wealth-holding. We ask the question—are the people who are rich today the sons and daughters of those who were rich in the previous generation? This question has been extensively investigated by Harbury and his collaborators who examined the estates of sets of fathers and sons (Harbury and MacMahon, 1973; Harbury and Hitchens, 1976). They found that there was a highly significant correlation between dying rich and having had a rich father. Inherited wealth remains an important determinant of the distribution of wealth at the top of the distribution, although its influence may be declining slightly. Harbury and Hitchins (1976) found that 58% of those who died wealthy had themselves inherited a large amount; so large in fact that had their fathers been a random sample of the male population the figure would have been less than 1%.

In the light of this evidence we are inclined to put more weight on inequalities of wealth caused by inheritance than on inequalities resulting from differences in lifetime accumulation. This leads us away from an annual wealth tax and towards the taxation of gifts and bequests. We shall now consider ways of reforming the taxation of transfers.

The first, and most obvious, change is that gifts *inter vivos* could be taxed at the same rates as apply to estates or gifts made within three years before death. A more important change, however, is to examine closely the rate structure. Too much attention is paid to the high marginal rates at the top end which gives rise to the myth of the terrible burden of death duties. The very high exemption level means that the bulk of wealth which is transferred either on death or by gift pays a very low average rate of tax. We feel that it is important to consider carefully the idea of including all transfers in the tax base. One way of doing this is by a comprehensive income tax which counts as income of an individual all receipts of gifts and bequests during the year. Since an individual may have little control over the timing of receipts of gifts and inheritances, his income defined in this way may fluctuate wildly from year to year. Under a progressive tax system this may mean that he would pay more tax than if he had received the same amount in equal instalments. This possibility has led to an acceptance of the need for averaging provisions under a comprehensive income tax. In Chapter 5 we discussed a better way of measuring an individual's lifetime comprehensive income which we saw was equal to the total use of resources over his lifetime. This can be measured by the sum of his consumption plus gifts and bequests made. So if we wish to impose an annual tax on a measure of the individual's lifetime use of resources, a better way of achieving this objective is to impose an annual tax on consumption plus gifts made during the year, the lifetime expenditure tax. Like the comprehensive income tax it includes transfers in the main personal tax base but the amount included refers to gifts made, not those received, and hence the donor can smooth the timing of gifts if he so wishes which reduces the need for averaging provisions.

There are three main virtues of the lifetime expenditure tax. First, it is genuinely a tax on an individual's lifetime income or uses of resources, and in that sense is superior to a comprehensive income tax. Second, it would widen the tax base quite considerably because all transfers (except for some very small exemption on gifts which had to be included) would come within the tax net. Third, since all transfers would be taxed such a scheme holds out the hope of a reasonably equitable way of taxing owner-occupiers. As we have seen, other attempts to remove the tax subsidy must fail because the concessions have already been capitalized,and existing home-owners do not have the resources to cope with the removal of the tax concessions to mortgage interest payments. But to tax the value of owner-occupied property transferred by gift or, more usually, on death is a relatively painless way of recouping some of the revenue. This proposal would generate enough revenue to enable a reduction to be made in the tax rate on earned income (or expenditure out of earned income), but it would impose very much heavier taxes on gifts and inherited wealth than currently exist. The extra revenue would arise because the 'typical' estate consisting, say, of a house and little else, would pay tax at full personal tax rates and because a much heavier tax burden would be imposed on medium-sized and large estates resulting from the abolition of the high exemption level. Even with a top marginal tax rate under the lifetime expenditure tax (L.E.T.) of 50% or 60% virtually all large estates would pay more tax than at present. Gifts would be included in the annual L.E.T. computation, and the value of the estate resulting from death could be considered as the expenditure of a separate tax year.

The main objection which will be raised to this proposal is that the tax burden on gifts and bequests is far too great. The reply to that is in two parts. First, we have seen that with good advice available to the wealthy, the tax collected from large estates in the past has been small, and our proposal would seek to prevent this occurring in future. Second, we regard it as a merit of the proposal that the average taxpayer who is an owner-occupier will find a large sum of tax collected on his estate. At the moment there are many families who know that at some point they can expect to inherit their parents' house, and we believe many of them would be prepared to trade off part of this windfall gain in return for lower tax rates on earned income.

To raise substantial revenue from transfer taxes requires the elimination of the sort of avoidance possibilities which we discussed above, and the extension of the tax net to catch a much larger number of taxpayers. The benefit is that less revenue need be collected from earnings or retirement savings, and tax rates can be reduced. We feel that this is an attractive prospect, and one which reflects the inherent superiority of L.E.T. as a tax on lifetime resources.

Small businesses

The proposals set out above would clearly impose a heavy financial penalty on the transmission of wealth from one generation to the next. This might be thought a severe burden on small businesses because it would not be easy to hand on majority ownership. Although it is evident that small firms would find great difficulty in obtaining cash to meet the transfer tax payments, we believe that the problems of small businesses can best be dealt with by reforms which do not involve special tax concessions which create anomalies and avoidance.

The current tax system already contains a formidable range of concessions to small businesses. Small companies pay a lower rate of corporation tax; the first £20,000 of capital gains made by the owner or director of a business who is over 65 (and has worked for the firm for ten years) is completely tax-free; transfers of certain business property can be reduced in value by 50% for the purposes of computing a capital transfer tax liability; and capital gains tax can be postponed when a business is transferred by gift. Despite these concessions there are still complaints that the tax system is biased against individuals trying to build up their own business. The Bolton Committee Report on Small Firms, published in 1971 (Cmnd. 4811), claimed that its basic philosophy on taxation was a 'wish to emphasise again that what is needed is a taxation policy which will restore initiative, encourage entrepreneurial activity and improve the liquidity position of small businesses. We believe that continued reduction in taxation of personal incomes and of estates would be most likely to achieve this result' (p. 200). The Committee's basic recommendations were for further special concessions to small firms, especially for estate duty purposes. Its specific suggestions included lower valuation of business property for estate duty purposes, lower capital gains tax rates for owners of small firms, tax privileges for savings by the self-employed to provide pensions, and changes in the legislation dealing with close companies. Close companies are companies under the control of five or fewer persons and where less than 35% of the shares are publicly held.

The first of these suggestions affects what happens on the death of the owner of a small business and the second and third relate to what happens when he decides to retire. It is difficult to believe that these are the moments at which it is most essential to restore initiative, encourage entrepreneurial activity, and restore the liquidity position of small businesses. We saw in Chapter 4 that the distinctive characteristic of small businessses in the U.K. is not that they die prematurely but that their average age is quite exceptionally high; this does not square with the view that transfer taxes are the major problem and as we have noted estate duty was never a very effective tax anyway. We argued that the real obstacle to the growth of small businesses in Britain was the institutionalization of savings, and it is to that problem that our proposals are directed.

How do these suggestions compare with our proposals for a lifetime expenditure tax and a cash flow corporation tax? Let us leave aside for the moment the taxation of the transfer of the business when the original founder hands on the firm, and consider the treatment of the firm when the founder is creating and building up his firm. Our proposals would mean that any money devoted to investment in the business would escape tax altogether. Tax would be paid only on money which he took out of the business to spend on his personal consumption. Since in the earliest, and most critical, stages of the firm's life the founder typically works very hard and lives frugally, our proposals would give most encouragement to the creation and expansion of new firms. There would be no capital gains tax and tax would be charged only when the founder took money out of the firm, in which case there would be no liquidity problems in meeting these tax payments. Saving for retirement would be tax-free and the cash flow corporation tax would mean that there would be no need for close company legislation (see Ch. 11), which, as the Bolton Committee pointed out, is costly both to the Inland Revenue and to the small firms concerned. The combination of a lifetime expenditure tax and a cash flow corporation tax offers substantial encouragement to the creation and growth of small businesses, and it does this without any 'special' concessions which can have such undesirable effects.

In return for these incentives to the establishment of small firms our proposals levy a heavy tax on the transfer, whether by gift or on death, of a business to the next generation. This is in sharp contrast to the attitude of the Bolton Committee which viewed estate duty as the major fiscal difficulty facing small firms. Our proposals would distinguish very clearly between those individuals who created firms and those who inherited them.

Would this inability to pass on intact to their heirs ownership of their firms act as a serious disincentive to founders of new firms? The Bolton Committee thought so, but there is very little evidence for such a belief. The most detailed examination of the question is the study by Boswell (1973) of 64 small companies. He found little evidence of the importance of the dynastic motive and even less of its desirability. The firms run by their founders performed better (in terms of profitability) than did those run by inheritors. The founders of business were less interested in handing them on to their children than were those who inherited the business themselves. Family succession can lead to serious management problems, and often occurs through lack of an alternative. Boswell studied 30 inheritors of family firms and found that as far as these were concerned 'positive enthusiasm to enter the firm seems to have been marginal' (p. 125). Moreover, firms run by the original founder who remains in charge well beyond normal retirement age suffer from 'gerontocracy' problems when the founder has lost his verve for business but is unwilling to retire because of problems of management succession. We agree with Boswell that 'it is hard to resist the conclusion that the best point at which to secure necessary changes—humanely as well as effectively—is when small firm bosses reach retirement or die. The method would be a combination of tougher inheritance taxation with public action to deal with transitional problems.' What is needed is *not* concessions on transfer taxation, but public action to develop a market in small businesses to enable ownership and control to be transferred without the destruction of the business. The stock-market achieves this already for larger firms. In return for this tougher inheritance taxation it would, under our proposals, be easier to build up a small firm in the early years than it is at present.

11

PRINCIPLES OF COMPANY TAXATION

IN the U.K. taxes on companies are more recent than personal income taxes. In the U.S. a corporate income tax first appeared in 1909, but the separate taxation of companies began in Britain only in 1947. Before then the taxation of corporate profits was integrated with the personal income tax, and special taxes on profits were used only as wartime measures to raise extra revenue. In 1947 the system was rationalized by raising the rate of profits tax and exempting individuals and partnerships from the tax altogether. In effect, in addition to income tax there was a separate tax on corporate profits. The system of corporation tax has changed at regular intervals, with major changes occurring in 1958, 1965, and 1973. The implications and significance of these changes we discuss below, but it is not surprising that they have produced a widespread feeling that it matters less what the system is than that it should be left alone. Unfortunately this is not possible. The reason is that the system is in total disarray. In 1974 there was a crisis of corporate liquidity; share prices fell to less than 30% of their previous peak levels, and the tax payments which were due at the beginning of 1975 would have led to serious financial difficulties for a number of major British companies. As a result, there was introduced in November 1974 a scheme of 'stock-relief' whose effect was, in conjunction with other allowances, to eliminate the corporation tax liability of U.K. manufacturing industry.

This scheme was described as temporary, and legally it takes the form of deferral of tax, although categorical but imprecise assurances have been given that the tax will never in fact be collected. But since its introduction little corporation tax has been paid (see Table 11.1), and most of that by financial companies (banks and insurance companies); and no permanent proposals have (in 1977) been produced. In effect, the Inland Revenue has given up collecting corporation tax from manufacturing industry while it thinks of what to do next. There is therefore a temporary problem of how to get out of this difficulty, and an underlying permanent problem of how to restructure the way in which companies are taxed so that similar difficulties do not occur in future.

TABLE 11.1

Corporation Tax Liabilities 1969–1976
(£ m.)

	1969	1970	1971	1972	1973	1974	1975	1976
Industrial and Commercial Companies	1528	1322	1156	938	1227	306	101	178
Financial Companies	270	290	342	372	769	784	973	1143
All Companies	1798	1612	1498	1310	1996	1090	1074	1321

The figures shown are estimates of mainstream corporation tax liability accruing in the year.
Source: Own estimates based on C.S.O., *National Income and Expenditure* (1976 and 1977).

Since we have come so close to abolishing Corporation Tax, an obvious question to ask is, 'Why tax companies at all?' A common reply, and indeed one that was used in the U.S. to justify the introduction of a corporate income tax, is that corporate status conveys certain privileges, and companies should pay for these privileges. In particular, companies have limited liability status, thus protecting their shareholders in the event of bankruptcy. At first sight this argument has some appeal, but on closer inspection it becomes less attractive. There is no reason to believe that the benefits of incorporation are proportional to profits (indeed the reverse might be the case) and one might as well argue for a licence fee for companies. More fundamentally, although limited liability is a very convenient form of contractual arrangement between shareholders and creditors, it is a voluntary agreement entered into by both sides. Before lending to the company the creditors know full well that the shareholders' liability is limited and can adjust the terms on which they are willing to lend accordingly. There is no reason to tax one party more than the other.

Why then do firms incorporate? For large firms the most important reason is that the existence of shares enables the ownership of the company to be divided among, and transferred between, indivi-

duals without affecting the scale of control of the firm. The process
of management can continue while the ownership of the company
is changing. There are two main tax inducements for small businesses to incorporate. The first is that if money is ploughed back
into the business the owner of an incorporated business can avoid
paying income tax at the cost of paying corporation tax plus, eventually, also capital gains tax. If his personal income tax rate is high
enough, incorporation will be worth while. The second reason is
that there are generous tax concessions for contributions to company pension funds, which are not available to a self-employed
business man on anything like the same scale. If the latter wanted
to save for retirement he might well find it profitable to incorporate
simply to take advantage of the tax privileges of a company pension. For large firms, however, taxation is not a significant factor
because incorporation is necessary for other reasons.

The mere fact that some firms are incorporated is not a very
strong argument for imposing a separate tax on them. Indeed,
insistence on treating companies as entities distinct from the individuals who own them has provided a tax shelter for retained earnings. Another argument which has been used is that companies can
afford to shoulder an extra burden, and that companies, as well as
persons, should pay their fair share of taxes. This argument is
completely mistaken. The effect of a tax is to reduce either leisure
or consumption (whether this year or in the future via a reduction
in savings) or both below the levels which would have been chosen
in the absence of the tax. Whether any given tax burden is distributed fairly can only be discussed by reference to the effects on the
different individuals in society. Companies are owned by individuals and it is meaningless to talk about the 'welfare' of I.C.I.
The fact that a company has a *legal* personality of its own quite
distinct from that of its managers, shareholders, and employees
cannot change the fact that a tax can only affect the well-being
of those who work for or own the company, or consume its
products.

The incidence of company taxes

Who then actually pays the corporation tax? Corporation tax is
normally levied on company profits, but it is important to distinguish two components which make up the figures which companies
report as their profits. One is a return on the capital which

companies use in conducting their business—the money they have borrowed to buy fixed assets, stocks, etc. In order to attract funds —either from lenders or from those who might wish to buy their shares—companies must offer a return on these funds comparable to that which investors could obtain elsewhere. Companies typically report their gross trading profits—the return they have made before deducting any of these financing costs—and their net profits, which are computed after subtracting the cost of interest payments on the money which they have borrowed, but before deducting the cost of servicing the capital which they have obtained from shareholders (the dividends which they have had to promise in order to secure these funds).

Many companies make a return on capital employed which appears to exceed, often by large amounts, the amount which they need to make to attract funds from investors. For example, in 1975 Rank Xerox reported a return on capital employed of 41·1%, and Marks & Spencer a return of 36·1% (figures drawn from the *Times 1000*), while the Monopolies Commission (1975) discovered that LRC International had obtained a return on capital employed in the manufacture of contraceptive sheaths which exceeded 100% over the period 1969–73. These returns are much greater than these companies would appear to have needed to make, or to promise, to obtain finance for their business. In a competitive economy, it would be difficult for firms to earn such high profit rates, since other people would be attracted into the same line of business by the prospect of these enormous returns: and although many companies seem to earn profits greater than the cost of capital there are few which are as profitable as these. But as these examples suggest, there are at least three reasons why companies might make above-normal profits. Rank Xerox is a company which exists to exploit a highly successful invention, and its profits represent the rewards of being first in the field with a new product (aided by patent protection). Marks & Spencer does not have any single invention which distinguishes it from other companies, but it is an exceptionally successful and efficient firm, which by virtue of effective management and carefully cultivated customer goodwill is able to earn higher profits than other retailers with whom it is competing. We might regard its profits as returns to successful organization. LRC's profits appear to be the rewards of the successful creation and maintenance of a near-monopoly in its products.

Economists describe the amount by which profits such as these exceed the cost of capital as 'pure profits'. Such profits can of course be negative for foolhardy ventures or badly managed firms. At any time some firms will be more successful than the average and others less successful, so that there will be a dispersion of realized rates of return around the cost of capital: lager producers will earn more when the summer is hot and umbrella manufacturers more when it is wet. But the major sources of pure profits are invention, organization, and monopoly, and we shall broadly describe them as returns to entrepreneurship, noting that in this title we are including activities which we should view with approbation—like successful invention—and others which we would wish to discourage—like the creation of monopolies. Real 'profits taxes' are normally partly a tax on pure profits and partly a tax on capital employed. We shall see that the British corporation tax is a combination of a tax on pure profits and a tax on capital. This latter tax ranges from a net *subsidy* to borrowings which are used to buy plant and machinery to a substantial tax on equity finance used to purchase commercial property.

We can therefore identify three main groups who may bear part of the burden of corporation tax. One is the people who supply entrepreneurship—Mr. Marks and Mr. Spencer and others who helped build up their organization, Mr. Carlson who invented the Xerox machine, and the owners of the Xerox Corporation which helped him develop it. A second is the people who supply capital to companies. This group overlaps somewhat with the first—the people who supplied capital to Marks & Spencer or Xerox in the early days of their development did very well out of it, though we might argue that by choosing to support these operations rather than others at a time when their potential was not universally recognized these individuals were themselves supplying entrepreneurship as well as capital. It is clear, however, that the people who own shares in Marks and Spencer now are not entrepreneurs in this or any other sense, and there is no reason to suppose that the return they earn on their investment will be higher than they would expect from any other shares they might buy.

This point is important. The present shareholders in this company are not growing fat on its above-average rate of return on capital. This return has been capitalized; the present owners of Marks & Spencer have bought the right to it from the founders, who were thus able to sell their shares and obtain the proceeds of their entrepreneurial activities. Similarly, the present stockholders in the Xerox Corporation are those who have bought the right to Mr. Carlson's invention from him and his original backers at a price which reflected the expectation of the profits which the company is currently earning.

We have so far only looked at the production side of these activities. The third group of people who may share the burden of corporation tax are those who buy goods and services which are produced by companies. If there is a tax on capital employed in the company sector, and people require a certain rate of return before they will invest in companies (because, for example, they can obtain that return by buying Government bonds or investing overseas), then the tax will have to be paid by those who buy goods which are produced by companies. Part of it may also fall on those who form companies to exploit their entrepreneurial activities.

It should be clear from this that the incidence of corporation tax depends in part on the structure of the tax. If it is a tax on pure profits only, then it falls in the first instance on those who supply entrepreneurship to companies—inventors, successful organizers, would-be monopolists. If, as we might suspect, the supply of such entrepreneurship is not too sensitive to its rewards then these entrepreneurs will pay the tax and that will be the end of the matter: but if they abandon entrepreneurship and enter routine employment instead then consumers will have to bear the burden of the tax, partly in higher prices to induce a little more entrepreneurship and more importantly through the loss of the ideas and efficiency which these people might otherwise have promoted (this is the 'excess burden' of this tax). Moreover, because of capitalization we can tax *past* entrepreneurship at rates as high as we like without the tax being shifted forward to consumers in this way or producing economic inefficiency of any kind. It is possible that if Mr. Marks had known that profits would be taxed at 52% he would not have bothered to think up Marks & Spencer, or that the current shareholders would have been less willing to pay so much to him for his business, but they have made their decisions and there is nothing that they can do about it now.

We should note that similar disincentives apply to entrepreneurship in the unincorporated sector: but there they arise from the effect of the personal income tax rather than the corporation tax. Since the rates of this may well be higher (and certainly will be if the invention is a very successful one), the disincentive brought about by the corporation tax may be less than that which exists in the economy generally from the effects of other taxes: so that although all activities of this kind are penalized the use of the corporate form as a means of exploiting invention reduces the tax burden imposed.

We can therefore see that a tax on pure profits is not without economic attractions—though these depend on the belief that desirable entrepreneurship will be inelastically supplied. (If people are deterred from seeking monopolies by the knowledge that the proceeds will be taxed, that is all to the good.) We shall describe a corporation tax which falls only on pure profits as a neutral tax. If a corporation tax is not neutral, it will fall also on those who supply capital to companies. The incidence of this part of the tax then depends on the response of firms and financiers to this change. If there are profitable investment opportunities elsewhere—and foreign investment is probably available to domestic investors and certainly to overseas investors—then firms will be unable to pass the burden of the tax back to investors. They will then try to substitute other factors of production for the now more expensive capital. To the extent that this raises costs and to the extent that they cannot substitute successfully they will have to share the tax between a reduction in any pure profits they may be making (which may be small or zero for many companies) and a higher price charged to the consumers of their products. If this happens, corporation tax will act as a general sales tax on the goods which companies produce (though at different rates on different goods). We may note that the openness of the economy to capital flows will be an important factor in determining the incidence of corporation tax. The greater this is, the greater the proportion of the tax which is likely to fall on consumers.

We have seen that the analysis of the incidence of corporation tax is a complicated issue—and indeed we have underestimated its complexity because we have examined only the most immediate consequences of the tax. There are likely to be further repercussions from the effects on income distribution of whatever the incidence may turn out to be. Nor have we considered adequately the problems we raised in Chapter 1—what is the alternative tax with which we are implicitly comparing the corporation tax? But in this simple framework it seems that incidence depends on empirical questions which are not easily answered, and it is not surprising that the subject has been in long-standing dispute. What we have suggested—and what has perhaps not received sufficient attention in that dispute—is that incidence is likely to be rather sensitive to the structure of the tax; and that the issue of whether the tax is or is not neutral is critical to this. We therefore turn to analyses of alternative tax structures, focusing on this issue.

But before doing so, we should notice that although corporation taxes do not emerge in a very satisfactory light from this discussion and non-neutral corporation taxes particularly badly, the analysis, suggests one argument for such a tax. This is that we have one already. To the extent that the tax falls on pure profits, and stays there, it will be capitalized in share prices; the value of Marks & Spencer is lower than it would be if there were no corporation tax, and this expectation has been reflected in the price at which shares in this company have changed hands in the past. To abolish the tax now would be to confer a windfall gain on these present shareholders. The force of this is weakened by the observation that few British companies are paying much corporation tax; but some (including Marks & Spencer) are, and more expect to in future.

Systems of company taxation

If a separate corporation tax is to be retained, it is important to choose a tax which does not conflict with the objectives of the personal direct tax system. There are two sorts of questions about company taxes we could ask. What are the different types of company tax systems? What are the economic effects of a tax on companies? It is clear that we cannot answer the second question until we know exactly what type of company tax we are talking about, and so we shall describe some of the main corporate tax systems which could be employed. It is useful to classify corporate tax systems in terms of how they tax distributed profits relative to their taxation of undistributed profits. When the corporate tax system in Britain was changed in 1965 and 1973, on both occasions the idea behind the change was to alter the relative tax burden on dividends and retentions. We shall follow this method of classifying company tax systems. An alternative approach is to look at systems in terms of their effects on the investment decisions of firms by asking the question: how does the tax system affect the pre-tax rate of return on an investment project required to induce firms to go ahead with the project? This is a question to which we shall return after having described the different systems of corporation tax.

If there are no taxes the cost of capital is simply the rate of return demanded by the supplier of finance, the rate of interest at which the firm can borrow, for example. In a competitive economy this cost of capital is independent of the particular method of finance which is chosen. While it may appear, for example, that borrowing secured on particular assets is 'cheaper' than other ways of raising new capital, such activities increase the risk, and hence the cost, attached to other financial instruments, such as unsecured loans or equity shares. Since there must be a lender for each borrower, the outcome will be one in which the 'price' of each kind of capital which the firm has will reflect the degree of risk attached to that particular asset, and the over-all cost of capital cannot be reduced by resorting to so-called 'cheap capital'. It follows from this that there is little to choose between alternative methods of financing when there are no tax considerations, and that such decisions will be very sensitive to tax systems which favour one method rather than another. When tax considerations do apply, a firm will use the cheapest source of finance first, though there are practical limits to this, especially when this source is debt or retained earnings.

Between 1947 and 1965 companies in Britain paid tax at the standard rate of income tax plus an additional rate of profits tax which, until 1958, was charged at a different rate on distributed profits than on retained profits. The differential rates were abolished in 1958 and profits tax was imposed at a uniform rate on all profits. In 1965 corporation tax was introduced and the U.K. adopted the *classical system*. This is perhaps the simplest system to understand and is often represented as embodying the principle that the tax liability of the company should be completely independent of that of its shareholders. It is the system employed in the U.S.A. and in Holland amongst other countries, and was in force in Britain until 1973. Under the classical system the company pays a flat rate of corporation tax on its taxable profits, and then the shareholders pay income tax on their dividends and capital gains tax on the gains which arise from corporate retentions. A company wishing to raise a given amount of finance may either retain profits, or distribute the profits as dividends and issue new shares, or borrow the money and pay interest charges on the loan. The classical system discriminates between the first two sources of funds unless capital gains are taxed at the same rate as unearned income, and it favours debt finance if, as is almost always the case, interest payments may be deducted against profits in assessing liability to corporation tax.

It is precisely this discrimination between dividends and retentions which, so it is claimed, constitutes the major objection to the classical system because it involves the 'double taxation of dividends'. The double taxation arises because dividends are subject to both corporation tax and income tax, whereas retentions are liable only to corporation tax. As we have seen, this argument ignores the fact that capital gains tax is payable on gains arising from retentions although of course it is perfectly true that the effective tax rate on capital gains is much less than the rate of income tax. Nevertheless, in 1973 the classical system was replaced by the *imputation system* in order to alleviate part of the 'double' taxation of dividends. The imputation system gives shareholders credit for tax paid by the company, and this credit may be used to offset their income tax liability on dividends. Part of the company's tax liability is 'imputed' to the shareholders and regarded as a prepayment of their income tax on dividends.

The company pays tax on its profits at the rate of corporation tax, and any profits which are subsequently distributed are regarded as having already paid income tax at a certain rate, which we may call the 'rate of imputation'. In Britain the rate of imputation is always set equal to the basic rate of income tax. Shareholders only have to pay additional income tax on their dividends if their marginal rates of income tax exceed the basic rate, while if their marginal rates are less than the basic rate they actually receive a refund from the Revenue. For example, a charity or pension fund will receive a refund of tax deemed to have been paid on their behalf by the company. An alternative method of alleviating the double taxation of dividends is to charge a lower rate of corporation tax on distributed profits than on undistributed profits. This is called the *two-rate* system.

An alternative system is simply to integrate the personal and corporate tax systems, and for tax purposes to regard shareholders as partners in a business. Under the *integrated system*, as it is called, each shareholder is deemed to have earned a fraction of the company's profits equal to the fraction of its shares which he owns. The effect of this is that the company's profits, both distributed *and* undistributed, constitute part of the shareholders' personal taxable income. Once a year each shareholder would receive a piece of paper from the company showing his taxable profits for the last year together with a tax credit for the tax paid by the company on his behalf. The taxable profits would be added to his personal income. A reform along these lines was suggested by the Carter Commission in Canada and was seriously considered in West Germany. In neither country, however, was it adopted, partly on administrative grounds and partly on the irrelevant legal argument that a company is distinct from its shareholders.

Taxes and investment

We shall consider first a project financed entirely by borrowing. Imagine a firm contemplating investing in a project which involves buying a piece of machinery and then using it together with labour and raw materials to produce output which is then sold. If the receipts from the sale of output more than cover *all* the costs involved then the project will earn profits for the firm, and the project will be given the go-ahead. What do the costs include? Obviously, they include the payments made for raw materials, fuel, and labour, but they also include the capital costs incurred. These will consist of two parts. The first is the interest payment on the loan taken out to finance the purchase of the machinery, and the second is the deterioration in the value of the machinery itself due to wear and tear caused by use, or to obsolescence caused by the invention of better machinery. This second element is the depreciation charge, and is called 'true economic depreciation'. It is important to note that it consists of the change in the value of the machinery during the firm's accounting period regardless of the way the value has changed. Since firms rarely sell machinery it is extremely difficult to value second-hand plant and so depreciation charges usually follow rather arbitrary rules, such as writing-off the cost of an asset in equal instalments over some assumed average life for assets of that particular type, and only approximate true economic depreciation.

If the receipts from the project exceed all its costs, including capital costs as defined above, then the project will earn a surplus for the shareholders of the firm and will always be a desirable investment, provided the surplus is positive. What matters is not the size of the surplus, but the fact that it is a surplus. A proportional tax on this surplus will still leave a positive surplus for the shareholders, and therefore will not affect investment decisions. In the case we examined investment was financed by borrowing and in that case capital costs consisted of interest payments on the borrowed money and depreciation of the capital equipment. As far as investment financed by borrowing is concerned a corporation tax which allows as deductions both interest payments and true economic depreciation will be neutral.

What happens if the project is not entirely financed by borrowing? The argument remains valid if the costs of different forms of finance can be fully deducted from profits for corporation tax purposes. For financing by new share issues this has never been true, since dividends are not a 'cost' for corporation tax purposes. Under the classical system, no part of dividends can be offset against liability to corporation tax; hence the discrimination against financing projects this way is very heavy and to the extent that such finance is necessary the required rate of return from the project is increased. With the imputation system, dividends are partially deductible for corporation tax purposes; £100 paid out as gross dividends reduces the final corporation tax liability by £34, while £100 paid out in interest or any other cost would reduce it by £52. Thus there is some increase in the required rate of return, but the effect is smaller than under the classical system.

If the investment is undertaken from retained profits, the position is more complex. The cost of internal finance depends on the personal tax rates of the owners of the company because they can avoid paying income tax on their returns by sheltering behind the combined burden of corporation tax and capital gains tax. It is possible that for some wealthy investors this double burden is less than their marginal rate of income tax which actually lowers the required rate of return on investment projects financed from retained earnings.

We shall now apply these principles to an analysis of how company taxes operate in Britain today.

12

COMPANY TAXATION IN THE U.K.

The present imputation system

SINCE 1973 company taxation in the U.K. has been based on the imputation system. To illustrate how the system works consider a shareholder who has received a cheque for £100 as his annual dividend. With a rate of corporation tax of 52% the company has had to use £208 of pre-tax profits to pay this dividend with the balance of £108 (52% of £208) going to the Revenue in corporation tax. Part of this corporate tax bill is in fact prepayment of income tax at the standard rate on dividends which is deducted at source, and this component is paid to the Revenue when dividends are distributed. Since this is usually before the date when companies are called upon to pay corporation tax on the year's profits, this element of tax is called advance corporation tax (A.C.T.), but in fact it is more properly regarded not as a company tax but as deduction at source of standard rate income tax on dividends. The remaining tax payments to the Revenue are described as 'mainstream' corporation tax. It is these payments which constitute the effective corporate tax burden, since the amounts which are described as A.C.T. would be paid, as income tax, even if corporation tax were completely abolished.

The essence of the imputation system is that when the shareholder receives his dividend cheque for £100 he is deemed to have already paid income tax at the basic rate on the dividend. If all shareholders paid income tax at the basic rate that would be the end of the matter. But some shareholders have higher marginal tax rates and others lower, and this complicates matters somewhat because we have to calculate the amount of extra tax or of refund which is due. To do this we ask the question—what dividend before tax would I need in order to finish up with £100 after payment of basic rate income tax? Suppose the basic rate of income tax is $33\frac{1}{3}$%. Then to end up with £100 after tax I would need £150

before tax. This is the notional pre-tax dividend which the shareholder receives, the 'grossed-up' dividend, and £50 is the notional
tax which he has paid.

If all this seems rather abstract to our shareholder then he
should think again, for with his dividend cheque for £100 will
come a piece of paper representing a tax credit of £50 exactly
equal to the notional tax we have just described. On his tax form
the shareholder must enter the notional pre-tax dividend of £150
(which is equivalent to the value of his dividend of £100 plus the
tax credit of £50) which will then be added to his other income to
calculate his total income tax bill. But since he is deemed to have
already paid the notional tax he can use the credit as an offset
against his income tax liability. If he pays tax at the basic rate, the
credit eliminates his liability and he can forget about the imputation system of corporation tax. If his marginal income tax rate is
60%, then his tax liability on the dividend is £90 minus the tax
credit of £50. He will have to send a cheque for the balance of £40
to the Inland Revenue. But if the recipient of the dividend cheque
were a charity or pension fund, and hence not liable to tax, the boot
would be on the other foot and the Revenue would have to refund
the tax credit of £50 to the shareholder. Of the pre-tax profit of
£208, a basic rate taxpayer would receive £100, an effective rate
of 52%, a charity would receive £150, a tax rate of 28%, and an
individual with an income tax rate of 60% would receive £60, an
effective tax rate of 71·2%.

We have discussed the example at length so that the reader
should understand the principles of the system and not be confused by the terminology used in the actual operation of the imputation system in Britain. It is complex because after they have
received their dividends some shareholders owe additional tax and
others are owed refunds. The system of tax credits is needed to
ensure that the correct amounts are paid.

In the U.K. the rate of imputation is always set equal to the basic
rate of income tax because the majority of shareholders pay tax
at the basic rate, and hence for a large number of dividend recipients no net payments or refunds are required. Although this may
seem appealing on administrative grounds, it is in fact a rather
restrictive provision. There is no obvious reason for taking the rate
of imputation to be the basic rate of income tax, and there are two
objections to it. First, it has the consequence that an increase in the

basic rate of income tax increases the tax burden on earned income but has no effect on the tax burden on dividend income of shareholders paying the basic rate, because the tax credit rises in line with the increased income tax liability, and actually benefits exempt shareholders, such as pension funds.

Second, the imputation system was introduced to reduce the fiscal discrimination between dividends and retentions, and hence between the different methods of raising finance. But the basic difficulty with the system is that it can lead to a neutral tax position only for those shareholders paying one particular rate of income tax. If we ignore capital gains tax this neutral position exists only for shareholders paying the basic rate. For other shareholders there will be discrimination in one direction or another. But the neutral tax rate does not coincide with a weighted average of the marginal income tax rates of shareholders, which is somewhat above the basic rate of tax and has been falling over the last decade or so (see King, 1977, App. A), principally because of the rapid growth in the shareholdings of institutions, such as pension funds, which pay little or no tax.

An additional complexity in the system is advance corporation tax. The Revenue does not wish to pay to shareholders any refunds of tax which it has not received from the company in the first place, and so each company is required to pay A.C.T. before any refunds can be made.[1] A.C.T. is equal to the total of the tax credits received by the company's shareholders. The rate of credit (and hence also A.C.T.) is defined as the ratio of the notional tax paid by the company on behalf of its shareholders to the dividends distributed, and so is always expressed in the rather strange form of 34/66, for example, in the case of a basic rate of income tax of 34%.

Tax changes in the U.K.

The tax treatment of dividends and retentions has oscillated since the last war, first favouring one and then the other. After the introduction of corporation tax in 1965 debt finance was very attractive, but new equity finance reappeared after the change in 1973. Issues of preference shares (a security with a fixed rate of

---

[1] A.C.T. can be offset against the company's eventual liability to corporation tax, but this relief is limited to the amount of relief due under the assumption that the company distributed all its taxable profits (which in recent years have been very low). Surplus A.C.T. may be offset against the corporation tax of the two previous years or carried forward.

interest which may if necessary be reduced, thus giving some of the flexibility of equity finance) were virtually killed off in 1965, and yet this sort of finance would have helped some companies with their liquidity problems in 1974.

It is not easy for a company to change its capital structure overnight to take advantage of changes in the tax system, and certain changes might be illegal. But there is one way in which a major change in capital structure can be effected, and that is by merger or take-over. A company with a suitable capital structure may appear an attractive partner for another firm even if the two companies have nothing in common by way of similar products or production methods. Other tax reasons for mergers are unrelieved tax losses or credit for foreign tax which cannot be used because the company has no domestic taxable profit. It is hard to imagine any industrial policy which would encourage mergers of this sort. We do not use the personal tax system to encourage the marriage of otherwise unsuitable partners, so it is hard to see why we would want to do this with companies. Yet we find British American Tobacco operating supermarkets and Consolidated Gold Fields building roads.

The main effect of the many changes in the corporate tax system has been to introduce fiscal considerations into decisions which there is every reason to believe are best left to companies themselves. The capital structure of a company and the method by which it finances its investment are matters which the tax system ought not to try to influence, and if it does it will create difficulties for itself. Divergencies from a non-neutral tax system give rise to the need for complex legislation to prevent abuse and avoidance through the conversion of income into whatever legal form happens to be taxed most lightly. Close company legislation is needed to prevent individuals retaining income in a company behind the corporate tax shelter. The idea of paying shareholders 'scrip dividends' (by giving them shares whose value was taxed as a capital gain) instead of cash dividends taxable as income was outlawed in 1975 when such dividends were deemed to be income for tax purposes. It is very difficult to distinguish clearly between capital and income and yet that is what is required if the present system is to work smoothly. Complaints by companies about the losses they have made on foreign currency loans illustrate how income and changes in capital values are not easy to separate. By repurchasing their own debt at below its nominal value companies can substitute tax-deductible interest payments for repayment of capital, with favourable tax consequences. Even the difference between debt and equity can be blurred, and in the 1960s there was extensive importation of the American device of the convertible loan stock, which is debt to the taxman and equity to the holder.

Any deviation from a neutral tax system will provide someone with an opportunity to invent methods of avoiding tax. The authorities then respond with legislation to prevent such abuse, and effort then goes into devising even more ingenious financial operations to save the company and its shareholders tax. £1 in tax saved is worth as much to the company as £1 earned by productive activity. Most of these side-effects of a non-neutral tax system were unintended and, if perhaps not enormously harmful to the economy, nevertheless constitute a diversion of resources of time and skilled manpower to pointless activities. The frequency of the changes in the tax system aggravates the situation.

Investment and the tax system

Applying our previous analysis to the U.K. tax system is complicated by the multiplicity of different ways in which depreciation is treated. For many years depreciation allowances have been becoming more and more generous, and 100% of all investment in plant, machinery, ships, and aircraft, can be depreciated immediately ('free depreciation'). Industrial buildings qualify for a first-year allowance of 54% (consisting of an initial allowance of 50% and the first year's ordinary depreciation allowance of 4%). In addition there are special cash grants to certain kinds of investment in the assisted regions. No allowances, however, are given for land and commercial buildings because they are expected to retain their value. First-year allowances can be offset against the profits of the three previous years, and can be carried forward in money terms indefinitely. There is a special form of relief for investment in stocks which we discuss below in the context of inflation accounting. The net result of this is that most investment by industrial companies qualifies for free depreciation and the bulk of the remainder for some form of accelerated depreciation. In addition, interest payments are tax-deductible which means that the tax system is considerably more generous than either of the tax bases discussed above. Provided tax allowances can be claimed, which for some companies recently has not been the case, then the existence of corporation tax at 52% is not a disincentive to invest at all.

In fact, for investment qualifying for free depreciation and substantially financed by borrowing, the higher the rate of corporation tax the stronger the inducement to undertake the project. Consider the following example. An investment of £200 will yield £30 per annum for sufficiently long that we can simplify matters by neglecting depreciation. Corporation tax is at 50%, so that the yield is 15% before tax and 7½% after tax. However, the company succeeds in borrowing £50 at 12% p.a. to finance the project: so that it must pay £6 in annual interest, leaving £24 return on the £150 supplied by its shareholders. This produces 16% before tax, 8% after tax. Since the cost of the borrowing is less than the yield on the investment, the rate of return on shareholders' funds is increased by this use of external finance.

Free depreciation improves the return dramatically. In the first year of the project the company can deduct the £200 invested from its taxable profit; so that provided it has sufficient profits on its other activities it can reduce its tax bill in that year by £100 (50% of £200). This reduces the amount which the shareholders need contribute from £150 to £50; since the returns and the interest cost remain the same, the net profit after tax is still £12, which is a 24% return on capital. In this example, free depreciation and interest deductibility together imply that the rate of return is higher after tax than it is before: 24% as against the original 16%.

It is easy to see that the *higher* the corporation tax rate, the higher the yield is. Suppose corporation tax went up to 60%. The taxpayer's contribution in the first year is now £120, and the shareholders need only provide £30. In subsequent years the Government takes 60% of the profit after interest of £24, leaving only £9·60 for the shareholders: but this means that the return on capital has actually risen to 32%.

The present system discriminates between investment in different types of asset and between investment in different sectors. Plant and machinery are favoured assets and commercial building is not. Stocks of both raw materials and finished goods received rather unfavourable treatment until 1974 and generous treatment thereafter. (Although knowing how generous the treatment is depends on successfully guessing what permanent form the 'temporary' stock relief scheme will eventually take.) The rationale for these differences is unclear, apart from a vague desire to encourage investment in manufacturing industry. But for a long time the sector which has paid conspicuously little corporation tax has been the property sector, as a result of the favourable tax treatment of debt finance. This is a strange state of affairs and we discuss below ways in which it might be remedied.

Inflation accounting

We have not so far paid much explicit attention to the question of how inflation affects the argument about which tax system to choose. In fact the only points at which inflation would have modified the picture would have been when we were defining the value of 'true economic depreciation' and of deductible interest payments. Here we have to distinguish between the change in the *money* value of capital equipment (a measure of depreciation based on historic costs) and the change in the *real* value of assets (true economic depreciation at current replacement cost). We must also distinguish between nominal interest payments and real interest payments. In times of inflation the real value of debt denoted in nominal terms falls over time, and interest payments contain an element of capital repayment. This is obvious to anyone who is paying interest on a mortgage who finds the burden of meeting interest payments progressively less onerous. The value of real interest payments is the interest calculated at the 'real' rate of interest (the money rate of interest minus the rate of inflation), and can be computed by subtracting from nominal payments the rate of inflation multiplied by the value of liabilities. This adjustment is described as allowing for the fall in the real value of net monetary liabilities.

Concern about the effects of inflation on the presentation of company accounts led the Government to appoint an Inflation Accounting Committee (the Sandilands Committee) in 1974. It reported in 1975 (Cmnd. 6225) and sparked off a debate which has continued pretty well ever since. For their starting-point the Sandilands Committee took as a definition of a company's profit 'the maximum value which the company can distribute during the year, and still expect to be as well off at the end of the year as it was at the beginning' (para. 98).

This is an adaptation of the Hicksian definition of income which we discussed in Chapter 5. We saw there how difficult it is to translate this definition into an operational concept, and much of the debate which has followed publication of the Sandilands Report reflects this. There are really two distinct questions: how should profits be measured, and how should this measure be adjusted for inflation? The Accounting Standards Steering Committee had proposed a system of current purchasing power (C.P.P.) accounting which started from the premiss that conventional historic cost accounting would measure profits correctly if there were no inflation, and therefore dealt only with the second of these issues. The Sandilands Committee rejected C.P.P. and attempted to answer both questions. While both are important, the major difficulties surround the first.

Once the answer to the first question has been arrived at, it is straightforward to apply an inflation adjustment. Most of the difficulties concern the proper way of measuring profits even in the absence of inflation. But there is no necessary reason why the figure arrived at by accountants as a company's annual profit should be taken as the appropriate figure for the company's taxable income. Accounting calculations are important and serve many useful purposes, but in view of our earlier discussion about how to define income it is far from clear that the tax authorities need to get embroiled in the debate on the Sandilands Report. Indeed it would be an advantage if they were not to, for the urgency for a permanent and sensible reform of the corporate tax system could then be separated from the issue of what conventions, if any, the accountancy profession could agree to.

There is no need to detain ourselves further with a discussion of all the technicalities contained in the 364 pages of the Sandilands Committee's Report. Essentially, the Committee argued for the adoption of replacement cost accounting, which it called 'current cost accounting', the effect of which would be to measure depreciation at current replacement cost and to take stock appreciation out of profits altogether. Stock appreciation is the increase in the value of a company's stocks owing to rises in the prices of the stocks. Thus when oil prices rose sharply in 1973–4, oil companies made large gains on their stocks of oil. What part of this gain is counted as profit is, or ought to be, the heart of the debate on inflation accounting. It was also proposed that balance sheets should record assets at their current values. This set of proposals was intended to replace the traditional historic cost approach to accounting measurements, and superseded the earlier recommendations of the Accounting Standards Steering Committee for the C.P.P. method.

Following publication of the Sandilands Report, the accounting bodies tried to work out the details of how it might be implemented, but the first attempt to do this (the Morpeth Committee Report) was rejected as being too complex. A much simpler proposal was published in late 1977. Known as the Hyde Guidelines, it suggested that a short statement be added to the conventional profit and loss account describing three adjustments for inflation on depreciation, stock profits, and gearing (the ratio of debt to the total value of debt and shareholders' capital). Proposals to update company balance sheets (which were the useful part of the Sandilands recommendations) now appear to have been abandoned.

This gearing adjustment has led to great confusion. It concerns the treatment of net monetary liabilities. As the Sandilands Committee pointed out, when defining real profits we have to take account of the effects of inflation on the real value of assets. It is not enough to base depreciation allowances on the historic cost of plant. But the Committee ignored the effect of inflation on the value of liabilities. If we are calculating the real profits of a company's shareholders it is illogical to make an allowance for the effects of inflation on the value of assets and to ignore any effect on liabilities. The liabilities in question consist principally of monetary liabilities to bondholders and other suppliers of debt finance. An adjustment for inflation must allow for both assets and net monetary liabilities. Yet many accountants have been slow to pick up this basic point, and the Hyde Guidelines have only confused the issue by proposing a gearing adjustment which would add back to profits that fraction of stock profits and the depreciation adjustment which could be said to have been financed from debt. But the fall in the value of net monetary liabilities is unrelated to whether the firm even holds stocks.

Why has this been the case? Although it is incontrovertible that shareholders gain, and hence the profitability of the firm is enhanced by the decline in the real value of monetary liabilities under inflation, the resistance to introducing this item is largely attributable to the realization that gains of this kind do not generate 'cash in the bank' in the same way as do some other components of profit. There is nothing inconsistent about this; profitability and liquidity are not the same thing, and profitability is not a flow of cash, but a change in the value of assets which offers a potential flow of cash in the future. Most owner-occupiers know this only too well because whereas it is certainly profitable to buy one's own home it imposes great strains on the liquid resources of the household during the first few years of the mortgage. What those who resist the inclusion of an item for the decline in the value of monetary liabilities are really saying, then, is that because profitability is not necessarily a good guide to the liquid resources available to a firm it is not the only, or even the best, measure of that firm's ability to pay dividends or taxes. We share this view, though it is a very confusing way of expressing it to argue that profitability is really something other than what it is. This suggests that taxation might be more appropriately based on a measure of cash flow than of profitability; this is what has happened in practice, and it is what we think should happen in principle also. We pursue each of these points in turn.

We should begin by noting that the question of what is a suitable corporate tax base is not the same question as how profits should be defined for accounting purposes. Moreover, if the tax system did take account of the effects of inflation on the monetary liabilities of companies, it would equally have to extend indexation to the taxation of the interest income of the bondholder. If we start on this road we have to go all the way; indexation is an all-or-nothing business. Failure to do this would create yet more loopholes and require further legislation to stop them up.

In 1974 companies were facing severe liquidity problems and the Chancellor decided that he could not wait until a permanent method of inflation accounting had been agreed upon before giving some tax concessions to the corporate sector. With most firms using historic cost accounts it was impossible simply to exempt stock appreciation from tax, and an arbitrary form of relief, stock relief, was introduced in November 1974, retrospective to 1973. Under this scheme companies could deduct for tax purposes the excess of the change in the book value of stocks over 10% of gross trading profits. The increase in the book value of stocks in any year consists of stock appreciation plus the value of physical investment in stocks. The figure of 10% of gross trading profits was held to be a rough average for the economy of the value of additions to stocks plus 'normal' stock appreciation, from which it was felt exemption from tax was not justified. In 1976 this was changed to 15% of trading profits after depreciation allowances. This is evidently a rough-and-ready justice which takes no account of the circumstances of individual companies. And at the margin stock relief permits purchases of stocks as a tax deduction, thus providing a bigger incentive to invest in stocks than was envisaged by the Sandilands Committee. But it pushes the current tax system nearer to what we shall call a cash flow corporation tax.

As we have seen, the corporation tax which exists in the U.K. today is far removed from a tax on company profits. A company earns profits on its productive assets but before paying tax it may deduct interest payments on loans taken out to finance the purchase of some of its fixed and working capital, and also any expenditure on investment on a wide range of assets (by taking advantage of free depreciation). On top of this stock relief mitigates the taxation of stock appreciation. The effect of these allowances is to reduce the size of taxable profits, thus lowering the burden of corporation tax. In fact the situation has been reached where for the 'average' industrial company corporation tax has effectively been abolished. Many of them have negative taxable profits while still being in a position to pay dividends, and are building up unrelieved tax losses which they will carry forward to offset future years' tax.

The fact that many companies pay no tax is hardly evident from published company accounts which often show in their profit and loss account a notional tax charge which takes no account of accelerated depreciation nor of stock relief. The effect of this accounting practice is that many companies, especially in manufacturing industry, show substantial tax charges in their accounts when in fact they are paying little or no tax at all. We have tried to extract from the published accounts of a number of leading British companies figures on the amounts of mainstream corporation tax which they actually paid. The results are shown in Table 12.1. (Readers who are unfamiliar with company accounts may be surprised that basic information such as how much tax companies pay is not readily available; those who are familiar with them will recognize the difficulty and unreliability of such estimates.)

Although it is true that on average companies pay little tax, there are substantial variations between firms, and there is great uncertainty about future tax liabilities. The Chancellor receives little revenue, but companies do not face a stable environment in which they can plan. Stock relief is temporary and there is no agreement on how the tax system should embody inflation accounting. There is a need for a simple and stable tax system, but it is clear that the current set-up must be changed, and we turn now to a discussion of possible reforms.

TABLE 12.1

Mainstream corporation tax paid by the 20 leading U.K. industrial companies, 1977

(£ m.)

Company	Profits, 1976	Tax payment, 1977
British Petroleum	1784	nil
I.C.I.	540	23
B.A.T. Industries	374	2
Rio Tinto-Zinc	279	nil
Esso	69	nil
Imperial Group	130	9
Courtaulds	43	nil
Grand Metropolitan	57	nil
P. & O. Steam Navigation	31	nil
Guest Keen & Nettlefolds	98	nil
General Electric Co.	207	42
Dunlop	73	nil
Reed International	75	nil
Bowater	78	nil
Distillers Co.	91	7
Bass Charrington	69	24
Allied Breweries	63	9
British Leyland	56[1]	nil
Ford Motor Co.	122	nil
Marks & Spencer	84	29
Totals	4323	145

Notes: Companies are largest 20 by capital employed from *Times 1000* (1976–7), excluding Shell, Unilever, Burmah, Rank/Rank Xerox.
Profits are latest full-year figures at 30 April 1977.
[1] Annual rate.
Source: Own estimates.

The Future of Corporation Tax

The simplest reform would be to abolish corporation tax altogether. We suggested above that if it did not exist we would not wish to introduce it, and since it contributes little revenue there is

something to be said for being rid of it. Attractive though it might
seem there are problems with this idea. Earlier we suggested that
the reason for retaining the corporation tax is that it exists already.
It may be true that the tax does not raise much revenue at the
moment but many companies may be expecting to pay taxes in the
future. Moreover, although on average the effective tax rate is
negligible, some companies are paying a lot of tax and others pay
nothing or have unrelieved tax losses. To abolish the tax now would
result in windfall gains and losses to individual owners of companies. There is also a desire to extract tax revenue from British
subsidiaries of foreign-owned companies and from those shareholders of British companies who are resident overseas. The easiest
way of taxing their profits is to have an independent corporation
tax.

We believe that the most desirable reform of the corporate tax
system would be to convert the existing mixture of what is, on the
one hand, excessively generous relief for investment financed by
borrowing and, on the other, only temporary relief for the effects of
inflation, into a tax based on cash flows. This is based on the use of
free depreciation which allows companies to deduct for tax purposes any investment expenditure as soon as the money is spent.
No distinction is made between expenditure on current items
(labour, materials, etc.) and the expenditure on capital goods. The
tax base is simply the difference between receipts from the sales of
goods and services (including the proceeds from selling plant or
factories) and the money spent on acquiring goods and services.
For this reason we shall describe such a tax as a *cash flow corporation tax*. The essence of the tax is that all receipts and payments,
whether they correspond to current or to capital items, enter into
the tax base and therefore there is no need to worry about how 'true
economic depreciation' should be calculated. Companies would be
taxed on their cash flow. However, it is important to note that our
definition of cash flow refers to that of the company, and does not
correspond to an alternative common usage of the term as cash
flow to the shareholders. We do not allow interest payments as a
deduction. Under the cash flow corporation tax expenditure on real
items can be deducted, but the returns to the suppliers of finance,
whether shareholders or creditors, cannot.

What would the effect of such a tax be? Imagine a firm contemplating a specific investment project which would cost £1 m.

With a cash flow tax it would be able to deduct the £1 m. spent on purchasing equipment against its profits on other projects, thus reducing its total tax payments. If the tax rate were 50% the reduction in taxes would be £½ m. The future profits of the project would also be reduced by 50% by such a tax, and so the net effect is that both the initial outlay and the subsequent returns are reduced by the same proportion, a proportion equal to the rate of tax. The tax scales down the size of the project financed by the company, but it does not alter the rate of return on the money invested in the project by the company. With a 50% tax rate then what the Government is saying is 'in any project in which you invest we shall compulsorily acquire a 50% stake, and we shall of course provide half the finance in return for half the profits'. The reason why this tax system can raise revenue is that it ensures that if firms are in a position to earn pure profits then the Government too will get a good share of the excess profits. It is for this reason that we argue below that the cash flow tax is well suited for tackling problems such as how to tax the profits on North Sea oil and gas extraction. We believe that it also represents the best way of tidying up the present mess into which corporate taxation has drifted by allowing for inflation in a simple manner without the need for complicated conventions on how to account for inflation. It taxes companies on those flows which are most important to the companies themselves, namely flows of cash.

In the above example it was crucial that the firm had available profits from other projects against which it could deduct investment expenditure on new projects. But a new or expanding firm might not have sufficient profits for this purpose, and such a possibility was an important element in the decision to replace accelerated depreciation allowances with cash investment grants in 1966. The problem can be partly met by allowing companies to carry forward tax losses, not, as at present, simply at their nominal value, but marked up by an interest factor to allow for the fact that they have to wait to get the benefit of the first-year tax allowances.

Because the tax is based on cash flows as and when they occur, there is no need to index for inflation. The distinction between capital and income would be irrelevant, and the effects of inflation would be allowed for automatically without the need for any special adjustment. It is important to stress the simplicity of this system in contrast to the complexity of the alternative methods of calculating taxable profits which have been suggested.

To convert the current tax system to a cash flow corporation tax would necessitate several changes, the net effect of which would probably be to raise the revenue collected from the corporate sector. The first modification would be to extend 100% first-year allowances to all capital expenditure in order to eliminate any distinction between current and capital expenditure. This would be an increase in the allowances currently granted for expenditure on buildings, land, and stocks. But since expenditure on stocks would be tax-deductible there would be no need for any special scheme of 'stock relief' and the existing relief could be abolished. Corporate capital gains would no longer be taxed at concessionary rates, and the proceeds from all sales of assets would be taxed at the full corporate tax rate. The other major set of changes is that no payment to the suppliers of finance would be allowed as a tax deduction. Interest payments would no longer be tax-deductible, and there would be no tax credit for corporate tax paid on dividends. Consequently, we would return to the classical system of corporation tax and abolish the tax deductibility of interest payments.

There are three difficulties with this proposal. The first is that to abandon the imputation system might be seen as a failure to take seriously the E.E.C. Commission's views on harmonization of member countries' tax systems. This is not an objection to which we give much weight because the proposals for harmonization have really been concerned with the cosmetics of the tax system not with any reality. Moreover, at the beginning of 1977 West Germany adopted a corporate tax system which was inconsistent with the Commission's ideas. We discuss the question of harmonization further at the end of the chapter.

The second problem would be the transitional difficulties faced by those companies which had responded to the incentive to use debt which exists under the current regime, and were highly geared. They would face problems if deductibility of interest payments were abolished overnight, and for this reason we suggest a transitional period of several years over which tax deductibility would be gradually phased out.

The final difficulty is the application of the new tax system to financial companies. The logical counterpart to abolishing the tax deductibility of interest payments is the abolition of the taxation of interest income. If this were done then any profit made by lending at higher interest rates money borrowed at lower rates would go untaxed. Yet this is exactly what financial companies do, and often the reason why they pay lower interest rates is because they do not charge market prices for the financial services which they provide. For example, banks do not pay interest on current accounts and in turn do not charge the full price for the banking services they provide. The pure cash flow corporation tax would not work for such cases, and special rules would need to be devised for financial companies. (The logical treatment is to regard an interest-free current account as representing a combination of an interest-bearing deposit and a charge for banking services. It has become clear that the tax treatment of these companies, of which the clearing banks are the most important, creates problems for any reform of the corporate tax system which deals with problems posed by inflation.)

One remaining point is the treatment of overseas investment. It would be wrong to grant 100% first-year allowances on investment made overseas for reasons to do with the rather complex rules dealing with overseas income and the related credit given against U.K. corporation tax for taxes paid abroad. A company operating abroad pays tax to the foreign government and only pays to the U.K. Revenue the difference between its liability to U.K. corporation tax on the overseas profits and the taxes which have been paid abroad. In other words, it only pays U.K. tax if this is greater than the amount actually paid abroad. It would be anomalous to allow a company which had both domestic and overseas activities to deduct its investment abroad against its domestic profits for tax purposes if the tax on its subsequent overseas profits ended up in the hands of the foreign government, and, because of the existence of credit for foreign tax, no tax was ever paid to the U.K. government. In these circumstances overseas investment can reduce a company's domestic tax liability! Yet in fact this is precisely what British companies can do at the moment by investing in plant and machinery abroad. An overseas investment is actually more attractive to a British company than to a foreign one. We presume this was an unintended side-effect of giving 100% first-year allowances. As long as we are obliged by international agreement to grant credit for foreign tax the easiest way to deal with the problem is to disallow overseas investment as qualifying for 100% allowances.

Harmonization

It is often suggested that one of the constraints on reforming our tax system is the need to keep in line with developments in other E.E.C. countries with whose tax systems we are supposed to be harmonizing. The question of corporate tax systems in member countries has received considerable attention from the E.E.C. Commission which has produced many documents on the subject, and, recently, a Draft Directive advocating that member countries aim to harmonize on the imputation system. This proposal is, however, unlikely to have a significant impact on what each member country actually does. One reason for this is that some years ago the E.E.C. appeared to favour the two-rate system before it turned its favours to the classical system, only to finish up by supporting the imputation system. It appears to have been swimming with the tide rather than setting the pace. Consequently, if one or more member countries seem determined to adopt a different system the proposals for harmonization might well be changed. At the beginning of 1977 West Germany adopted a system of corporate taxation which was inconsistent with the recommendations of the Commission. Holland seems determined to retain the classical system with no imputation credit being given at all.

The Commission's concern with harmonization is inspired by a concern about free movement of capital and possible tax barriers to this caused by additional taxes being levied on dividends flowing from one member country to another (although there are rather more serious obstacles to the free movement of capital such as the fact that it is usually illegal). In its proposals, therefore, attention is directed entirely at the taxation of distributed profits. Harmonization, it is suggested, should be on the imputation system, with tax credits extended to individuals in other member countries. Any refunds due would be paid by the authorities of the country in which the underlying profits were taxed, not by the authorities of the country of residence of the shareholders. An additional withholding tax would be levied on dividends except where paid to known residents of a member country, or residents of a country which has negotiated an appropriate double tax treaty.

This concern with distributed profits ignores the fact that the effects of a corporate tax are very much bound up with the taxation of undistributed profits and the allowance available for depreciation. Moreover, the corporate tax system cannot be considered in isolation from the personal tax system with which it interacts. Perhaps harmonization, like indexation, is an all-or-nothing business.

The taxation of North Sea oil and gas

The flow of both oil and gas will bring benefits not only to the balance of payments, but also to the U.K. Exchequer. The magnitude of this contribution is too large to ignore and so we shall briefly describe the main features of the methods used to tax the profits arising on North Sea operations. The size of its importance can be seen by the fact that the Government expects to receive £5 billion in revenue at constant 1976 prices from the taxation of North Sea activities over the years 1976–80 (*Economic Progress Report*, Aug. 1977).

The profits accruing to the companies in the North Sea contain a supernormal component consisting of rent on the right to exploit the oil and gas fields. In order to recover some of these profits the Government has imposed a special tax system on North Sea activities. This system contains three elements. The first tax is a royalty levied at $12\frac{1}{2}\%$ of the value of deliveries of oil. The second element is a new tax called petroleum revenue tax (P.R.T.). It is charged on the receipts from sales of oil and gas (except for contracts made with the British Gas Corporation before 30 June 1975) less the expenses incurred in finding it, extracting it, and bringing it ashore. Royalty payments are an allowable expense.

P.R.T. has some features of the cash flow corporation tax which we described earlier in this chapter; for example, interest payments will not be an allowable deduction because they are a return to the suppliers of finance not a cost of obtaining the oil. But there are a number of differences. Firstly, P.R.T. is charged on each field separately, and the fact that interest deductibility applies to activities outside the North Sea arena means that the taxation of North Sea profits has to be isolated from the rest of the company's activities, the so-called 'ring-fence' approach. Secondly, capital expenditure is treated as an allowable cost, as in the cash flow tax, but companies may deduct not only the value of this expenditure but 1.75 times the expenditure (described as an 'uplift' of 75%). This odd state of affairs seems to have arisen from a feeling that disallowing interest payments as a deduction required some alternative compensation, even though logically there was a perfectly good argument for disallowing interest payments. In addition there is a special relief to ensure that the rate of return on marginal fields is adequate to ensure their development. This takes the form of an oil allowance per field of 1 million tons of oil a year which will be exempt from P.R.T., subject to a cumulative total of 10 million tons per field. Clearly, the fixed allowance will be of proportionately greater value to small fields than to large ones. There are also discretionary powers for the Secretary of State for Energy to refund royalties if a field is becoming unprofitable, and for the P.R.T. charge to be cancelled if the return on a field after royalties and P.R.T. is less than 30% in historic cost terms. The final tax charge is corporation tax which is charged on the usual basis with both royalties and P.R.T. payments counting as allowable costs.

This rather complicated system has two objectives. First, to ensure a 'reasonable share' in the economic rent obtained by the exploitation of North Sea oil and gas. Second, to ensure that marginal fields are not discriminated against. The difficulties encountered in designing a tax system to achieve these objectives derived from the need to fit the new scheme into the existing corporation tax. The deductibility of interest payments under the latter necessitated a new charge, and levying royalties on the value of sales, taking no account of costs, provides a disincentive to exploit marginal fields. These problems would be overcome by the replacement of all three of the taxes on North Sea profits by the cash flow corporation tax. Indeed this kind of operation illustrates very well the attractions of a cash flow tax because the difficulties involved in defining income and depreciation resulting from investment in exploration as well as physical plant and machinery are enormous. In the U.S.A., where the taxation of oil and gas activities has been a problem for very much longer, the appropriate definition of depreciation has caused considerable problems and controversy. A cash flow tax avoids all these problems and, as we have seen, means that the Government shares in the supernormal profits of the enterprise leaving the average rate of return on the company's investment unaffected. A tax of this kind implies no discrimination against marginal fields, and no special relief would be needed. Because profits on oil and gas will be abnormally large the right approach might be to set up a ring-fence around North Sea activities and apply a cash flow corporate tax to these operations at a specially high rate. As we have seen, the imposition of a tax of this kind does not have any effect on firms' investment decisions, and the effect of the tax is simply to extract a certain proportion of whatever surplus the companies make. It can siphon off into

Government coffers whatever fraction of the pure profits the oil companies make on their North Sea operations the Government cares to choose, and it can achieve this without distorting investment decisions. To obtain the revenue which the current system of royalties, P.R.T., and corporation tax, is expected to produce would require a rate of cash flow corporation tax of the order of 70%.

THE DISTRIBUTION OF THE
TAX BURDEN

OUR concern in this chapter is with the way in which the tax burden is distributed between individuals. We have noted in particular contexts that all taxes are ultimately taxes on individuals, and it is in this connection and only in this connection that considerations of equity enter the analysis of taxation. It simply makes no sense to talk about 'fairness' between sectors of the economy, or industries, or between the personal and corporate sectors. But these aspects of distribution may be very relevant to the effects of the tax system on efficiency and to the way in which the tax burden is distributed between people with different tastes or between wage-earners and the owners of capital.

The theory of public finance has traditionally distinguished between *vertical* and *horizontal* equity in taxation. Vertical equity is concerned with how tax liabilities are arranged among people whose circumstances are acknowledged to be different; with the distributive and redistributive implications of taxation, with the 'rich' and the 'poor'. Horizontal equity is derived from the application of the axiom that similar individuals should be treated similarly. This axiom seems compelling, though it may conflict with other objectives. (Two men are in a lifeboat with only enough water for one. The only horizontally equitable outcome is that both die.)

In practice, horizontal equity is most frequently violated when administrative arrangements are unsatisfactory; when tax impinges heavily on some transactions but can be avoided on others; when tax is paid principally by the honest, or those without effective tax advisers or the readiness to reorganize their affairs so as to minimize their liabilities; when borderlines between activities or commodities cannot be satisfactorily defined. A high proportion of popular complaints about the tax system results from inequities of this kind. We have seen serious difficulties here in the U.K. income tax. They arose to a scandalous extent with the old estate duty and are beginning to do so with capital transfer tax also.

The difficulty of principle in applying horizontal equity is that the identification of 'similar circumstances' raises awkward problems of fact and of values. In general, most people seem to take the view that the tax (and benefit) system should recognize differences where they are involuntary but not where they are a matter of choice. We want to take account of differences in endowments of wealth or skill but would resist more favourable treatment of those who are unlucky enough to have expensive tastes, although this approach is not (and cannot be) pushed very far. The most pressing problem of horizontal equity is to decide how the tax system should take account of household composition and arrangements in defining 'similar circumstances'. This is difficult because these matters involve both choice and necessity. Is having children more akin to losing a leg (which it is agreed should reduce the contribution one is expected to make to national revenue) or to buying a Rolls Royce (which it is agreed should not?). We shall not attempt to answer this question.

In fact the principle of horizontal equity has very little practical utility. Any discussion can be turned into a debate as to what is meant by 'similar circumstances' or 'similar treatment'. If in our previous example the two men in the lifeboat had tossed a coin to see who survived some people might claim that horizontal equity had been achieved. The introduction of a random element in taxation would generally be regarded as unacceptable; but there is a real difficulty in defining what exactly is involved in either 'similar circumstances' or 'similar treatment'. We therefore adopt a rather more practical approach and begin by examining the definition of the tax unit: the relationship between the tax treatment of individuals and that of households. We then look at empirical evidence on the effects of the tax system on vertical equity and consider what economic analysis can contribute to the definition and resolution of the issues involved.

The tax unit

The problem of the tax unit is to decide how households should be taxed relative to individuals. This issue arises for all direct personal taxes, but we shall discuss it with primary reference to an income tax. The present British tax and social security system encourages the poor to cohabit, those on average incomes to marry, and the rich to get divorced. Since it is difficult to imagine any social philosophy which would intend this combination of outcomes, we should begin by examining the underlying principles.

The simplest treatment of the tax unit is not to have one; to adopt an *individual basis* which 'looks through' the household and taxes its members as separate individuals. The difficulty with this system is that households do in fact exist (Though they do not necessarily take the form of husband, wife, and children. In fact in 1975 the Family Expenditure Survey showed that only one household in seven consisted of the 'typical' husband, wife, and two children (see Table 13.1)). To ignore the fact that the needs and financial affairs of households differ from those of single individuals gives rise to some curious results. The alternative is a *unit basis*, under which there can in principle be a wholly separate schedule for a household, though in practice it will normally bear some straightforward relationship to that imposed on single people. There are two principal variants: the quotient system and the dependency principle.

TABLE 13.1

Household composition of participants in the family expenditure survey, 1975

	Numbers	%
One man	408	5·7
One woman	1033	14·3
Single-parent families[1]	189	2·6
Couple[2]	2011	27·9
Couple and one child	684	9·5
Couple and two children	1034	14·4
Couple and three or more children	591	8·2
Three adults	452	6·3
Other	801	11·1
Total	7203	100·0

[1] A household consisting of one adult and one or more children.
[2] One man and one woman.

Source: *Family Expenditure Survey* (1975), H.M.S.O. App. 7.

The *quotient system* aggregates the whole income of the household and then subjects it to a rate schedule which differs from the schedule for single people in that every point on the scale has been multiplied by some figure, known as the quotient. Thus if a basic rate of tax of 34% operates on incomes above £1,000 and rises to 40% when taxable income exceeds £6,000, a quotient of 1·7 would imply that a couple would pay 34% tax on joint income in excess of £1,700 and reach the 40% rate only when their income was above £10,200. The same result is obtained if you divide the joint income by the quotient, find the corresponding liability for a single person, and then multiply that figure by the quotient. This method of calculating the tax liability of the unit explains why it is called the quotient system. The effects of this system clearly depend very much on the figure which is chosen as the quotient. The figure 1 amounts to simple aggregation of the two incomes; 2 ensures that no couple loses and most gain a tax advantage by marriage, whatever their incomes, and if their incomes are very unequal this benefit can be very large. The method can be extended to allow for children; thus in France, where the scheme is observed in its purest form, the quotient for a married couple is 2 and this figure is increased by 0·5 for each child in the family.

The British system rests on the *dependency principle*. The wife's income is simply treated as if it were the husband's, and in recognition of the burden which she imposes on him he receives a specially enhanced personal allowance. Social pressures have led to two important modifications. A wife is entitled to a single personal allowance against her own earned income; and a couple can opt for separate taxation of their earnings (but because they lose the married man's additional allowance it is rarely advantageous to do so; see p. 25).

The case for the individual basis rests on the view—which many people hold rather strongly—that they are individuals and their tax position should depend on their own earnings and circumstances and not depend on the earnings and circumstances of others, even those others with whom they may choose to live. But it is difficult to overlook the fact that in many cases the interdependence of these factors is absolutely fundamental. It is clear that we would wish to discriminate between the millionaire's wife who has no income because she stays at home to oversee the servants and the inebriate woman who sleeps under the arches at Charing Cross, although on paper their personal financial circumstances may appear to be identical. And it is very easy to reduce tax liabilities by transferring investment income from one spouse to the other. This will cost a lot of tax revenue; and it is not very desirable that fiscal consideraations should interfere with the domestic arrangements of a household. It is only necessary to envisage the conversation which runs ' "Why don't you transfer your property to me, darling, and we shall pay much less tax" "I love you, darling, but not as much as that" ' to see some of the difficulties.

The basis of the quotient system is the belief that the living standard of a couple is determined by their joint income, and the quotient is a means of relating that to the level attainable by a single individual. But a major difficulty is that the underlying premiss is not really valid. A couple in which the husband earns £10,000 per year and the wife nothing is typically much better off than two spouses each earning £5,000 per year. This is partly because there are costs to earning income—not only the cost of bus fares to work and the leisure foregone, but also costs which arise from the need to eat convenience foods and tolerate more dust on the furniture. These are costs which rise quite rapidly if there are dependent children. Additionally, the second couple will normally be at the peak of their joint earning capacity, while the former couple are probably not. Households where the wife does not work are treated very generously indeed under the quotient system, and it is difficult to believe that modern social attitudes would sustain either this outcome or a move away from, rather than towards, an individualistic viewpoint. This generosity to wives who stay at home also has the consequence that there is little incentive for the wife to work; every penny she earns is subject to tax at the marginal rate applicable to the household. Since this aspect of labour supply is, as we noted in Chapter 3, one of the most sensitive to the operation of fiscal incentives and disincentives, this objection is a serious one.

While the philosophies underlying both the individual and the quotient bases retain some validity, the dependent basis has become an anachronism. It dates from an era in which Soames Forsyte was the representative taxpayer, and there is now very little to be said for it. But neither of the principal alternatives is wholly convincing. The basic difficulty is that in constructing an appropriate tax unit we are trying to achieve a number of essentially irreconcilable objectives. There is a basic conflict between the principle that the occurrence of marriage should not affect tax liabilities much, or at all (which tends to favour an individual basis), and the principle that arrangements within marriage should not affect tax liabilities much, or at all (which tends to favour a unit basis). There is also a conflict between the wish to respect the rights of an individual to independent treatment and the desire to relate liabilities fairly to the whole of an individual's circumstances.

On this issue we see no real alternative to a pragmatic approach which seeks some suitable compromise between these different considerations, recognizing that compromise may change as social attitudes do. We should begin by identifying the principal faults in the present U.K. system. Firstly, it is much too generous to working couples without dependent children. A couple in this position receive a married allowance of £1,455 and a personal allowance of £945, so that their first £2,400 of joint income is tax-free. Compare this with the position of two single people—who receive between them allowances of £1,890—or with a married couple with two dependent children who prevent the wife from working, who will receive tax allowances of around £1,900 and child benefit of £130, which is equivalent to a total tax allowance of around £2,300. It is difficult to see any good reason why the tax and benefit system should treat the first of these couples so much more favourably and the comparison would make much better sense if the additional allowance for the married man were lower and child benefit higher. But this differential allowance has actually been substantially increased in recent years, apparently in a rather muddled attempt to help families. Since about half of all recipients of the additional married man's allowance have no dependent children, and the benefit derived is unrelated to the number of children in the families of those who do, the objective could have been attained more cheaply and effectively by increasing child allowances or child benefit.

The second anomaly in the present system is the effect of the aggregation of investment income in increasing the tax bill of people with substantial investment incomes who marry. If two people each with investment incomes of £20,000 p.a. marry, their joint tax bill rises by almost £7,000. While the plight of this couple will not bring many tears to the eyes, the irrationality of the heavy penalty on marriage is evident.

The third problem is the various elements of sex discrimination involved in the remains of the dependency principle. Many women find it offensive that their husband is required to prepare, sign, and answer for a return of their income, and some men resent being expected to proffer complete details of and be liable for tax on income which they have no legal right, and may feel no moral right, to receive or know of. These objections are much weakened by the existence of an opportunity for husband and wife to seek separate assessment.[1] (This should not be confused with separate taxation, which is a distinct option: separate assessment does not affect total liability, while separate taxation normally will.) But it is also true that if A is married to B, and their respective incomes are X and Y, then their tax liabilities, both individually and in aggregate, depend on which of A and B is male and which female. (For example, if X is £5,000 of earned income and Y £1,500 of investment income, they pay total tax of £1,715 if A is male and £1,394 if A is female, at 1977–8 rates.) While the frequency with which problems of this kind arise is now small, it is curious that a Parliament which has outlawed sex discrimination in general should nevertheless sustain a tax system with these properties.

A realistic basis for reform would, we think, involve taxing earnings on an individual basis and investment income on a unit basis. This intermediate position (which we describe as partial income splitting) avoids the major difficulties associated with the extreme versions of either principle. It also corresponds to the way in which income arises, and is treated, in many households, and it could deal with the main deficiencies of the present system as we have detailed them above. The most important change is that the additional married man's allowance should be phased out; a consequence would be that individual taxation of earnings would become the norm rather than the exception. At the same time child benefits would be increased so that families with two or more children would be at least as well off as at present (the revenue gained would, if it were thought desirable, permit an increase in child benefit of over £3 per child per week, which is an increase of well over 100%). Personal allowances would be given against earned income only, but unconditionally to those over 60; this would end sex discrimination at the price of depriving those under 60 with no

[1] Though this opportunity is denied to poor claimants of family income supplement.

earnings of a personal allowance. This would pave the way for investment income to be aggregated and then split evenly between husband and wife. Thus households would be taxed as if their property were shared equally between the two spouses regardless of the way in which it is in fact distributed.

Similar principles seem appropriate for taxing the income of children. Their earnings might be taxed on an individual basis, which means that in practice they would not be taxed; there is no feasible alternative. The tax treatment of the investment income of children has become a political football, kicked from one end of the pitch to the other depending on which party has the ball. Both convenience and common sense suggest that until children are old enough to achieve independent economic status their investment income should be treated as the income of their parents.

If a shift is made in the direction of an expenditure tax, then the individual basis loses some of its appeal, and Kaldor (1955) has argued that a quotient system would then be the most appropriate. After all, a natural way to define a household is as a group of people who incur expenditure on a unit rather than an individual basis, and it is very reasonable to apply the same principle in taxation. And it is even easier for spouses taxed as individuals to arrange their savings and dissavings so as to minimize their joint liability than it is for them to organize their investment income. But the objections to the quotient system apply with equal force under expenditure-based taxation. A couple's standard of living is not related to their joint expenditure alone, but will depend on whether that expenditure is derived from the income of only one of them or equally from both; and the strong discouragement to wives to work which results from the over-generous treatment of non-working wives and which applies under a quotient-based income tax arises equally well with a quotient-based expenditure tax.

Indeed the arguments and conclusions which we have rehearsed in the income tax case are not modified much if expenditure taxes are used instead. Earned income might be taxed on an individual basis, savings and dissavings on a unit principle. It may seem somewhat odd to have an expenditure tax which discriminates between types of income, but if we think of the lifetime expenditure tax as a tax on lifetime receipts (as we know we can) the logic becomes more apparent. It poses no practical problems either; the reader who turns back to the expenditure tax form (Fig. 6.2, p. 92) will see that some items (earnings, pensions) would require that an individual should enter his own receipts, while others (gifts, dividends, sales of securities, etc.) would ask for half the joint total to be entered. The most difficult case is trading receipts, where the distinction between earned and investment income is blurred; this is a familiar difficulty under the present tax system (which is not to say that it is easily or satisfactorily solved).

Any treatment of the tax unit must be related to the social habits of a particular time, and must change as those social habits change. A unit basis supposes that units can be identified and are fairly stable. Adopting marriage as the basis of definition works well in the U.K. at present. If large numbers of couples live together in continuing household units—as is the case in Sweden—or a high proportion of marriages end in divorce—as in the U.S.A.—then a unit basis, of any kind, becomes harder to sustain. Both these trends are increasing in Britain; if this continues an individual basis is likely to be the final outcome and it would then be a desirable outcome.

Taxation and distribution: evidence

There are many difficulties, both practical and conceptual, in assessing the effects of taxes on income distribution. A frequently used method of illustrating the distribution of income, and the effect of factors which alter it, is to draw a Lorenz curve. Such curves are illustrated in Fig. 13.1. They are constructed as follows. We order the entire population in line, starting from the poorest and ending with the richest, and we move along the line, measuring at each stage the proportion of the total population which we have encountered and the proportion of the community's total income which they receive. Thus in Fig. 13.1 we plot on one axis the cumulative percentage of total population, and on the other the cumulative percentage of total income. If income were evenly divided, the poorest 25% of the community would receive 25% of its income, and the Lorenz curve would be the diagonal straight line OA. Since income is not equally divided, the poorest 25% earn less than that and the Lorenz curve lies below the diagonal line of perfect equality. The further away from the diagonal it is, the greater the extent of inequality in distribution.

We show in Fig. 13.1 the Lorenz curve of 'original income', which is basically taxable income excluding state benefits; and of 'final income', which takes account of the effect of all taxes and benefits. The Lorenz curve of final income is at all points closer to the diagonal line of perfect equality than that of original income, so that the combined effects of the tax and benefit system is an unambiguous reduction in inequality.

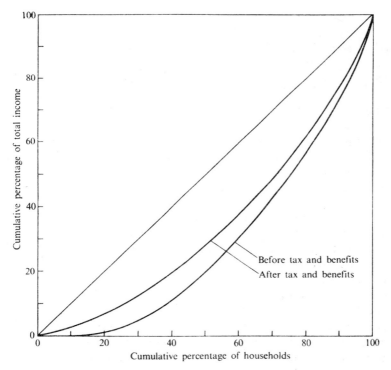

Fig. 13.1. The distribution of income before and after tax and benefits, 1975

We should like to consider the ways in which the different elements of the tax system contribute to this over-all result. We shall define a tax as *progressive* if the proportion of an individual's income which is paid in tax increases as his income increases; if the rich pay relatively more than the poor. It is easy to see that progressive taxation leads to an inward shift of Lorenz curves such as those in Fig. 13.1 and so reduces inequality. This definition of progressivity is not universal but it is the most natural and the most common.

If we are to examine how the tax burden is spread over different groups, we need to decide what criteria to use in defining these groups. How do we determine whether a particular household is 'rich' or 'poor' and how much richer or poorer it is than others? We might measure this by income, or expenditure, or wealth, or some combination of these: the same issues arise as those which we raised in our discussion of measures of taxable capacity in Chapter 5 and as we discovered there it is not a question to which there is a simple or single right answer. But we suggested there that expenditure had some advantages as a measure for these purposes, and we think a useful way of measuring the way the tax burden is distributed over rich and poor is to see how tax payments vary at different expenditure levels. We cannot do this with the available data, and instead use 'final income'—income after all taxes and benefits —as the next best measure and our principal criterion.

But this raises another issue. We want to see how taxes are distributed over ranges of income or expenditure. Should the ranges be defined as they are after the tax and benefit system has done its work, or as they would be before the effect of redistributive taxes and social benefits? Do we measure progressivity in relation to final income or to original income? There is a case for looking at both. Imagine a tax system which penalized 'rich capitalists' so severely that they ended up worse off than 'poor workers': there is a sense in which such taxes are progressive and there is a sense in which they are not. It would seem odd to say that a heavy tax on the scrag ends of meat which the impoverished capitalists were forced to eat was a progressive measure though we might not be convinced that this curious tax system was regressive, rather than progressive, in its over-all effect. The ambiguity is a genuine one, and we illustrate both possibilities below by describing progressivity relative to both original and final income.

This discussion relates purely to matters of definition, and the reality of what is going on is not affected by the way in which we choose to present our data. But these issues are not usually spelt out in analyses of tax progressivity, and since statements that certain taxes are progressive or regressive have some persuasive force it is important to be clear what we mean by them. As we see below, the question of whether British indirect taxes are or are not regressive turns on the answer to the problem we have just raised—should we measure regressivity in relation to original or final income?

Empirical information on the effects of taxation on distribution —such as that in Fig. 13.1—is regularly published by the C.S.O. in *Economic Trends*. The figures which underlie it are both much criticized and much used. We should note a number of difficulties. Firstly, the basis of classification is the household unit (so that when we described the construction of the Lorenz curves of Fig. 13.1 it was households, or heads of households, who were standing in line). This means that no account is taken of household composition or needs; a single person is categorized with a family of six with the same income, although it is clear that the former is likely to have a higher standard of living. This problem can be avoided by presenting separate analyses for each household type—which the C.S.O. does—or tackled by devising some 'equivalent scale' for comparing different households.

The analysis also makes naïve assumptions about tax incidence. Commodity taxes are assumed to fall entirely on the consumers of the goods in question; corporation tax is simply ignored because its incidence is so difficult to establish. Similar American studies have employed a range of assumptions about incidence (Okner and Pechman, 1974) and shown that the results are rather sensitive to such assumptions. To improve on this crude view of incidence it is necessary to use a very fully specified model of the whole economic system. This attempt has been made, though in a very preliminary way, by Whalley and Piggott (1977), who suggest that Fig. 13.1 may slightly understate the redistributive effect of the tax system. The C.S.O. studies also omit death duties and capital gains tax on the argument that they are taxes on capital. This seems to confuse two distinct questions: 'What is the base of the tax?' and 'What measure of economic position should one use in assessing the distributional impact of a tax?' and it would be helpful if the analysis were extended to include these taxes (which presumably fall mainly on high-income groups).

We illustrate in Figs. 13.2 and 13.3 the effects of the three main elements in the U.K. tax and benefit system—cash benefits, direct taxes, and indirect taxes. The basis of construction of these curves is as follows. We saw in Chapter 1 that the analysis of tax incidence requires some counterfactual hypothesis about alternative ways in

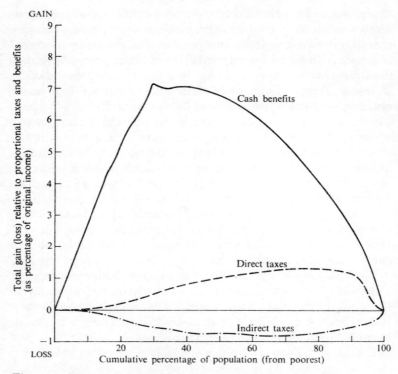

Fig. 13.2. Tax progressivity, relative to original income, 1975
(i.e. income before all taxes and benefits)

which public revenue would have been raised or disbursed. In
analysing progressivity, we make the counterfactual assumption
that each tax (or benefit) is distributed in direct proportion to
income, so that relative incomes before and after the tax (or benefit)
are unchanged. We then compare the actual distribution of the tax
burden with this hypothetical distribution, and compute the net
gain or loss by the poorest 10%, 20%, etc. as a proportion of aggregate income. Thus Fig. 13.2 shows that the poorest 30% of the
population were substantially better off as a result of the allocation
of cash benefits than they would have been if these had been allo-
cated in proportion to income, and that their net gain amounted to
about 7% of the original income of the whole population. Thus if
we evaluate the effects of the benefit system on this group, relative
to the population as a whole, we observe substantial progressivity.

The poorest 30% also gained, in relative terms, from the effect of direct taxes, but this gain was much smaller; the further the curve corresponding to a particular tax (or benefit) is above the horizontal axis (which represents proportional taxation) the greater the degree of progressivity, while a curve lying below that line illustrates a regressive tax. Both cash benefits and direct taxes are unambiguously progressive in incidence.

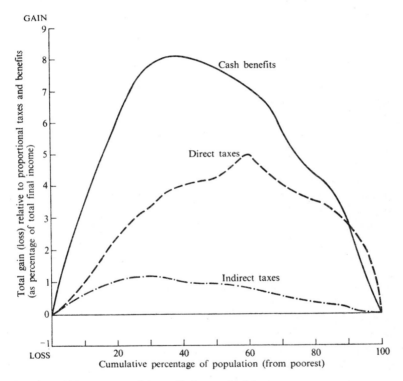

Fig. 13.3. Tax progressivity, relative to final income, 1975
(i.e. income after all taxes and benefits)

Indirect taxes are regressive in Fig. 13.2, but this pattern emerges only because that diagram illustrates their incidence in relation to original income. Since many people have very low original incomes—they are wholly dependent on pensions or national insurance benefits—but do have some expenditure, their indirect tax bill forms a very high proportion of their original income (indeed it could quite easily exceed 100% of it). Seen from final income, as in Fig. 13.3, indirect taxes are progressive—they absorb a higher proportion of the income of the rich and it is almost certain that indirect taxes rise more than proportionately with total expenditure. This results mainly from the zero-rating provisions of V.A.T. (see Chapters 8 and 14) and the existence of food subsidies (which are treated as negative taxes). For similar reasons, direct taxes appear more progressive in Fig. 13.3 than in Fig. 13.2. People with small original incomes may nevertheless pay some income tax on their pensions, while the relative affluence of high-income earners is much reduced if we base our comparison on their income after tax rather than their income before tax.

The net effect of all taxes and benefits, however, is clearly progressive, in relation to both original and final income. How great is the reduction in inequality which results? If we are to answer questions of this type, we need some measure of inequality. A frequently used measure is the area between the Lorenz curve and the diagonal, which is known as the Gini coefficient. While this may seem an attractive idea, the Gini coefficient is a purely statistical artefact with no real underlying economic meaning (Newbery, 1970; Sen, 1974). Some commentators (for example, Nicholson, 1974) have sought to make a virtue of necessity by claiming the Gini coefficient is therefore 'objective' in some way that other measures are not, but this is like saying that since we cannot agree on what constitutes beauty we should measure height instead. We prefer an approach suggested by Atkinson (1973a). In effect, Atkinson asks the question: 'Imagine a rich man and a poor man with half his income. How much commission would we pay Robin Hood to transfer £1 from the rich to the poor?' The answer will depend on our view of inequality. But by answering questions of this kind, we can construct a measure of the costs of inequality. For each transfer of income from rich to poor we would be willing to give up some of the amount transferred as 'commission' in this way. We can envisage a continuing series of such transfers which eventually bring us to a wholly egalitarian outcome, and measure the amount of income which we would be willing to give up in order to bring about this result. This total amount is the 'cost of inequality': the reduction in aggregate income which we would accept in order to achieve complete equality in its distribution.

The size of these costs depends on how much we are offended by inequality. If we were not much worried by it, then the commission we might agree to pay to secure a transfer from rich to poor would be rather low: the efficiency loss we would accept for distributional improvement would be small. By contrast the American philosopher, Rawls, who argues that justice requires that society maximize the welfare of its least advantaged member (Rawls, 1971), would be happy with the arrangement if anything at all reached the hands of the poor. (This is a rather extreme characterization of Rawls's position, though one which is popular with economists.) Because there are different views of equality and its nature and desirability, there can be no unique measure of inequality but a scheme of this kind enables us to express a range of possible views. We consider three possibilities in Table 13.2. A '10% commission

TABLE 13.2

The effects of tax and benefits on inequality, 1975

	10%	50%	90%
c (commission rate)	10%	50%	90%
ε	0·15	1·0	3·32
Original income			
Actual average	3386	3386	3386
Equivalent, equally distributed	3215	1880	224
'Cost' of inequality	171	1506	3162
Effect on 'cost' of			
Cash benefits	−62	−761	−912
Direct taxes	−40	−261	−674
Indirect taxes	−8	−85	−275
Income after tax and benefits			
Actual average	2506	2506	2506
Equivalent, equally distributed	2445	2107	1205
'Cost' of inequality	61	399	1301

Technical note: ϵ is the corresponding 'elasticity of the social marginal valuation of income'; see Atkinson (1975), Stern (1977). Thus for each distribution (y_i) we have computed $\{\Sigma y_i^{1-\epsilon}\}^{1/1-\epsilon}$ where $\epsilon = \dfrac{\log(1-c)}{\log 0·5}$.

Source: Own calculations based on data in *Economic Trends* (1976).

rate' implies that we would favour a transfer from a high-income individual to an individual with half that income only if the gain by the latter was at least 90% of the loss of the former, so that we attach equal social value to £1 in the hands of a man earning £10,000 a year, 90p for someone who earns £5,000 and 73p for a man whose income is only £1,250. The radical 90% rate implies that £1 for the £10,000-a-year man and 1p at £2,500 a year are rated equally, so that the range of views covered by the 'commission rates' we use in Table 13.2 is rather wide. (Stern (1977) suggests that the value implicit in the present U.K. tax system is about 75%, but the argument is a somewhat speculative one.)

Table 13.2 shows the 'costs of inequality' and the effect of taxes and benefits in reducing them, under these alternative assumptions. Under the conservative '10% rate' view of inequality, the cost of the inequality of original income is estimated at £171 per head. The actual average income is £3,386 per head: we should be prepared to see this reduced by £171 to £3,215, or by around 5%, if the distribution associated with the lower average income was completely equal, so that each household received an income of £3,215. Correspondingly, we should be prepared to give up egalitarian ambitions and accept the distribution of original income if the result were to raise average income by 5%. The radical approach implicit in the third column demonstrates a very different view; one which would give up over 90% of existing national income if the distribution were equalized. We estimate the (lower) costs of inequality in the distribution of final income in a similar way.

Although the costs differ under different assumptions, the effect of taxes is rather similar in each case. The costs of inequality are greatly reduced by the effects of taxes and benefits; the reduction is between one-half and three-quarters in all cases. Cash benefits are the most important influence on this, with direct taxes next in significance; but indirect taxes operate so as to reduce inequality, though only slightly, under each assumption. The effective reduction in inequality which the tax system brings about is much greater than Fig. 13.1 suggests, because that diagram (and the associated Gini coefficient) does not weight sufficiently what happens at the extremes of poverty and wealth, while our welfare measures do acknowledge that this is of prime importance in analysing inequality.

Taxation and distribution: principles

How should the tax burden be distributed between different individuals and households? We shall discuss this question as if the only tax in the economy was an income tax, but this is simply for expository convenience; an income tax schedule relates tax liability to income received, but as we saw in our discussion of empirical evidence on tax incidence the relevant question is the way in which the burden of all taxes is related to a somewhat broader concept of the individual's resources than his taxable income.[1] But the income tax is for those in work the most important and most flexible influence on the distribution of tax liabilities.

We have defined a progressive tax schedule as one in which the proportion of income which is taken in tax increases with income. This definition implies that the *average* rate of tax should increase with income. It is a common error to think that this means that the *marginal* rate of tax should also increase with income (as it in fact does in the U.K. and most other countries), but this is not the case. A tax system is progressive if, and only if, the marginal rate of tax is higher than the average rate of tax: if you pay a higher rate of tax on any *additional* earnings than you do on your current earnings. Figure 13.4 illustrates one possible relationship between average and marginal rates of tax. On incomes less than A, both marginal and average rates of tax are increasing. At incomes above A, the marginal rate of tax begins to fall, but because it is so high the average rate of tax continues to rise. Only at incomes beyond B, where the marginal tax rate falls below the average rate, does the average rate start to fall: this tax schedule is progressive throughout the range OB.

The schedule shown in Fig. 13.4 is not a very likely one, but the case illustrated in Fig. 13.5 is important. This shows a tax schedule in which a certain amount of income, OX, is exempt from tax, and earnings in excess of that are taxed at a rate of OY. Someone whose income barely exceeds OX pays virtually no tax, and hence his average tax rate is very low (although his marginal rate is OY). As income increases, the fraction of it which is taxed becomes larger and larger, until for those with very substantial incomes the allowance OX is hardly significant and their average rate of tax is nearly

[1] Readers of recent literature on 'optimal income taxes' will realize that the lifetime expenditure tax discussed in Chapters 5 and 6 is much closer to the taxes analysed there than are real-life income taxes.

equal to OY. If the personal allowance is paid as a 'tax credit' to those with incomes too low to make full use of it (i.e. those with incomes below OX), then the schedules of average and marginal rates are extended as shown by the dotted lines. This is a *linear tax schedule*, and it is completely described by two parameters; the basic allowance OX (which we shall assume is greater than zero) and the tax rate OY.

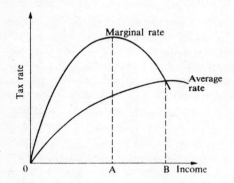

Fig. 13.4.

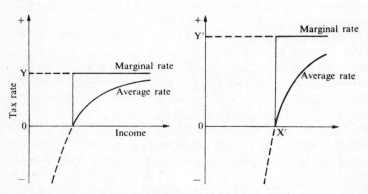

Fig. 13.5. Alternative tax schedules   Fig. 13.6.

A linear tax system is progressive, since the average tax rate increases steadily with income. The slope of the schedule of average rates gives the rate at which the average rate rises, and is an indication of the degree of progressivity of the schedule. If OX and OY are both increased, as to OX' and OY' in Fig. 13.6, then the curve of average rates becomes steeper and the rate structure is more progressive. For most taxpayers the present British tax system with its personal allowance and wide basic rate band is a linear one (if we ignore its interaction with national insurance contributions and means-tested benefits).

The appropriate structure for a tax schedule was extensively discussed in the nineteenth century, in an era when the view was widely held that the utilities enjoyed by different individuals could be measured and compared in much the same way as their heights. Debate raged between the principle of equal sacrifice (by which tax should be computed so as to impose equal utility losses on all), the principle of equiproportional sacrifice (everyone should lose the same fraction of their utility), and the principle of minimum aggregate sacrifice (the total utility loss of the community as a whole should be minimized). The objective of minimum aggregate sacrifice might have won the day, were it not rather easy to show that if one adds the assumptions (i) that everyone has the same capacity to enjoy income; (ii) that utility increases with income but at a decreasing rate; (iii) that the tax schedule does not modify behaviour in ways which would change incomes before tax (there are no disincentive effects), the conclusion is that everyone should have the same income, net of tax: 'the crowning height of the utilitarian principle, from which the steps of a sublime deduction lead to the high tableland of equality' as Edgeworth put it (1897, p. 553).

Since neither the objective nor the assumptions are very plausible, this analysis received as little attention as it deserved; and until recently economists had little constructive to say about tax schedules. But this ignores an important problem. Progressivity requires high marginal tax rates; but as we saw in Chapter 3 it is precisely this aspect of the tax system which generates disincentive effects. Thus there is a basic conflict between equity and efficiency considerations in the design of tax schedules, and it is important to understand the interrelationships and the empirical information which is needed to determine these issues. While few people would now happily accept the utilitarian objective or the assumption of identical tastes, it is nevertheless necessary to express some view on the consequences of drawing tax revenue from people at one income level rather than another. We might start by characterizing two extreme positions. In one, the Government is simply indifferent to the source of its tax revenue; a pound is a pound and valued equally whether it is in the wallet of a rich man or a poor man. The other extreme, which we have already attributed to Rawls, only looks at the welfare of the least advantaged; the fate of others matters only in so far as their activities have effects on him (which mainly take the form of generating tax revenue for his benefit). In effect, one position ignores considerations of income distribution altogether; the other thinks of nothing else. It is possible to go beyond either of these extreme viewpoints; to argue that inequality built Versailles and commissioned Beethoven's late string quartets and is desirable for its own sake, or that inequality is so offensive that the rich should be made worse off even if no one else's standard of living rises as a result. But many people might be willing to agree that an appropriate stance was somewhere between these two.

Even the Rawlsian view, however, implies less than perfect egalitarianism. Under it, public policy is concerned with the interests of the rich only in their function as milch cows for the poor, valued only for the tax revenue they provide. But the interests of the poor require that tax revenue from the rich be maximized, and this is not achieved by 100% rates. People who find themselves paying 100% of income, or additional income, in tax are unlikely to trouble to earn much of it; and we would obtain more tax revenue if we retained some incentive by allowing them to keep part of their earnings for themselves. In fact it is possible to go beyond this and show that the marginal tax rate faced by the man with the highest income should, under an optimal rate schedule, be zero. The argument hinges on the point that tax revenue depends on average rates of tax but disincentives on marginal rates. If we lower the *marginal* tax rate on the richest man, we reduce disincentive effects on him without reducing the amount of tax which he (or anyone else) pays. So if these disincentives are of any significance, earnings will increase and so will tax revenue. It does not matter if we attach no value to the welfare of this man, so that we give no weight to the increase in his post-tax income. So long as we do not actually wish to see him made worse off, whether anyone else benefits or not, the increase in tax revenue allows lower average tax rates on everyone else and an unequivocal all-round gain. This argument should not be taken absolutely literally. We cannot have different tax rates for each individual, and it tells us nothing even about the appropriate tax rate on the second-richest man. But it does show that even a firm belief in progressive taxation does not imply that marginal, as distinct from average, rates should increase with income.

A rather similar argument may be applied at the opposite end of the distribution: the marginal tax rate faced by the lowest income group should also be very low. This is not the same as saying that the average tax rate on the lowest income group should be very low —as most people would agree it should—since it is quite possible to have low (or negative) average rates of tax on low incomes but high marginal rates. We saw in Chapter 7 that this is precisely what the 'poverty trap' and a number of proposed social security reforms entail. The case for low marginal rates is different, and derived from efficiency rather than distributional considerations. The problem with reducing marginal tax rates on low incomes, as Chancellors have discovered, is that it reduces the average tax rate faced by absolutely everyone, and so is extremely costly in revenue. Proposals to reintroduce a 'reduced rate band' have had to face this difficulty. We can offset this by lowering the tax threshold, so that the lower rate is payable from a lower level of income; the problem with this is that while it has desirable effects on incentives and reduces the 'poverty trap' it raises the amount of tax payable by people with low incomes who are now brought into the system as a result of the reduction in the basic allowance. But at the lowest levels of income there is no one 'below' who will be caught up in the tax net; and it is therefore possible to reduce marginal rates of tax without compromizing distributional objectives.

These conclusions—that marginal tax rates should be low at both the highest and the lowest levels of income—contrast sharply with what most people have previously believed (ourselves included). They also suggest a pattern different from that observed in the U.K. and most other countries—where, as we saw in Chapter 3, the *highest* marginal rates are found at the top and bottom of the income distribution (because of higher rates in one case and the poverty trap in the other). But the arguments which lie behind them are in fact rather familiar, and we have only focused rather sharply on points which have been widely if indistinctly appreciated. High marginal tax rates on the largest incomes bring in very little revenue, and are not worth pursuing if they have any adverse consequences. Measures of support for low-income families achieve rather less than nothing if their receipts are recouped by high marginal rates of tax. But it is of particular interest that the conclusions reached remain valid over a rather catholic range of views about the ethical importance and empirical significance of distributional factors and tax disincentives—for any, in fact, between the extreme Rawlsian and extreme output maximization positions we have described.

But this is not quite as encouraging as it might appear. A major difficulty with these arguments is that although they tell us about marginal tax rates at the very top and very bottom of the income scale, they tell us little about the rates in between, even at income levels rather close to these extremes. In answering this question, the relative weights which are given to disincentives and to distribution are absolutely crucial. But it is important to see that the answer is likely to go in the same direction at both ends of the scale. If we think disincentive effects are probably not too substantial, or that equality of after-tax incomes is very important, then we would want to select rather high *marginal* tax rates throughout the intermediate range. We would be anxious to narrow the gap between the poor and the very poor, the rich and the very rich, and would not be unduly concerned by the disincentive effects which stem from the high marginal tax rates necessary to do it. We would in this way compress the whole distribution of income after tax. If, on the other hand, we attach a lot of emphasis to incentives and are not much worried about the resulting distribution, then we would choose low marginal rates throughout. It does not follow from this that the marginal rate would, in either case, be the same throughout the distribution, and in general the appropriate tax structure is a rather complicated function of the two underlying objectives— distribution and incentives—and the distribution of earning capacities in the population. But since this information is not easily obtained, and a linear tax schedule has obvious administrative advantages, it is worth examining further the properties of such a system.

Some insight can be gained from the experience of Britannia,

TABLE 13.3

Income distribution in Britannia

Income (£)	No. of house-holds	Cum. no. of house-holds	Cum. % of all income	U.K. system Marginal rate of tax	Average rate of tax	Employers system	Union system
< 1200	1309	1309	4·6	Zero tax assumed throughout			
1500	1391	2700	10·6	40	10	13	3
2000	1294	3994	18·7	40	18	20	13
2500	749	4743	23·6	40	22	23	20
3000	888	5631	31·3	40	25	26	24
3500	816	6447	39·7	40	27	28	27
4000	724	7171	48·1	40	29	29	29
4500	646	7817	56·5	40	30	30	31
5000	532	8349	64·3	40	32	32	33
5500	425	8774	71·1	34	32	32	33
6000	248	9022	75·4	34	32	32	34
6500	213	9235	79·4	34	32	33	36
7000	177	9412	83·0	34	32	33	36
7500	135	9547	86·0	40	32	34	37
8000	89	9636	88·0	40	33	34	37
8500	71	9707	89·8	45	34	34	38
9000	78	9785	91·8	45	34	35	38
10 000	50	9835	93·3	50	36	35	39
11 000	39	9874	94·5	55	37	36	39
12 000	32	9906	95·6	60	39	36	40
13 000	23	9929	96·5	60	40	36	40
14 000	16	9945	97·2	65	42	36	41
15 000	11	9956	97·6	65	44	36	41
16 000	9	9965	98·1	70	45	37	41
17 000	7	9972	98·4	70	47	37	41
18 000	4	9976	98·6	75	48	37	42
19 000	4	9980	98·8	75	51	37	42
20 000+	20	10 000	100·0	75/83	55I	→39	→45

a small and little-known oil sheikdom in the North Sea. Its population comprises 10,000 households, all childless married couples, and their income, which is entirely derived from oil revenues, has been deemed to be earned income for tax purposes. The average income, and its distribution among households, are, however, believed to be very similar to those in Britain. (We adopt this device in order to avoid complications of analysis and data which are not very relevant to the main points at issue here.) The income distribution in the island is shown in Table 13.3; until recently, they applied the same schedule of tax rates and national insurance contributions as in the U.K., which they had discovered in a copy of the *Daily Mail Tax Guide* left behind by a visiting oilman.[1]

A Royal Commission was appointed to consider tax reform. The Britannian trade unions, in evidence, proposed the abolition of both higher rates of tax and national insurance contributions, and their replacement by a personal allowance for all couples of £1,400 and a basic rate of tax of 45%. The Commission was at first surprised at the apparent moderation of this suggestion, but the following facts were pointed out. Under the reform, all islanders with below-average incomes would pay less tax: about 6,000 of the 10,000 households. (Some Commissioners were surprised to learn that if a distribution is skewed, as the distribution of incomes is, then more than half of all workers earn less than average.) The lower the household income, the greater the benefit. Of the remaining 4,000 Britannians with above-average incomes, 98% would pay more tax (including nine-tenths of the former higher rate taxpayers). The only beneficiaries in this group would be the 70 islanders who earn more than £14,000 per year, and the reduction in their tax bill was computed at 0·8% of total tax revenue. The amount transferred to those with below-average earnings was five times as great.

The Britannian employers' federation was horrified by these proposals and by the proposed 45% tax rate with its possible disincentive effects. They presented a counter-proposal, with the same tax structure but for a £1,000 tax threshold and a 39% basic rate; they pointed out that while the union proposals would increase the marginal tax rate faced by virtually all taxpayers their scheme would reduce it for virtually all taxpayers. They acknowledged that an effect would be that all Britannians with below-average incomes would pay more tax and everyone with above-average earnings would pay less: but they asked the Commission to recognize that if the increased incentives in their scheme raised national income by 3% across the board then everyone in Britannia would be better off.

The Commission's secretariat confirmed that the facts were as stated by both unions and employers, and that both schemes would produce the same tax revenue as the existing system. The secre-

---

[1] The tax guide had been printed in 1977 before the budget of November 1977 and was based on a personal allowance of £1,295 for a married couple rather than the £1,455 to which it was retrospectively increased.

tariat were assuming, as they always did, that none of the changes would affect behaviour in any way. They drew Fig. 13.7 to illustrate the possibilities. While there was disagreement on the Commission as to which proposal should be recommended, they were unanimous in concluding that either would be much superior to the *status quo*.

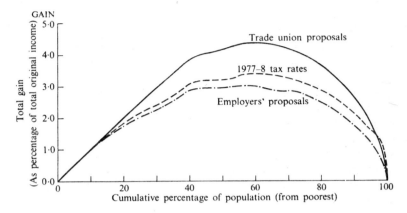

Fig. 13.7. Britannian tax reform proposals

These examples illustrate that there is no inconsistency between a linear tax schedule and substantial progressivity—indeed we can have a completely egalitarian outcome if the basic allowance is equal to average income and the marginal tax rate is 100%, though it is not likely that this is a good idea. What is even more startling, however, is the demonstration of the essential irrelevance of the existing higher rates of tax to the issue of tax progressivity. This seems surprising because the confusion of the properties of average and marginal rates is really very widespread. The fact that someone is paying a marginal rate of tax of 75% or 83% demonstrates that he is facing a substantial disincentive to work, a strong temptation to convert his income into other forms, and that he is likely to be rather disenchanted with the way the tax system affects him; but it does not necessarily mean that he is paying a lot of tax, because that is a function of his average rather than his marginal rate. The mathematical properties of rate schedules imply that this average rate an individual pays depends not on his own marginal rate, but on the marginal tax rates of everyone below him in the income distribution. As Table 13.3 shows, although the marginal tax rate exceeds 50% for those with incomes in excess of £9,300, it is necessary to earn almost £20,000 before the average rate of tax reaches that level. There are approximately ten times as many people in the former category as in the latter: a system of steeply escalating marginal rates imposes high marginal rates on relatively many in order to impose high average rates on relatively few.

Returning from Britannia to Britain, we should consider two other constraints on the progressivity of a tax system. The first of these relates to administrative feasibility. We have shown in Chapters 3 and 4 that the highest rates of tax in the U.K. do not work, and it is very improbable that they could be made to work. This might not be too important if they were uniformly ineffective, but this is not the case; the result of this (and the general result of procedures which are administratively impracticable) is that the outcome is erratically and unfairly effective. But it is difficult to assess what the maximum marginal tax rate that can work reasonably well in practice is likely to be. The top rates in most developed countries lie in the range from 50% to 70% but many of these suffer to greater or lesser degree from the difficulties which the top British rates face, while Scandinavian countries seem to be reasonably effective at administering rates not much below those in Britain.

The second constraint is the possibility of migration. The simplest framework for analysing this is the Rawlsian one, in which we attach no weight to the welfare of Rod Stewart (a distinguished pop star and tax exile) or his friends, and regret his going only for the tax revenue which is lost with him. Even this consideration may have a surprisingly substantial effect on a well-designed tax system. Mr. Stewart is presumably influenced by a comparison of his net-of-tax incomes at home and abroad; his incentive to migrate is related to his average tax rate rather than to his marginal rate, which distinguishes this from other incentive effects. The issue then hinges on the sensitivity of migration decisions to after-tax income. There is little systematic evidence on this. Recent trends in migration from the U.K. are shown in Table 13.4. 'Professional and managerial' emigration might be compared with an annual output of 67,000 university graduates at a cost of £451 m. (in 1973-4; *Annual Abstract of Statistics*, 1976). The trends are rather striking, but are probably as much influenced by the declining significance of emigration to 'old Commonwealth' countries by non-professional groups as by changes in relative incomes; there has also been an increase in the proportion of 'professional and managerial' immigrants. The most relevant study known to us (Psacharopoulos, 1976) suggests that a 10% change in net income might induce a 3% rise in emigration. This figure is very tentative, especially since the international study on which it is based suggests that Britain (as a low-income English-speaking country) is peculiarly vulnerable to migration. But a 10% change in net income (corresponding, say, to a change from 50% to 55% in the average tax rate faced by the affected groups) might lead to an increase of 3,000 in annual emigration; if these emigrants took with them an expected present value of tax revenue (net of associated public expenditures) of £50,000 the resulting loss from emigration would be £150 m. p.a. These back-of-envelope calculations do no more than suggest the difficulty of systematic appraisal; but it does seem possible that the orders of magnitude are such that this consideration ought to be a significant influence on tax policy.

TABLE 13.4

Emigration from U.K.

('000s)

Year	Occupational category		Total
	Professional and managerial	Manual and clerical	
1966	32·6	64·9	110·9
1971	35·1	51·2	97·7
1976	50·3	36·2	98·5

Source: Population Trends (1977).

We must now bring out explicitly two assumptions which have been underlying our analysis. We have assumed that all income is earned. At high levels of income this is only the case to a very limited extent, though the discussion of incentives applies equally to earnings which although classed as investment income are in fact the return to business activities. While incentives—of a different kind—also affect investment incomes, it is clear that the factors which should influence the taxation of income or expenditure from inherited wealth are rather different and the reasons for limiting top marginal rates are less compelling. We should note, however, that the arguments on migration and on feasibility apply to un-earned incomes also; and that it is probably on employment in-comes that the present top rates of tax are less easily avoided and come closest to working as intended.

The second assumption is that the value of people's work is approximated by what they are paid. If they are paid more than their work is worth, there will be losses to everyone else if they are induced to do more such work: if they are paid less, then the argu-ment operates in the reverse direction. At low and medium ranges of income, our assumption is not too bad; but for high-income earners the position is more complicated, and the relationship between the value of work and the way in which it is remuner-ated becomes much more tenuous. We should also note that the work they do will often be intrinsically attractive and disincentive effects consequently less serious. These groups will include people in the City who occupy sinecures or perform services of no social value; they will also include people in positions where the com-petent exercise of their functions can generate benefits far greater than anyone would consider paying them. If under Sir Arnold Weinstock the productivity of G.E.C. is $\frac{1}{2}\%$ higher than it would be under the best alternative manager, then the benefits of this are £10m. per year and one such individual can compensate for the entire boards of several merchant banks. The direction of bias in this area is therefore unclear.

We conclude that the definition of the tax base—the issue we discussed in Chapters 3–5—is more important in determining the effective progressivity of taxation, especially at high-income and expenditure levels, than the shape of the rate structure. The diffi-culty in constructing rate schedules is that substantial progressivity requires that average rates should be much higher at high-income levels than at lower ones; but this requires high *marginal* rates on those in between. If the majority of income-earners are concen-trated in a rather narrow range—and about 98% of all units have incomes below £10,000 per year—then these marginal rates may have to be distinctly high and will have to be imposed on people who are not the primary target of redistributive taxation. High marginal rates at the top lead to many of the adverse consequences of progressive taxation without having much real effect on distribution, because the number of people who face correspondingly high *average* rates as a result is very small.

14

THE TAX SYSTEM AS A WHOLE

Is Britain over-taxed?

WE have devoted a good deal of attention to the structural deficiencies of the British tax system. We have not, however, considered explicitly the view that these structural deficiencies would not be very important if the rates of tax were not so high. This argument has considerable validity. The base of the American income tax, for example, is probably more defective than that of the U.K., but because tax rates are much lower at all income levels the anomalies, loopholes, and distortions which result are less significant. Is the real problem that the British are simply over-taxed?

Since there are few people who do not believe that they personally are over-taxed, we must search for some more objective yardstick. A natural one to use is an international comparison; is the tax system required to raise more revenue in Britain than in similar countries overseas? Table 14.1 sets out what figures we have on this matter. It shows the ratio of total tax revenue to G.N.P. in 1974 for 15 major O.E.C.D. countries. The highest tax ratios are to be found, not surprisingly, in the Scandinavian countries, followed, perhaps more surprisingly, by several of the successful postwar economies, the Netherlands, Belgium, Germany, and France. In this league table Britain comes eighth out of the 15 countries. Nor was 1974 an atypical year. If we examine the U.K.'s position in the league table of tax ratios of the same 15 countries for each year between 1965 and 1974, we find that in the ten-year period covered by the table, the U.K. never came higher than fifth and never lower than ninth.

International comparisons can be misleading, and all we can do is to point to some of the difficulties which arise. The decision as to whether a certain payment is or is not a tax is often an arbitrary one. For example, help to families may take the form either of extra tax allowances, which reduce taxation, or of cash payments,

TABLE 14.1

Level of taxation in selected countries, 1974

(Tax revenues including social security contributions as % of
G.N.P. at market prices)

	All taxes	Taxes on			
		Spending	Income	Social security contributions	Other
Denmark	46·7	14·8	26·4	2·7	2·8
Norway	45·3	16·6	14·0	13·2	1·5
Netherlands	45·2	10·5	15·5	17·4	1·7
Sweden	44·2	11·9	21·4	8·5	2·3
Belgium	38·1	10·8	14·3	12·0	1·1
Germany	37·6	9·5	13·3	13·3	1·6
France	37·5	12·7	7·2	15·7	1·9
UNITED KINGDOM	35·6	9·6	15·4	6·1	4·5
Canada	34·8	11·2	16·6	3·2	3·8
Ireland	32·4	15·5	9·5	3·8	3·7
Italy	31·9	10·8	6·5	13·3	1·3
U.S.	28·9	5·3	13·0	6·7	4·0
Australia	27·2	8·0	14·9	—	4·3
Switzerland	26·2	5·6	11·2	7·4	2·0
Japan	22·2	3·8	10·5	4·6	3·3

Individual figures may not sum to totals because of rounding errors.

Source: Revenue Statistics of OECD Member Countries 1965–74, O.E.C.D., Paris
(1976), Tables 1A and 4.

as with child benefits in Britain. The latter are often regarded as
Government expenditure rather than negative taxation, thus making it difficult to compare tax ratios in cases when countries adopt
different forms of family support. The same argument applies to
investment incentives which may be given either as tax allowances
or as investment grants. A less obvious, but probably more important, source of difficulty is the treatment of pension contributions.
In many Continental countries state pensions are much higher
(relative to average earnings) than in Britain, and occupational
pensions correspondingly less developed. Contributions to these
state schemes are financed by social security contributions and not
by payments to private schemes. In Table 14.1 the former are

regarded as taxation and the latter not. If social security contributions were excluded the U.K. would move from eighth to fifth place in the league table of tax ratios. On the other hand, there are very good reasons for regarding social security contributions as equivalent to a tax on earned income, as we have argued in Chapter 3. Contributions to health insurance may take the form of voluntary, semi-compulsory, or compulsory contributions to private or state schemes, or may simply be incorporated in general taxation: such payments may sometimes count as taxes and at other times not, but the practical difference is often very slight.

It is possible to quibble endlessly about these problems of definition (in a way which suggests that the underlying question has not been carefully formulated), and some people are willing to do so (Bracewell-Milnes, 1976, and the references therein). But it is difficult to avoid an impression that there are three main groups of developed countries for these purposes: Holland and the Scandinavian countries, other Western European countries, and a somewhat disparate group containing Japan, Switzerland, and the U.S.A. These groupings reflect different attitudes to the value of public services and the role of the state in promoting social welfare, and Britain's placing in the second group seems an appropriate reflection of prevailing ideologies. It is true that if Britain were to move into the first or third of these divisions (and we shall not say which we think is which) the problems confronting the tax system would be rather different; but it is clear that such a decision should be taken on the basis of a much wider assessment of gains and losses than those which result from dissatisfaction with the tax system. Nor do we think it probable that either of these shifts will occur.

Although the U.K. tax ratio can only be described as average, the sources of the revenue it produces are superficially somewhat different. The most striking feature of Table 14.1 is the small dependence of the British system on social security contributions, but if one believes that it is more appropriate to include these with taxes on income then the only difference between Britain and other countries is the slightly smaller reliance in this country on taxes levied on consumption spending.

A broader tax base?

We have seen that the revenue required from the British tax

system is not out of line with that raised in other European countries. We have argued, however, that most of the undesirable effects of taxation are the result of high marginal rates of tax, and we should consider whether it might be possible to effect substantial reductions in *marginal* rates without correspondingly large reductions in average rates and hence in total tax revenue.

In the immediate future, this will indeed be possible. The reason is the emergence of a new, substantial, and apparently painless source of tax receipts—the taxation of revenues from North Sea oil. We discussed the structure of these taxes in Chapter 12, but the important points to note here are two. First, the likely revenues are very substantial. Anticipated receipts are £1,000 m. per annum in 1976 prices in the period up to 1980 and £3,500 m. in 1976 prices in 1985. These compare with a yield from income tax in 1975–6 of £15,000 m. (figures from *Economic Progress Report*, Aug. 1977, and *Inland Revenue Statistics*, 1976). Second, these taxes have no significant adverse economic effects; if they did not exist, then either the return which oil companies earned on North Sea investment would be ludicrously high, or else these reserves would be sold in U.K. markets at prices well below the true cost of supplying them. The real cost to the British economy of using North Sea oil reserves is not the cost of extracting them, but the much greater amount for which these oil products could be sold on world markets.

There is therefore a unique opportunity to maintain existing levels of public expenditure while making major reductions in existing taxes. This opportunity is a temporary one, since it depends not only on sustaining North Sea oil production at the levels reached in the early 1980s but also on continued success of the cartel of oil producers (O.P.E.C.) in maintaining prices for oil products which are much in excess of the costs of exploiting the rather expensive North Sea reserves. It would therefore be foolish to make other than short-term plans on the basis of continuing major revenues from this source, and it is more sensible to regard the period in which they are available as an opportunity to make longer-term structural reforms rather than an opportunity to defer them.

We consider, then, whether the U.K. tax base can be expanded in some other, more permanent, way. At first sight, the opportunities for this seem considerable. Less than half of all U.K. income is subject to income tax, and little more than half of all consumers' expenditure is subject to V.A.T. Table 14.2 sets this out in some detail. In a well known *jeu d'esprit*, *The Economist* (24 Apr. 1976) has suggested that all income tax allowances might disappear and the basic rate be cut to 15%. But proposals of this kind do not survive scrutiny. Much the most important allowances are the basic personal allowances. If these were removed, the result would be a very substantial redistribution to those with above-average incomes from those below. We saw above how the degree of progressivity of a tax system could be altered by varying the parameters of a linear tax schedule: the proposal in *The Economist* eliminates all progressivity by abolishing the personal allowance altogether. We therefore look at untaxed components of incomes.

TABLE 14.2

The U.K. tax base: income tax and V.A.T.

Income tax, 1973–4 (Aggregate figures, £ m.)		V.A.T, 1975 (Average household expenditure, £)	
Total income	60 803	Total expenditure	54·58
Untaxed income		Zero rated items	
Social benefits and benefits in kind	2730	Fuel, light, and power	2·99
		Children's clothing	0·40
Pension fund contributions	3050	Travel	1·39
Exempt superannuation benefits, etc.	1307	Books, magazines, etc.	0·87
		Rent, rates, etc.	6·06
Income from owner-occupation	2329	Zero rated food	10·83
Life insurance relief	417		———
Other deductions	1700		22·54
Net income	49 270		———
Incomes below personal allowances	4137		
Personal allowances	20 090		
Taxable income	25 043		
Tax payable	8045		
Average rate:			
on taxable income	32·1%		
on total income	13·2%		
(Basic rate 1973–4	30·0%)		

Sources: Inland Revenue Statistics (1976), Table 4; *Economic Trends* (June 1976); C.S.O., *National Income and Expenditure* (1976).

Source: Family Expenditure Survey (1975) (N.B. *F.E.S.* categories do not correspond exactly to V.A.T. categories, so figures are approximate).

While it would be desirable to bring social security benefits within the scope of the tax system, the revenue gains from doing so would not be large, since it would be necessary to make upward adjustments to the rates of benefit at the same time. It is certainly possible to impose tax on contributions to pension funds and the income which they earn; but the problem of unfunded schemes seems intractable, and these would certainly become more common if funded schemes were taxed; while to the extent that the measure was effective it would simply be likely to lead to an increase in the contributions of both employer and employee, which is not very different in effect from a general increase in taxation.

The most serious possibilities for broadening the income tax base are (i) to modify the present favourable treatment of owner-occupied housing; (ii) to withdraw subsidies from life insurance policies; (iii) to tax capital gains as ordinary income. The first of these is certainly capable of producing substantial revenue: tax relief on mortgage repayments cost £865 m. in 1975–6 and to tax the 'imputed income' from owner-occupied property (see p. 60) might raise £1,000 m.–£2,000 m. depending on the level at which the notional 'rents' for such property were set. But these figures should be viewed sceptically. We have suggested that, given the capitalization of these tax benefits, the case in equity for withdrawing them has little merit; that considerable hardship would be caused to many people; and that we should hesitate to make such changes except in the context of a general review of housing policy. And if the objective of change is to rearrange the tax burden in a way which is likely to provoke less public hostility, we need spend little time considering this particular alternative.

We can more readily envisage removing the present tax relief on life insurance premiums and taxing more effectively the funds of such companies (see p. 63). We can also tax capital gains more heavily, though this would require that the top rates of tax on investment income be reduced to realistic levels, while to admit a case for indexation of capital gains would turn these revenue gains into revenue losses. There is much to be said for changes in the way life insurance and capital gains are treated, but the likely revenue gains are not very large. A figure of £500 m. for life insurance and of £250 m. for capital gains would be optimistic estimates, and these would allow the basic rate of income tax to be reduced by less than 2%.

If we turn to V.A.T., the two most important categories of exemption are housing and food. It would be possible to bring housing within the scope of V.A.T. by imposing it on rents and on new construction. But as we have seen, there is already a very heavy indirect tax on housing (rates), and our usual caveats about piece-meal changes in the housing market apply. There is a long tradition in Britain of slightly hysterical opposition to the taxation of food; the origins of these sentiments lie in controversies over the relative political roles of agriculture and commerce and the desirability and effects of Imperial Preference in tariff policy which have no contemporary relevance. It is now suggested that food is a necessity; but very little of the food which would not be eaten if it were 8% dearer is in the least necessary and other taxed goods such as clothing are 'necessary' in exactly the same (limited) sense. The substantive argument for exempting food is that such exemption is progressive in its distributional effects; the rich spend a smaller proportion of their incomes on food than the poor. (The main category for which this is not true—meals away from home—is subject to V.A.T.)

In Fig. 14.1 the circles and crosses show the cost to households at various income levels of paying standard rate V.A.T. on all currently exempt items (including fuel and light, children's clothing, travel, books and newspapers, but not housing). The two lines shows the gains which would accrue to households if the income tax thresholds were raised by £76 for a single person and by £135 for a married couple, while the basic rate of tax was reduced by 0·34%. These changes in income tax have been chosen to provide the best offset to the distributional impact of abolishing zero rating, and as Fig. 14.1 shows they do approximate it very well indeed. This illustrates two points. First, as we noted in Chapter 8, the distributional flexibility of a linear tax schedule is considerable; simply by altering its two parameters we can reproduce the distributional effect of zero rating with some precision. Second, it shows the kind of tax change which would be possible if we aimed to reduce marginal rates of tax by broadening the tax base in this way, assuming we are not aiming to change the progressivity of the tax system; the reduction in marginal tax rate of 0·34% which can be achieved is small.

The main feasible methods of broadening the tax base might allow the basic rate of income tax to be reduced by, say, 2%–3%: if

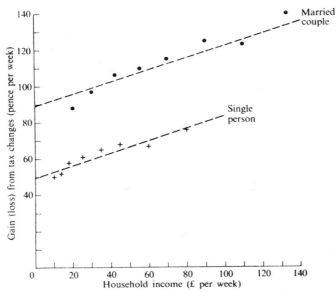

• Loss to married couple at different income levels if zero rating abolished
+ Loss to single person at different income levels if zero rating abolished
— — — Gains from changes in income tax at different income levels

Fig. 14.1. The effects of abolishing zero rating for V.A.T.
  Notes: Based on estimated equation
    $$\text{V.A.T.} = 0.498 + 0.383D + 0.0034\,Y \qquad R^2 = 0.98$$
        $$(0.103) \quad (0.024) \quad (0.0003)$$
    V.A.T. = weekly loss from abolition of zero rating by house-
    hold (*D*)
    D = ; 0 for one-person household, *D* = 1 for two-person
    household
    Y = weekly income (£)

we taxed food and fuel, and taxed life insurance policies and capital
gains more effectively. This reduction may be worth having but is
not spectacular. We conclude that major improvements in the U.K.
tax system must come from more fundamental structural reforms.

Conclusions

We have tried to ask of each part of the tax system 'What are the
underlying principles here?' This may appear to conflict with the
typical administrator's motto 'We start from where we are'. It is
often believed that this 'practical' approach removes the need to

give thought to where, in the long run, we are aiming to go. It is true that the practical man who knows where he is, and has not given any thought to where he is going, may appear more in command of his situation than the academic theorist who knows where he wants to go but is unsure of how to get there; but both of them end up comprehensively lost. It is in this way that we have finished up where we are.

The mess into which the present British tax system has drifted has been documented in earlier chapters. Anyone who came to it for the first time would regard the present system with some incredulity. There is a maze of taxes on different kinds of income, each tax with its own rules for determining taxable income and liability. The interaction between these taxes is difficult to comprehend, and, because of this, is rarely brought out into the open when tax changes are discussed. To take one obvious example of the general problem; in addition to income tax there are distinct and separately administered surcharges on each of employment incomes, investment incomes, and income from self-employment. The first of these is levied non-cumulatively on current earnings of less than a stated amount, the second cumulatively on current earnings of more than a stated amount, and the third cumulatively on preceding year earnings in excess of one amount and less than another amount. No one would design such a system on purpose and nobody did. Only a historical explanation of how it came about can be offered as a justification. That is not a justification, but a demonstration of how seemingly individually rational decisions can have absurd effects in aggregate.

There are more important examples than this one, but it illustrates how pragmatism which is not motivated by an over-all view of the principles and operation of the tax system as a whole is not a principle of good administration, but a recipe for unnecessary complexity and excessive administrative costs. We expect that some readers of this book will think that the objections to the existing British tax system we have made carry some weight, but might be more appropriately met by measures which stop short of any radical reappraisal of the principles of taxation. The idea of a lifetime expenditure tax may seem appealing but perhaps many of the benefits of such a reform might be obtained by some further concessions to savings within the context of the existing income tax. If they think this, they have completely misunderstood our whole argument. It is true that some of the deficiencies we have noted could be ameliorated by further *ad hoc* modifications of the shambles we have portrayed. It is certain, however, that these modifications would lead to still greater complexity in the tax system and to further abuses, anomalies, and loopholes, few of which will be anticipated.

The only prospect for an efficient tax system, whether efficiency refers to its economic effect or to the cost-effectiveness of its administration, is to adopt one which is based on a small set of clear principles, and which departs from them only in a number of limited and clearly recognized ways. The alternative to this course is to devise particular rules for each situation as and when it arises, and since we cannot define or anticipate all possible situations or even fully appreciate the consequences of our last decision, these rules are bound to proliferate indefinitely.

'Income Tax', ruled Lord Macnaghten, 'is a tax on income', and this has been the principle, if one may call it that, underlying direct taxation in the U.K. since the days of Pitt. But, as we saw in Chapter 5, it is not a very useful principle for practical purposes, because income is not an easy concept to define precisely nor to measure objectively. The fact is that in many circumstances there is only a tenuous relationship between monetary transactions and whatever it is that one means by income, and any attempt to pretend otherwise leads either to the kinds of difficulties we have described in earlier chapters, or to the forced adoption of cash flows as the measure of taxable income.

The case against the existing structure of the U.K. tax system and for the kind of reforms we have proposed rests on an accumulation of arguments rather than on a single decisive argument, and we are reluctant to summarize the main points of our thesis. Nevertheless, some points deserve special emphasis. Perhaps the most important is that the redistributive elements in the present tax structure rely heavily on high tax rates on those with large incomes from employment. But high earnings are not an important source of wealth inequality in the U.K., so that these taxes fall heavily on those engaged in productive sectors of the economy without achieving much in the way of substantial redistribution. The tax system is rightly criticized on both counts; the conflict between equity and efficiency in tax policy appears very acute. Although this trade-off is a real one, preoccupation with *rates* of tax and concern with the appearance of the tax system rather than its reality have led to excessive emphasis on it; and to a futile process in which political parties have sought to compensate for the deficiencies in the structure of taxation by changes in the rates. We believe that with a better-conceived tax base and lower rates we can achieve both greater equity and greater efficiency in tax policy.

The second substantial problem is that the taxation of investment income is in need of a major overhaul. It is is not simple, it is not fair, it is not effective, and it is characterized by rates of tax which reach heights which are tolerable only because they are not intended seriously. It is difficult to believe that at least some objectives could not be achieved better in other ways. These two arguments might seem to point to a shift from the taxation of income to the taxation of wealth, and this has evident attractions. But we are forced to conclude that a wealth tax which raises substantial revenue is not a practicable proposition, and to go down this road is to continue on the path of increased complexity and reduced effectiveness in taxation.

We have also been concerned by the arbitrariness of the present tax treatment of savings, and the resulting effects on the pattern of savings. We believe that this, and not the exaggerated problem of the burden of transfer taxes, is the real obstacle to the development of small business in the economy; and that the costs of the tax system's promotion of the increased institutionalization of capital flows have been high. Finally, everyone recognizes that the British tax system has become much too complicated; and we have argued that the only way out of this is to try to relate it more explicitly to some well-defined set of principles.

It is these considerations which lead us to propose a major shift of the tax base in Britain away from the taxation of income and earnings and towards the taxation of spending and transfers, and we have framed specific proposals for this in the form of a lifetime expenditure tax.

We have seen that effective tax reform requires both a knowledge of long-run objectives and a plan for taking the first steps in the desired direction. A major object of this book has been to consider the possibility of adopting a cash flow basis for taxation, not simply as an unfortunate expedient which we are obliged to adopt in a wide variety of practical situations, but as the underlying principle. We have suggested that in the day-to-day administration of the tax system, we have gone quite far along this road already, but in an unsystematic fashion. Unfortunately, a major source of confusion and complexity in taxation has been the failure of our intellectual categories to keep pace with what we actually do.

Nevertheless, we believe that a shift from an accruals basis to a receipts basis, and hence the movement from an income base to an expenditure base in personal taxation and from a profits base to a cash flow base in the corporate sector, provides much the most promising direction of reform. A lifetime expenditure tax corresponds to two common-sense feelings which we hope are widely shared. First, that the amount of tax which an individual pays should be based on actual receipts and payments of cash, and not hypothetical calculations about accruals of income which do not correspond to any transactions in which he may have been involved. Second, that the yardstick for determining how much tax an individual ought to pay should be the amount which he spends on himself or chooses to bestow on others. It may be idealistic, but not unreasonable, to hope that such a reform would elicit support from different quarters. On the one hand, a lifetime expenditure tax would make it easier for individuals to save in whichever form they wished, and in particular would encourage the development of small businesses. On the other hand, it would for the first time represent a serious attempt to tax spending out of inherited wealth, and the transmission of wealth from one generation to the next. More agreement on the form of the tax system would remove the need for the long series of piecemeal changes and policy reversals which we have seen over the last twenty years.

Political decisions about the introduction of an expenditure tax are likely to be dominated by a view about who gains and who loses from this change. More reasonably, there will be those who find the case for a lifetime expenditure tax attractive in principle, but who hesitate on distributional grounds. We ourselves have often heard the argument, 'An expenditure tax would favour the rich because the rich can afford to save'. But the rich also dissave and, as we have seen, spending out of inherited wealth currently escapes much of the weight of taxation falling on spending out of earned income. There is as yet no detailed empirical study which would enable us to form an opinion about the distribution of gains and losses which would arise from the introduction of L.E.T. Nor do we believe the distributional effects would be very noticeable in comparison to those engineered by other recent tax changes and by changes in the housing market, and we would expect them to be small compared to the effects of inflation in the last few years. The introduction of L.E.T. would mean little change in the amount of tax paid by the average taxpayer, nor indeed could there be much difference without a change in the level of public expenditure. Since, however, the argument for L.E.T. is one based on the structure of the tax system, we believe that under L.E.T. it would be easier to have an intelligent debate about how much redistribution we want the tax system to bring about. This depends on the answer to a fundamental but very simple question: how high should the tax threshold and the standard rate of tax be?

Our long-run objective is, therefore, a lifetime expenditure tax. To achieve this objective a number of steps ought to be taken now. The first is the abolition of cumulative P.A.Y.E. and a move towards a non-cumulative system with annual returns from all taxpayers. This would enable us to begin the process of rationalizing the tax and social security systems and to sort out the present unsystematic reliefs to savings, and to envisage the wider changes of abolishing capital gains tax and extending the range of registered assets described in Chapter 6. Such a reform would also allow serious consideration to be given to local taxation and the financing of devolution. The second immediate change would be the transformation of the existing corporation tax into a cash flow tax on the lines set out in Chapter 12. This would involve transitional problems, but these would be no more acute than those experienced in the many previous changes of corporation tax.

We should end with a plea for realism in expectations of what can be achieved by tax reform. The changes we have advocated can only be implemented over a long period of time. They will not transform the British tax system into an instrument of economic progress or social change; though we believe that they will make it simpler, fairer, and more efficient, and reduce the number and extent of its unintended ramifications. They will not satisfy those who are looking for measures which can be adopted in the next budget which will revive small business, restore incentives, effect irreversible change in the distribution of wealth and power, or achieve whatever else was featured on last week's 'Money Programme'. The ill-considered expedients which are constructed to meet the demands of those with large ambitions and little time will leave their objectives as far from realization as ever and the tax system a little more complicated than it was before. We see the British tax system as a chronically diseased patient; but one who, obsessed by the last symptom he happened to observe, disregards considered medical advice and insists on being completely cured by next week. There is never any shortage of quacks willing to minister to his needs; and he never gets even slightly better.

FURTHER READING

WE have not given references for the information on tax rates and benefits which we have used frequently in the text. Tax rates can be found in the Reports of the Commissioners of Inland Revenue and Customs and Excise; but these are necessarily somewhat out of date. The most convenient up-to-date source (for direct taxes) is probably the annual *Hambro Tax Guide*, which provides a non-technical survey of the principal features of tax legislation. The Department of Health and Social Security publishes a *Supplementary Benefits Handbook* which gives the rates of and rules for supplementary benefits. There is no equivalent source for other social benefits and the most practical method of finding out about them is to contact the local office of the Department of Health and Social Security.

Chapter 1

The theoretical issues underlying our analysis of the British tax system are not dealt with in a wholly satisfactory manner by any of the current textbooks on public finance. Much of the material is contained in journal articles and the level of discussion makes them inaccessible to many students and the general reader. A good introduction to the subject will be found in the volume of essays published by the Brookings Institution (1974). The classic textbooks on public finance remain those by Musgrave (1959) and Shoup (1969). A more recent book by Musgrave and Musgrave (1976) is very good although its institutional material is aimed at American students. For a British account see Prest (1975).

Chapter 2

Statistics about the tax system are contained in a volume published annually called *Inland Revenue Statistics* and in the Annual Reports of H.M. Commissioners of the Inland Revenue. There are several commercial guides to the income tax system and each year *Money Which* provides useful advice on how to fill in your tax return. Sabine (1966) is a history of income tax in the U.K., while Johnston (1965) describes the operations of Inland Revenue.

Chapter 3

On the incentive effects of taxation there is a helpful introduction by Break in the Brookings Institution volume (1974). More technical surveys of the disincentive effect of income tax on work decisions have been written by Stern (1976) and Godfrey (1975). For a detailed analysis of the American evidence, including an account of the results of the New Jersey negative income tax experiment, see the volumes by Cain and Watts (1973) and Pechman and Timpane (1975). Some econometric results for Britain based on a research project at Stirling University are discussed in Brown, Levin, and Ulph (1976). The effects of inflation on the tax system are dealt with in Chapter 6 of the Meade Report and a wider discussion of indexation can be found in Liesner and King (1975). A survey of progress towards indexation in other countries is O.E.C.D. (1976). The redistributive role of taxation and the determinants of the distributions of income and wealth are analysed in Atkinson (1975). The definitive study of the distribution of wealth in Britain is Atkinson and Harrison (1978).

Chapter 4

It is difficult to find in one volume a coherent account of the theory and practice of the taxation of investment income and savings. Titmuss (1962) discusses some of the main issues but this study is now obviously rather out of date. A formal analysis of the effects of the British tax system on incentives to save and invest is contained in Chapter 4 of the Meade Report.

Chapter 5

The best-known and most detailed proposals for a comprehensive income tax are those put forward in Canada by the Carter Commission (1966). The concept of income is discussed by Hicks (1939) and Simons (1938), but the best survey is that by Kaldor (1955, Appendix). A collection of some of the more important contributions on the subject has been edited by Parker and Harcourt (1969).

Chapter 6

The two most cogent cases for an expenditure tax are the classic exposition of Kaldor (1955), arguing from the theoretical viewpoint, and the case put by Andrews (1974) on practical grounds. Two official reports explaining how an expenditure tax would work have been produced abroad, in the U.S.A. (U.S. Treasury, 1977) and in Sweden (Lodin, 1976). Administrative aspects of reforming the British tax system by introducing self-assessment have been examined by Barr, James, and Prest (1977).

Chapter 7

An excellent introduction to the social security system in Britain and possible directions for reform is Atkinson (1969). Although it is somewhat outdated it repays reading. An outline of the system of means-tested benefits is given in National Consumer Council (1977), and statistical information is provided in *Social Security Statistics* and Reports of the *Family Expenditure Survey* (both annual). The most recent study of the causes and characteristics of poverty is that by Fiegehen, Lansley, and Smith (1977), and a good general discussion of the problem may be found in Atkinson (1975). On schemes of fundamental reform (social dividend/tax credits/negative income tax) see Meade (1972) and the Report of the Select Committee on Tax Credit (1973).

Chapter 8

Statistics on the collection of indirect taxes are contained in Customs and Excise Reports. The distinction between direct and indirect taxes is at best an arbitrary one, and for further reading on the theoretical issues contained in this chapter the reader is referred to the notes on Chapters 3 and 10. An introduction to the theory of optimal indirect taxation is Sandmo (1976).

Chapter 9

The broad issues of the relationship between central and local taxation are discussed in the paper by Netzer in Brookings Institution (1974). In the U.K. context the most helpful sources are the Layfield Committee Report (H.M.S.O., 1976), Cripps and Godley (1976), and Institute for Fiscal Studies (1973).

Chapter 10

The best information on the distribution of wealth in Britain is to be found in Atkinson and Harrison (1978); see also the various Reports of the Royal Commission on the Distribution of Income and Wealth. The principles of taxing capital are discussed in Sandford (1971). For the theoretical and practical arguments for and against a wealth tax, see the *Report of the Select Committee of the House of Commons on Wealth Tax* (H.M.S.O., 1975), Flemming and Little (1974), and Sandford, Willis, and Ironside (1975).

Chapters 11 and 12

A detailed analysis of corporate tax systems and their effects on firms' financing and investment decisions may be found in King (1977). For the debate on inflation accounting the reader is referred to the Report of the Sandilands Committee (1975) and the review article by Kay (1977.)

Chapter 13

Each year *Economic Trends* contains an article examining the impact of the tax system on the distribution of income. The methodology behind these studies is assessed in contributions contained in Atkinson (1976). The theoretical literature on the distribution of the tax burden is extremely technical. The pioneering contribution was that by Mirrlees (1971). A less technical but still demanding paper is Atkinson (1973b); for the theory of the measurement of inequality see Atkinson (1973a) which contains a very useful non-mathematical discussion of the main concepts.

Chapter 14

Discussions of how the tax systems should be changed are not difficult to find. The most comprehensive survey of the British tax system and possibilities for reform is the Meade Report. A rather different view of reform is Field, Meacher, and Pond (1977) which concentrates on the tax system and poverty. A recent report on reforming the U.S. tax system is U.S. Treasury (1977), and another interesting American study is that by Break and Pechman (1975).

REFERENCES

ALLEN REPORT (1965). Committee of Inquiry into the Impact of Rates on Households, Cmnd. 2582, H.M.S.O., London.

ANDREWS, W. D. (1974). 'A Consumption-Type or Cash Flow Personal Income Tax, *Harvard Law Review*, 87.

ATKINSON, A. B. (1969). *Poverty in Britain and the Reform of Social Security*, Cambridge Univ. Press, London.

—— (1972). *Unequal Shares*, Allen Lane, London.

—— (1973a). 'On the Measurement of Inequality', reprinted with non-mathematical summary in A. B. Atkinson (ed.), *Wealth, Income and Inequality*, Penguin, London. (Originally published in *Journal of Economic Theory*, 2, 1970.)

—— (1973b). 'How Progressive Should Income Tax Be?', in M. Parkin (ed.), *Essays on Modern Economics*, Longman, London.

—— (1975). *The Economics of Inequality*, Oxford Univ. Press, London.

—— (ed.) (1976). *The Personal Distribution of Incomes*, Allen & Unwin, London.

—— and HARRISON, A. J. (1978). *The Distribution of Personal Wealth in Britain*, Cambridge Univ. Press, London.

—— and MEADE, T. W. (1974). 'Methods and preliminary findings in assessing the economic and Health Services consequences of smoking, with particular reference to lung cancer', *Journal of the Royal Statistical Society*, Ser. A, **137**.

—— and TOWNSEND, J. L. (1977). 'Economic Aspects of Reduced Smoking', *Lancet* 3 Sept. 1977, No. 8036, vol. 2 for 1977.

B.I.M. (1974). British Institute of Management, M.S. Report 18, *Business Cars in the UK*, London.

BARR, N. A., JAMES, S. R., and PREST, A. R. (1977). *Self Assessment for Income Tax*, Heinemann, London.

BAUMOL, W. J. and BRADFORD, D. F. (1970). 'Optimal Departures from Marginal Cost Pricing', *American Economic Review*, **60**.

BEVERIDGE, W. (1942). *Social Insurance and Allied Services*, Cmnd. 6404, H.M.S.O., London.

BOLTON COMMITTEE (1971). *Small Firms: Report of the Committee of Inquiry on Small Firms*, Cmnd. 4811, H.M.S.O., London.

BOSWELL, J. (1973). *The Rise and Decline of Small Firms*, Allen & Unwin, London.

BRACEWELL-MILNES, B. (1976). *The Camel's Back*, Centre for Policy Studies, London.

BREAK, G. F. (1957). 'Income Taxes and Incentives to Work: An Empirical Study', *American Economic Review*, **47**.

—— and PECHMAN, J. A. (1975). *Federal Tax Reform: The Impossible Dream?*, Brookings Institution, Washington, D.C.

BROOKINGS INSTITUTION (1974). *The Economics of Public Finance*, Brookings Institution, Washington, D.C.

BROWN, C. V. (1968). 'Misconceptions about Income Tax and Incentives', *Scottish Journal of Political Economy*, **15**.

——, LEVIN, E., and ULPH, D. T. (1976). 'Estimates of Labour Hours Supplied by Married Male Workers in Great Britain', *Scottish Journal of Political Economy*, **23**.

BUREAU OF THE CENSUS (1976). *Historical Statistics of the U.S.*, U.S. Department of Commerce, Washington D.C.

BUSINESS MONITOR M3 (1977). *Company Finance*, Department of Industry, Business Statistics Office, H.M.S.O., London.

CAIN, C. and WATTS, H. (1973). *Income Maintenance and Labour Supply*, Markham, New York.

CARTER COMMISSION (1966). *Report of the Royal Commission on Taxation*, Ottawa.

CHAWLA, O. P. (1972). *Personal Taxation in India*, Somaiya Publications, Bombay.

C.I.P.F.A. (Annual). *Return of Rates*, Chartered Institute of Public Finance and Accountancy, London.

CRIPPS, T. F. and GODLEY, W. (1976). *Local Government Finance and its Reform*, Department of Applied Economics, Cambridge.

CUSTOMS AND EXCISE (1976). *Report of the Commissioners*, H.M.S.O., London.

DEATON, A. S. (1975). *Models and Projections of Demand in Post-war Britain*, Chapman & Hall, London.

DIAMOND, P. A. and MIRRLEES, J. A. (1971). 'Optimal Taxation and Public Production', *American Economic Review*, **41**.

DIAMOND COMMISSION (1976). Royal Commission on the Distribution of Income and Wealth, Report No. 3, Cmnd. 6383, H.M.S.O., London.

—— (1977). Royal Commission on the Distribution of Income and Wealth, Report No. 4, Cmnd. 6626, H.M.S.O., London. 3

EDGEWORTH, F. Y. (1897). 'The Pure Theory of Taxation (III)', *Economic Journal*, **3**.

ERRITT, M. J. and ALEXANDER, J. C. D. (1977). 'Ownership of Company Shares: A New Survey', *Economic Trends*.

F.E.S. REPORT (1975). *Report on the Family Expenditure Survey*, H.M.S.O., London.

FIEGEHEN, G. C., LANSLEY, P. S., and SMITH, A. D. (1977). *Poverty and Progress in Britain 1953–73*, National Institute of Economic and Social Research Occasional Paper xxix, Cambridge Univ. Press, London.

FIELD, F., MEACHER, M., and POND, C. (1977). *To Him Who Hath: A Study of Poverty and Taxation*, Penguin, London.

FIELDS, D. B. and STANBURY, W. T. (1971). 'Income Taxes and Incentives to Work: Some Additional Empirical Evidence', *American Economic Review*, **41**.

FLEMMING, J. S. and LITTLE, I. M. D. (1974). *Why We Need a Wealth Tax*, Methuen, London.

GODFREY, L. (1975). *Theoretical and Empirical Aspects of the Effects of Taxation on the Supply of Labour*, O.E.C.D., Paris.

GODWIN, M. R. (1976). 'Compliance Costs of VAT to the Independent Local Retailer', unpub. thesis, Bath Univ. Library.

GOLDTHORPE, J., LOCKWOOD, D., BECKHOFER, F., and PLATT, J. (1970). *The Affluent Worker. Industrial Attitudes and Behaviour*, Cambridge Univ. Press, London.

GOODE, R. (1976). *The Individual Income Tax*, Brookings Institution, Washington, D.C.

HANNAH, L. and KAY, J. A. (1977). *Concentration in Modern Industry*, Macmillan, London.

HARBURY, C. D. and HITCHENS, D. M. (1976). 'The Inheritances of Top Wealth Leavers', *Economic Journal*, **86**.

—— and McMAHON, P. C. (1973). 'Inheritance and the Distribution of Personal Wealth in Britain', *Economic Journal*, **83**.

HAY-M.S.L. LTD. (1976). 'An Analysis of Managerial Remuneration in the U.K. and Overseas, a Report' (background paper for the Diamond Commission), H.M.S.O., London.

HICKS, J. R. (1939). *Value and Capital. An Inquiry into some Fundamental Principles of Economic Theory*, Clarendon Press, Oxford.

H.M.S.O. (1942). *The Taxation of Weekly Wage Earners*, Cmnd. 6348, London.

—— (1972). *Taxation of Capital on Death* (Green Paper), Cmnd. 4930, London.

—— (1974). *Wealth Tax* (Green Paper), Cmnd. 5704, London.

—— (1975). *Report of the Select Committee of the House of Commons on Wealth Tax*, H.C. 696–1, London.

—— (1976). *Local Government Finance*, Report of the Committee of Inquiry (Chairman F. Layfield), Cmnd. 6453, London.

—— (1977). *Local Government Finance*, presented to Parliament by the Secretary of State for the Environment and the Secretary of State for Wales, Cmnd. 6813, London.

—— (1977). *Devolution: Financing the Devolved Services*, Cmnd. 6890, London.

HOBBES, T. (1651). *Leviathan or, the Matter, Forme and Power of A Commonwealth Ecclesiasticall and Civil*, Andrew Crooke, London.

HORSMAN, E. G. (1975). 'The Avoidance of Estate Duty by Gifts *Inter Vivos*', *Economic Journal*, **85**.

ILERSIC, A. (1973). 'Grant Determination and Its Distribution' in Institute for Fiscal Studies, *Proceedings of a Conference on Local Government Finance*, I.F.S., London.

INSTITUTE FOR FISCAL STUDIES (1973). *Proceedings of a Conference on Local Government Finance*, I.F.S., London.

JOHNSTON, A. (1965). *The Inland Revenue*, Allen & Unwin, London.

KALDOR, N. (1955). *An Expenditure Tax*, Allen & Unwin, London.

—— (1956). *Indian Tax Reform*, Ministry of Finance, India.

KAY, J. A. (1977). 'Inflation Accounting—A Review Article', *Economic Journal*, **87**, 300–11.

—— and PARKIN, A. (1978). 'Taxation and Life Insurance in Britain', mimeo.

KING, M. A. (1977). *Public Policy and the Corporation*, Chapman & Hall, London.

—— (1978). *Profits in a Mixed Economy*, Macmillan, London.

LAYFIELD REPORT, *see* H.M.S.O. (1976).

LEE, P. N. (ed.) (1976) Statistics of Smoking in the United Kingdom, Tobacco Research Council, London.

LIESNER, T. and KING, M. A. (1975). *Indexing for Inflation*, Heinemann Educational Books, London.

LIFE OFFICES ASSOCIATION (1976). *Life Assurance in the U.K., 1971–75*, London.

LODIN, S. O. (1976). *Progressive utgiftsskatt-ett alternativ?* Finandsdepartementet, Statens offentliga utredningar 1976:62, Stockholm.

MEADE, J. E. (1972). 'Poverty in the Welfare State', *Oxford Economic Papers*, **24**.

MEADE COMMITTEE (1978). *The Structure and Reform of Direct Taxation*, Allen & Unwin, London.

MERRETT-CYRIAX ASSOCIATES (1971). *Dynamics of Small Firms*, Research Report for the Bolton Committee, H.M.S.O., London.

MILL, J. S. (1865). *Principles of Political Economy* (6th edn.), Longman, London.

MIRRLEES, J. A. (1971). 'An Exploration in the Theory of Optimum Income Taxation', *Review of Economic Studies*, **38**.

MONOPOLIES COMMISSION (1975). *Contraceptive Sheaths*, H.C. 135, H.M.S.O., London.

MUSGRAVE, R. A. (1959). *The Theory of Public Finance*, McGraw-Hill, New York.

—— and MUSGRAVE, P. B. (1976). *Public Finance in Theory and Practice* (2nd edn.), McGraw-Hill, New York.

NATIONAL CONSUMER COUNCIL (1977). *Means-Tested Benefits: A Discussion Paper*, National Consumer Council Report, London.

NEWBERY, D. (1970). 'A Theorem on the Measurement of Inequality', *Journal of Economic Theory*, **2**.

NICHOLSON, J. L. (1974). *The Distribution and Redistribution of Income in the U.K.*, in D. Wedderburn (ed.), *Poverty, Inequality and Class Structure*, Cambridge Univ. Press, London.

NORDHAUS, W. D. (1975). 'The Political Business Cycle', *Review of Economic Studies*, **42**.

O.E.C.D. (1976). *The Adjustment of Personal Income Tax Systems for Inflation*, Paris.

OKNER, B. A. and PECHMAN, J. A. (1974). *Who Bears the Tax Burden?*, Brookings Institution, Washington, D.C.

OPINION RESEARCH CENTRE (1977). 'A Survey of the Motivation of British Management', London.

PARKER, R. H. and HARCOURT, G. C. (eds.) (1969). *Readings in the Concept and Measurement of Income*, Cambridge Univ. Press, London.

PARR, M. and DAY, J. (1977). 'Value Added Tax in the United Kingdom', *National Westminster Bank Review*.

PECHMAN, J. A. and TIMPANE, P. M. (eds.) (1975). *Work Incentives and Income Guarantees: The New Jersey Negative Income Tax Experiment*, Brookings Institution, Washington, D.C.

PRAIS, S. J. (1976). *The Evolution of Giant Firms in Britain*, Cambridge Univ. Press, London.

PREST, A. R. (1975). *Public Finance in Theory and Practice* (5th edn.), Weidenfeld & Nicholson, London.

PSACHAROPOULOS, G. (1976). 'Estimating some Key Parameters in the Brain Drain Taxation Model', in J. N. Bhagwati (ed.), *The Brain Drain and Taxation*, North Holland, Amsterdam.

RADCLIFFE REPORT (1954). *Report of the Royal Commission on Taxation of Profits and Income*, No. 2, Cmnd. 9105, H.M.S.O., London.
RAMSEY, F. A. (1928). 'A Mathematical Theory of Savings', *Economic Journal*, **38**.
RAWLS, J. (1971). *A Theory of Justice*, Clarendon Press, Oxford.
REVELL, J. (1965). 'Changes in the Social Distribution of Property in Britain during the Twentieth Century', paper given to Third International Conference of Economic History, Munich, 1965.
—— (1967). *The Wealth of the Nation; the National Balance Sheet of the United Kingdom, 1957–1961*, Cambridge Univ. Press, London.
RICHARDSON REPORT (1964). *Report of the Committee on Turnover Taxation*, Cmnd. 2300, H.M.S.O., London.
RUBENSTEIN, W. D. (1974). 'Men of Property: Some Aspects of Occupation, Inheritance and Power among Top British Wealth-holders', in P. Stanworth and A. Giddens (eds.), *Elites and Power in British Society*, Canbridge Univ. Press, London.

SABINE, B. E. V. (1966). *A History of Income Tax*, Allen & Unwin, London.
SANDFORD, C. T. (1971). *Taxing Personal Wealth*, Allen & Unwin, London.
—— (1973). *Hidden Costs of Taxation*, I.F.S., London.
——, WILLIS, J. R., and IRONSIDE, D. J. (1975). *An Annual Wealth Tax*, Heinemann Educational Books, London.
SANDILANDS (1975). *Report of the Inflation Accounting Committee*, Cmnd. 6225, H.M.S.O., London.
SANDMO, A. (1976). 'Optimal Taxation—An Introduction to the Literature', *Journal of Public Economics*, **6**.
SELECT COMMITTEE ON TAX CREDIT (1973). *Report and Proceedings of the Committee*, H.M.S.O., London.
SEN, A. K. (1974). 'Informational Bases of Alternative Welfare Approaches; Aggregation and Income Distribution', *Journal of Public Economics*, **3**.
SHOUP, C. S. (1969). *Public Finance*, Weidenfeld & Nicolson, London.
SIMONS, H. C. (1938). *Personal Income Taxation*, Univ. of Chicago Press, Chicago.
STANWORTH, P. and GIDDENS, A. (eds.) (1974). *Elites and Power in British Society*, Cambridge Univ. Press, London.
Statistical Abstract of U.S. (Annual). U.S. Department of Commerce, Washington, D.C.

STERN, N. H. (1976). 'Taxation and Labour Supply—A Partial Survey', in *Proceedings of a Conference on Taxation and Incentives*, I.F.S., London.

—— (1977). 'The Marginal Valuation of Income', in *The Proceedings of the Association of University Teachers of Economics*, Edinburgh, 1976, ed. M. J. Artis and A. R. Nobay, Basil Blackwell, Oxford.

TITMUSS, R. M. (1962). *Income Distribution and Social Change*. Allen & Unwin, London.

U.S. TREASURY (1977). *Blueprints for Basic Tax Reform*, U.S. Govt. Printing Office, Washington.

Vision (1977). No. 75, Feb.

WHALLEY, J. and PIGGOTT, J. R. (1977). 'General Equilibrium investigations of U.K. tax subsidy policy', in *The Proceedings of the Association of University Teachers of Economics*, Edinburgh, 1976, ed. M. J. Artis and A. R. Nobay, Basil Blackwell, Oxford.

WHEATCROFT, G. S. A. (1965). 'Proposals for a System of Estate and Gift Taxation', in G. S. A. Wheatcroft (ed.), *Estate and Gift Taxation: A Comparative Study*, Sweet & Maxwell, London.

WORSWICK, G. N. D. (1971). 'Fiscal Policy and Stabilization in Britain', in A. Cairncross (ed.), *Britain's Economic Prospects Reconsidered*, Allen & Unwin, London.

INDEX